SO-ALC-949

A Fly Fishing Guide to Rocky Mountain National Park

The most comprehensive and fully illustrated guide available, covering the best flies and techniques for over 150 destinations in the Park

by
Steven B. Schweitzer

Photography, illustrations and text by the author unless otherwise noted

Watercolor illustrations by Rick Takahashi

Fishing fly photography by Mark Tracy

PIXACHROME Publishing • Northern Colorado

For more information about this book, visit the online companion at www.flyfishingrmnp.com.

INTERNATIONAL STANDARD BOOK NUMBERS:
ISBN-10: 0-9844123-0-1
ISBN-13: 978-0-9844123-0-3

TEXT AND PHOTOGRAPHY COPYRIGHT:
Steven B. Schweitzer, 2010-2015 All rights reserved.

FISH ILLUSTRATION COPYRIGHT:
Rick Takahashi, 2010. All rights reserved.

EDITORIAL REVIEW:
Josh Rickard, Kerry Evens, Dick Shinton, Erik Wagg

CONTRIBUTORS:
Health and Safety: Kerry Evens, Chief Flight Nurse, North Colorado Med Evac, RN, BSN, CFRN, CEN
Fish watercolor illustrations: Rick Takahashi
Fishing fly photography: Mark Tracy

STREAM, RIVER AND LAKE DATA:
Chris Kennedy
U.S. Fish and Wildlife Service
Colorado Fish and Wildlife Assistance Office

PUBLISHED BY:
Pixachrome Publishing
Northern Colorado, USA
www.pixachrome.com

PRINTING BY:
Printed in Canada - Friesens Corporation, Altona, Manitoba, Canada

No portion of this book, either text or photography, may be reproduced in any form, including electronically, without the express written permission of the publisher.

LIBRARY OF CONGRESS CATALOGING-IN-PUBLICATION DATA:
Schweitzer, Steven B.
    A Fly Fishing Guide to Rocky Mountain National Park / by Steven B. Schweitzer
        p. cm.
    Includes index.
ISBN-13: 978-0-9844123-0-3
ISBN-10: 0-9844123-0-1
Library of Congress Control Number: 2010939973

DESIGN AND LAYOUT:
Page layout created with Serif PagePlus X5. Line art illustrations created with Serif DrawPlus X4. www.serif.com.

PHOTOGRAPHY and EDITING:
Primary Camera: Nikon D70
Primary Lens for most shots:
    18-70mm f/3.5-5.6
Tele Lens: 28-200mm f/3.5-6.5
Wide Angle: 12-24mm f/3.5
Prime: 50mm f/1.8
Panoramic head: Nodal Ninja SPH-1
Photo and HDR Editing:
    Adobe Lightroom 3 and Photoshop CS5
Panoramic Editing: Ulead Cool 360 and Serif PanoramaPlus X4

TOPOGRAPHIC MAPS:
All topographic maps were created with DeLorme Topo USA® 8.0 software with permission. www.delorme.com.

FRONT AND BACK COVER DESIGN:
Design by Cortland Langworthy
Relish Studio, Inc.
www.relishstudio.com

FRONT COVER:
Mike Kruise fishing the Cache La Poudre
Photograph by Steven B. Schweitzer

A NOTE OF SAFETY REGARDING BACK-COUNTRY TRAVEL AND FLY FISHING:
With the exception of just a few roadside locations, fly fishing destinations listed in this book require various levels of physical activity including hiking, back-packing and off-trail travel. Every attempt has been made to discuss the potential hazards and level of physical activity required. It is the responsibility of the users of this book to assess their own capabilities and physical limitations, and learn the necessary skills required for safe hiking and back-country travel. The author and publisher disclaim any liability for injury or other damage caused by hiking, back-country travel and any other activity discussed in this book.

The author has made every effort to ensure the accuracy of the information contained within this book. From time-to-time, the information within can become out-of-date and require updating. If you find information in this book that requires revision, please notify the publisher for correction in future printings. As always, your comments and suggestions are encouraged and welcomed.

Email comments to *info@flyfishingrmnp.com*

Acknowledgements

Over the past decade, countless hours were invested and trail miles trekked collecting photos and research for this book. But that's only the beginning and frankly, the easiest part. There were many, many people involved, some behind the scenes and some with a more forefront part. All were equally responsible for this publication and are due a large dose of my humble respect and acknowledgement for their contributions. The book quickly evolved from an idea, to a project, to a labor-of-love, to sometimes an overwhelming goal. Through it all the people below pushed me forward.

A hats off, bow down thanks goes to **Chris Kennedy** of the U.S. Fish and Wildlife Service who provided decades worth of fish survey and destination data for nearly every water in the Park. It became the essential core for planning fishing and hiking research for this book. It is also the basis for the table in the Appendix entitled *Creeks, Streams, Rivers & Lakes in Rocky Mountain National Park*. Without the data, I wouldn't have known where to start and frankly, the value of this book is minimized.

When I needed illustrations, I asked noted author and local artist **Rick Takahashi** to assist. You get to see miniature reproductions of his full color original watercolor renditions. The full-sized originals are beautiful beyond words. Thank you for your artistic contribution, Tak.

When the idea came about that flies should be included in the book, I recruited the photographic talents of **Mark Tracy**. His attention to detail and unending pursuit of the perfect photograph of something so small would probably go unnoticed unless mentioned here. His fishing fly photography goes without compare. Thank you, Mark, for providing your incredible photography talents.

An old publishing adage says a cover will sell the book. **Cortland Langworthy** is not only a top-notch motion and still graphic artist, but an avid fly fisherman as well. Thank you Cort, for your incredible talent and of course, humor that only I get.

Contributors to the fly pattern section are notable in their own right, being some of the finest innovative fly tyers in the world. I selected them as people who knew the area and could offer patterns specifically useful for the Park: **Brad Befus, Tyler Befus, Kirk Bien, Charlie Craven, Frank Drummond, Tim Drummond, Eric Ishiwata, Joe Johnson, Larry Jurgens, Mike Kruise, Mark McMillan, Al Ritt, Richard Ross, Dick Shinton, Marty Staab, Harrison Steeves, Scott Stisser, Rick Takahashi, Hans Weilenmann and Brian Yamauchi.** Thanks to each of you for your innovative contributions.

A special thanks goes to **Kerry Evens** for her contributions to the health and safety section of the book, leveraging her 20+ years of emergency medical nursing as a flight nurse.

Several folks were instrumental in providing editorial review. A special thanks goes to **John Shewey**, who provided general publishing guidance and advice on writing for the fly fishing audience. This took many sessions where we observed proper fly fishing protocol by sampling the world's finest aqua vitae. Thanks, John, for the writing advice and tutorials on how to savor the single malts.

A special thanks also goes to **Pat Dorsey**, who provided counsel on writing fly fishing books – thanks Pat, for your *very timely* and sage advice.

A note of thanks to **Delorme**, who graciously gave permission to reproduce topographic maps and trail profiles.

Self-publishing and self-marketing a book is a daunting process. Many thanks goes to **Terry Wickstrom** and **Chad LaChance** for providing radio and TV time. Without each of you, I wouldn't have had the access to these types of media channels.

Editing a self-published venture such as this requires many sets of eyes to make it right. Significant editing time was invested by **Jerry Hubka, Josh Rickard, Dick Shinton, Rick Takahashi** and **Erik Wagg**. A million thanks to each of you for making this book usable and readable.

Finally, a great bit of thanks goes to all my hiking and fishing buddies who ventured with me along the trails over the years. Those not mentioned above include: **Scot Bley, Chris Bowell, Cort and Dickie Langworthy, Kurt and Teresa Legerski, Ed LeViness, Sean Miller, Max Moree, Betsy Porter, Whitley Porter, Josh Rickard, Neil Sudaisar, Dana Turner, and Liz Yaeger.** *(Many of those mentioned in the paragraphs above also logged trail miles with me).*

Contents

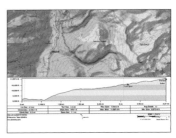

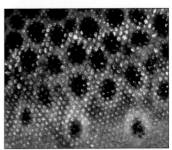

Contents

Figures and Tables

Tables

Figures

Errata and Etcetera

Correction to errors and omissions can be found by visiting the book's website at http://www.flyfishingrmnp.com. Additional material mentioned in this book can also be found at the book's website.

On an overcast day, Park guide Dick Shinton takes a day for himself and works the pocket water in one of his favorite streams. Fishing a hopper-dropper is an effective combination for pocket water like this.

How to Use This Guide

Key to Symbols and Icons Used in this Book

- 𝝅 - Easy (Slope Grade 0-3)
- 𝝅 𝝅 - Moderate (Slope Grade 4-7)
- 𝝅 𝝅 𝝅 - Challenging (Slope Grade 8-11)
- 𝝅 𝝅 𝝅 𝝅 - Very Challenging (Slope Grade 12-15)
- 𝝅 𝝅 𝝅 𝝅 𝝅 - Extremely Challenging (Slope Grade 16+)

- ♿ - Location Meets Accessibility Requirements

- 🐟 Brook Trout
- 🐟 Rainbow Trout
- 🐟 Brown Trout
- 🐟 Colorado Cutthroat Trout
- 🐟 Yellowstone River Cutthroat Trout
- 🐟 Greenback Cutthroat Trout
- 🐟 Cutthroat Trout (of hybrid genetics)

Using the Trail Maps and Profiles

Trails are highlighted in aqua-blue on a topographic map. Below each topographic map is a trail profile, marked with key destinations along the route. The trail profile matches the highlighted trail on the topographic map. Using the topographic map and trail profile together will give a clear picture of what to expect when hiking to a destination. Maps are provided as reference - do not solely rely on them for navigation. Some maps have been rotated to fit the trail for best viewing. Please note the map orientation indicator in the lower right-hand corner of each topo. Use commercially available topographic maps for all navigation. All data is known to be accurate at the time of printing.

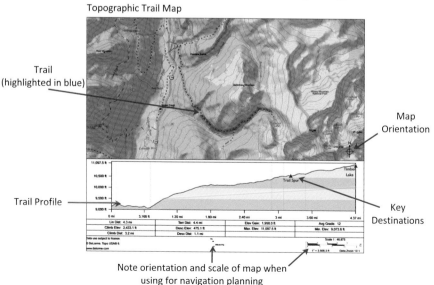

Note orientation and scale of map when
using for navigation planning

Foreward

About the Author

Steve Schweitzer spent over 10 years hiking and fishing in Rocky Mountain National Park, collecting notes and photographs for the book. He is a frequent contributor to leading fly fishing periodicals and contributing writer and illustrator for the book "Drag-Free Drift - Leader Design and Presentation Techniques for Fly Fishing". He is co-founder of the popular fly fishing website www.globalflyfisher.com.

Photo by Steve & Sue Violette

I am very fortunate to live only a half-hour from Rocky Mountain National Park. The Park is the playground that allows me to enjoy three of my favorite outdoor activities: hiking, backpacking and fly fishing.

A book was not the goal as I began logging notes after every trip to the Park. I took detailed notes to help me capture thoughts, techniques that worked, techniques that didn't, unusual events and interesting sidebars about the day, in an effort to learn the Park in an intimate way and become a better fly fisher. I meticulously logged things like water temperature, weather, hatch activity and flies I used - over 20 data points. I developed my own database and reporting tool to make sense of it all. After the first five years of notes and 100 trips in the Park, I realized I had the foundation that would be beneficial to others seeking to fish the Park. I now have a decade's worth of notes and have been to every destination discussed within - with exception of one very remote location. Hence the genesis of this book.

This book is not a hiking guide, although plenty of discussion is made around it, since it is the primary method to get yourself to fishy water. There are plenty of excellent hiking guide books specific to the Park which discuss the trails in more detail for the photographer, fauna or flower seeker. Using a hiking guide book in conjunction with this book will give you more than you ever desired to know about locations in the Park.

This book is a destination guide, focusing only on water that is known to contain fish. No discussion is given on water that has been identified as not containing year-round populations of fish. Ten years of research included countless day trips and overnight backpacks to fishy destinations with a fly rod and a camera. Many evenings each year were spent poring through Fish And Wildlife Service (FWS) creel data graciously provided to me by Chris Kennedy. Beyond the brief paragraphs about the fishing destinations, I provide a summary of the FWS data and my research analysis in the form of several tables found in the back of the book.

The tables are designed to answer the visiting angler's primary question: "Where shall I fish today?" The answer lies in assessing 1) how much time do you have to fish?, 2) do you want to fish a lake or stream?, 3) what kind of fish do you want to pursue?, and 4) are you physically capable of hiking to the destination? The tables include several data points on 350 lakes and stream destinations and are presented in such a way to help you answer the question above. Note that not all locations contain fish. As of the publication date of this book, just over 150 locations have known populations of fish and are the focus of the contents of this book. About half of the fishable locations in the Park are off trail, demanding as little as a wonderful meander in an open meadow to extremely difficult travel over uneven terrain or through dense vegetation, most always with significant altitude gain. Don't wander too far off trail if you aren't familiar with a compass and detailed topographic map. Again, the tables in the back of the book will help you assess waters that suit your physical capabilities, hiking experience, travel time and fishing goals. Once you find water that is within your reach, refer to the narrative to gain additional insight in fishing the destination.

I would be remiss if I didn't discuss the rigors and dangers of hiking in the Park. As most who are familiar with the area know, a bluebird morning could change in a heartbeat, yielding to heavy downpours, lightning or even hail. As a conservative estimate, I experience inclement weather on 70% of my trips in the Park. Many times, I took cover to avoid the pounding of chilly hail or ceased casting my fly rod as lightning struck too close for comfort.

I have made every attempt to clearly describe the nature and difficulty of hiking to the destinations and to frankly *warn* the reader of what to expect. Altitude does funny things to the strongest of wills; don't bite off more than you can chew. If it's your first time in the Park, or in any elevation for that matter, take it easy the first day or two. Choose a modest fishing destination that will help you gauge if you can attempt a more rigorous hike. It's not ideal to find out five miles in that the trail is too much for you, realizing you have five miles back to the trailhead. That will ruin an otherwise well-planned day of fishing!

I have have hiked and fished the Park with a wide variety of friends from all walks of life; I am eternally grateful to all of them for sharing the day with me. They will attest that I contend fishing isn't the goal, rather it's about getting there. (As you peruse the photos in this book, you'll get a clear sense the Park is immensely beautiful, supporting my assertion it really isn't about the fishing.) The Park is stunningly spectacular and catching a trout only makes it better. There *were* occasional days when I have walked away without a fish to hand. I am reminded as I hike the trail back out, of the perfect day nonetheless. So really, I have never wasted time going to the Park. I have added to my collection of memories, photographs and incredible encounters with nature.

I have experienced a curious fox that approached me at camp during dinner, witnessed pine martens chasing squirrels around trees, seen moose cocking their head in bewilderment as I float-tubed *their* remote lake, pikas begging for handouts, marmots following with curiosity, several hundred elk accepting me as part of the Moraine, grouse protecting their young from my presence, a rare turkey startled at seeing me, coyotes ignoring me, bears (and me) keeping distance, eagles and hawks soaring above - you get the idea - the list is endless. The moral of this story is you don't get to experience all the other hidden wonders of the Park unless you make a point to. I am reminded of my favorite quote, which perfectly sums it up:

> *"The streamside paths are the tramplings of the uninspired herd, follow them and your rewards will be commensurate."*
> - the late Sheridan Anderson, author of Curtis Creek Manifesto

So, get out there. Get off the beaten path. Experience all that Rocky Mountain National Park has to offer. Catch a fish or two and be safe in the process.

Steve Schweitzer
Berthoud, Colorado
September 2010

Map of Rocky Mountain National Park

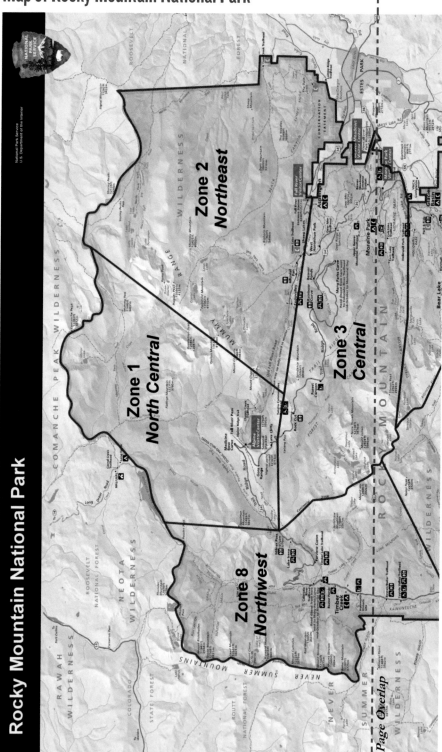

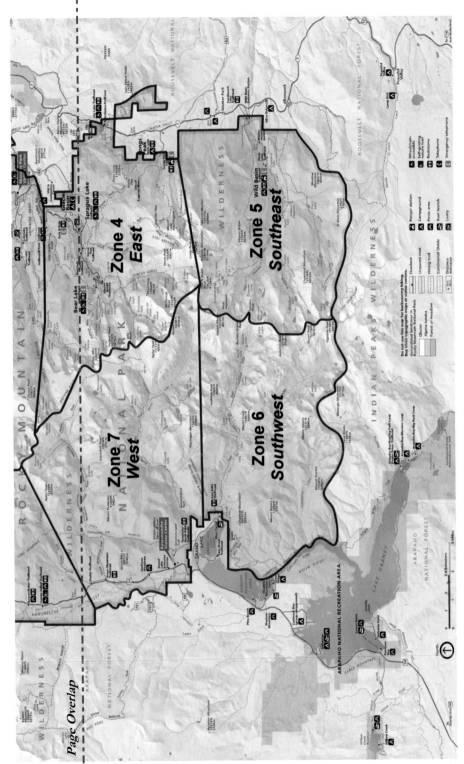

Section I
Park Overview

Rocky Mountain National Park

Before The Land Was A National Park

The land known today as Rocky Mountain National Park (RMNP) was first settled by nomadic hunters some 11,000 years ago, maybe even before. Archaeologists have found traces of 15th century nomadic hunters, principally the Utes and Arapahoes, in the Moraines, Estes Park and Grand Lake areas. They left well-worn trails, pottery shards, pine pole wickiups, discarded hunting tools and even a few legends that are still told today. Their favorite cross mountain trails (primarily in search of food) included what is known today as Trail Ridge Road and through Forest Canyon. During more recent history, Ute Indians were particularly attracted to the green valleys and crystalline waters. The Utes and Arapahoes dominated the area until the late eighteenth century.

In 1803, the land comprising RMNP was acquired as part of the Louisiana Purchase supported by a persistent Thomas Jefferson and a reluctant Congress. Despite the mixed opinions, the U.S. Purchased the land for the (then) exorbitant sum of six million dollars. Prior to the purchase, the land was controlled by France under Napoleon's command, primarily as a fur and trade speculation. Napoleon, being an ocean away, realized he could not protect the claim to the land from the Spaniards to the south and the new settlers to the east. He eagerly sold the land to the U.S., believing it would never amount to anything.

Pioneering settlers and trappers moved west during the mid-eighteen hundreds, supported by the thirst of the U.S. Government to "discover" these new lands due to the lure of bountiful natural resources (lumber and water) and game stock for food and fur, primarily beaver. As settlers populated the area, they eventually displaced the natives, partly by force and partly by the natives' need to move in search of natural resources and land not claimed by white men. Eventually, by the end of the eighteen hundreds, the land comprising the Park was settled by a few prominent families in the towns of Estes Park and Grand Lake.

The Park's Beginnings

During the latter half of the nineteenth century, several conservation and preservation groups, pioneered by the likes of Theodore Roosevelt, John Muir and local naturalist, guide and inspiring nature writer Enos Mills, worked diligently to convince law makers to create the nation's tenth national park. Enos Mills was the most influential, writing over 2,000 letters, presenting 42 lectures, providing 430 photographs of the Park, and authoring 64 newspaper and magazine articles to promote the idea of Rocky Mountain National Park.

Enos Mills came to the Longs Peak area at the age of 14 under medical advice to seek the clean mountain air, citing from his doctor that he would not live to adulthood if he didn't move from the plains of Kansas. He built a small cabin near the base of Longs Peak and from there began his lifelong campaign to shepherd the surrounding lands into a national park. Mills often gave credit to the writings and a chance encounter with John Muir, as a chief influence to become, who we today, call "the father of Rocky Mountain National Park."

On January 26, 1915, President Woodrow Wilson signed the Rocky Mountain National Park Act, and the Park was born. Ironically, John Muir died only a month prior on Christmas Eve 1914. Before his death, Muir wrote to Mills "I will glory in your success *[referencing Mills' efforts to form RMNP]*. Strange that the government is so slow to learn the value of national parks." Just prior to the signing, Congressman Albert Johnson of Washington suggested the Park would make a good leprosarium, a national leper

History

Rocky Mountain National Park's opening day dedication ceremony took place in Horseshoe Park on September 4, 1915. (source: Denver Public Library, Western History Collection, Rh-259. Photo: Harry Mellon Rhoads)

reservation. The Denver Post quickly replied to the Congressman's off-base suggestion, saying "that pinhead from Washington" misunderstood the purpose of a national park.

Early Park stewards realized the advertising benefit of having abundant natural resources to attract visitors. As example, a trout hatchery was built along Fall River Road, providing millions of trout for the Park's waters. And in 1913, elk were transplanted from Montana to reintroduce them into the Park, where they were previously depleted due to over-harvesting. Prior to formalized national park management, rangers in the 1920's lured wildlife roadside by placing salt blocks at strategic locations. They believed the tamed animals served an educational purpose to the visiting public. Superintendent L. Claude Way was quoted saying "The frolicking lambs are especially interesting to travelers and convince a great majority of them that the Kodak furnishes more real and lasting pleasure in game hunting than the gun."

Geography

Rocky Mountain National Park covers 265,758 acres, or 415 square miles. For comparison, the U.S. National Park system has 391 national parks covering 84.3 million acres which attracts 275+ million visitors annually. Rocky Mountain National Park is the seventh-most visited park in the U.S. National Park system, on par with Yellowstone

Rocky Mountain National Park

National Park, despite being only 12% of its size. Today, mostly due to commemoration of the natives by the early white settlers, the Park contains the most concentration of Indian names for geographic features in one small area in the U.S.

Figure 1. - Annual Visitors to Rocky Mountain National Park, 1915 through 2008.

Annual Visitors to RMNP
1915 through 2008

Source: National Park Service data

Annual Visitors and Fishing Days

Each year, three million people visit the Park, with over 70% of the Park's attendance occurring during the months of June through September. As Figure 1 shows, annual attendance has been affected over the years by wars, economic downturns and most recently, the tragic September 11, 2001 terrorist attacks.

While high traffic during the summer months seems daunting, it is estimated that only 2% to 3% of all visitors come to fish its waters. On an average day, that equates to just a few hundred fishers per day. What this means to the fisherman is a solitary day fishing relatively uncontested waters. With this prize however, comes a price; long lines at Park entrances and finding parking at the trailheads. You, along with day hikers, photography buffs, rock climbers, naturalists, families and artists use the trails to get away for a few hours. Finding parking at the Bear Lake trailhead after 9 AM on a weekend during the summer months is nearly impossible. It's best to park at the remote lots and take the bus to the Glacier Gorge or Bear Lake trailhead. However, it's not that easy for other trailheads which have limited space and no bus service to a remote lot. Warning served; if you want to fish during the summer months, be prepared to get to the trailhead well before 9 AM

Table 1. - Visitor Percentages by Month - Rocky Mountain National Park.

Winter	%	Spring	%	Summer	%	Fall	%
December	2%	March	3%	June	15%	September	15%
January	2%	April	2%	July	22%	October	8%
February	2%	May	6%	August	19%	November	3%

Source: National Park Service data

Visitor Facts

to get a parking spot. This even applies to some of the more remote trailheads such as Corral Creek, North Fork and Wild Basin. This isn't such bad news, though. Getting an early start often yields the best fishing of the day.

Trails and Roads

The Park has 355 miles of trails rated from easy to extremely challenging. Over 260 miles are open to private and commercial horse use. The Park has 82 miles of paved roads and 28 miles of unpaved roads.

Trail Ridge Road is the most direct road connecting the east and west sides of the Park. It winds 48 miles from the junction of US 36 and US 34 in Estes Park to just past the Kawuneeche Visitor Center on the west side of the Park. The road got its name as it was built on the trails the Ute and Arapaho Indians used to

Trail Ridge Road offers drive-by vistas seen no where else in the Park.

hunt and gather from the land long before it became a national park. When finished in 1932, the design of the road never exceeded 7% grade with much of it being 5% grade. This design made travel on the road easy for foot travelers, those on horseback and those driving motor vehicles. Today, bicyclists find the road an invigorating exercise circuit. Eight miles of the road is above 11,000 feet with the road peaking at 12,183 feet, making it the highest continuously paved road in the U.S. Ten miles are above tree line.

With the high elevation comes frequent snow, wind and rain. The road is generally open from the last week of May until the third week of October. However, the open and close dates change yearly since they are dependent upon seasonal snow fall and ice conditions. It is best to check the Trail Ridge Road status line by calling (970) 586-1222, or by visiting http://www.cotrip.org/roadConditions.htm. The website provides road conditions for the Park and area as well as major roads throughout the state.

Park Entrances and Fees

The Park entrance fee, as of 2011, is $20 per automobile and is valid for seven consecutive days inclusive of the day of purchase. A Rocky Mountain National Parks Pass costs $40 and is good for one year from the date of purchase. For $10 more, the $50 Rocky Mountain National Parks Pass is combined with the Arapahoe National Recreation Area Annual Pass and is good for one year from the date of purchase. An annual National Parks Pass is $80 which allows entrance into all U.S. National Parks and Federal Lands. Seniors can purchase a $10 lifetime National Parks Pass, which is quite a bargain in itself. Those with disabilities are eligible for a free National Parks pass. Entrance fees change from time-to-time, so it's best to check the most current fees by visiting http://www.nps.gov/romo/index.htm or by calling (970) 586-1206.

Rocky Mountain National Park

Accessibility (Handicap Access)

While the Park is noted for its rocky and rugged terrain, accessible trails have been constructed in areas of stunning beauty.

Coyote Valley Trail (at the trailhead of the same name) in the Kawuneeche Valley is a 1-mile trail that regularly offers moose and elk sightings. It follows a braided section of the Colorado River which contains brook and brown trout.

Sprague Lake offers an accessible back country campsite and plenty of fishing around its perimeter for eager brook trout, brown trout and an occasional rainbow.

Lily Lake has ample parking and a mile long accessible trail well suited to fishing for greenback cutthroat found in the lake.

Other sites providing wheelchair access include Beaver Ponds Boardwalk and sections of Bear Lake Trail.

Back Country Camping and Permits

The Park has 269 back country sites. Permits are required for all overnight camping in the Park. Permits currently cost $20 per reservation and can be obtained by calling (970) 586-1242 (Summer Hours: 7am - 7pm daily) or by writing:

Backcountry/Wilderness Permits
Rocky Mountain National Park
1000 Highway 36
Estes Park, CO 80517

While more shy than elk or deer, Rocky Mountain Bighorn Sheep can be seen climbing around rock out-croppings and at the edge of grassy areas flanked by rocky nearby cover. Look for bighorn sheep at higher and cooler altitudes most of the summer.

Regulations

Be sure to include your name, address, zip code and telephone number. Request the back country sites you wish to reserve and the number in your party. The $20 fee doesn't need to be sent in at the time of requesting reservations. It can be paid when visiting any back country office to pick up your back country permit. Written requests for permits can be made anytime after March 1 for the current year. Phone-in reservations are limited to March 1 - May 15 each year and after October 1, for dates within that calendar year. It is best to visit any back country office a day or two prior to your trip to obtain the back country permits best suited to your travel itinerary.

Accessing many of the remote locations discussed in this book requires back country camping for at least an overnight stay. Fees and rules may change. It is best to visit the Park's website at http://www.nps.gov/romo/index.htm and search for the Back Country Camping Guide for the most current and up-to-date information.

Fishing Licenses and Fees

A valid Colorado fishing license is required for all persons 16 years of age or older to fish in Rocky Mountain National Park. No other permit is necessary; however, special regulations exist. A summary of the current regulations at the time of print follows. It is your responsibility to know the current regulations and obey them. Current regulations for the Park and all Colorado fishing can be found at: http://wildlife.state.co.us/Fishing/.

- Each person shall use only one hand-held rod or line.
- A second rod stamp is not honored in Park waters.
- Only artificial lures or flies with one (single, double, or treble) hook with a common shank may be used. *("Artificial flies or lures" means devices made entirely of, or a combination of, materials such as wood, plastic, glass, hair, metal, feathers, or fiber, designed to attract fish.)* NOTE: This does not include:
  a) any hand moldable material designed to attract fish by the sense of taste or smell
  b) any device to which scents or smell attractants have been externally applied
  c) molded plastic devices less than one and one-half inch in length
  d) Foods
  e) traditional organic baits such as worms, grubs, crickets, leeches, minnows, and fish eggs, and
  f) manufactured baits such as imitation fish eggs, dough baits, or stink baits.
- Fly fishers may utilize a two fly rig, where one hook is used as an attractant.
- While in possession of any fishing equipment, bait for fishing (insects, fish eggs, minnows, or other organic matter) or worms is prohibited.
- Children 12 years of age or under, however, may use worms or preserved fish eggs in all park waters open to fishing except those designated as catch-and release areas.
- No bait or worms are allowed in catch-and-release waters.
- Use of lead sinkers (or other lead fishing materials) is strongly discouraged.

Possession Limits

This is general information only. A complete listing of regulations is available at Park visitor centers and ranger stations. Possession Limit means the numbers, sizes, or species of fish, fresh or preserved, a person may have. These provisions have Park-wide application and are detailed below.

- Possession Limit: eight (8) fish, six (6) must be brook trout

Four bull elk keep their distance from the author and his wife as they snowshoe around the Park in February of 2007.

- Rainbow, brown, Colorado River, and generic cutthroat trout: two (2) fish, 10" or greater
- Greenback cutthroat trout: zero (0), greenback cutthroat trout fishing is strictly Catch and Release (CnR) only
- Brook trout: six (6), eight (8) if no other species present, any size
- Brook trout bonus: ten (10), 8" or less

As you can see, the brook trout possession regulations encourage harvesting a few once in awhile. This is a good practice for the species, as brook trout reproduce quickly and provide unnecessary competition for other species, particularly native species such as Colorado River cutthroat and greenback cutthroat. In lakes like Box Lake, brook trout are so plentiful that stunting (big heads, small bodies) occurs due to overpopulation with a limited forage base. So, don't feel bad about keeping a few brook trout every so often when fishing the Park. You can't beat a fresh brook trout dinner.

I have, on rare occasions, kept a brook trout or two for a stream-side dinner whilst camping at a remote back-country site. However, since no open fires are permitted in the Park, and due to the mess a fish can make in a pan, I limit this luxury to when I know I won't be inviting any large critters later, such as bears. As a good rule of thumb, it's best to leave the brook trout feast to the kitchen table.

For all other species in the Park, practicing CnR is strongly recommended, even if the regulations permit keeping a modest amount.

Pets

Many fisherman, me included, like to take dogs with them as they hike and fish. There is no better fishing companion; dogs and fishing just go together. However, pets are not allowed on Park trails, period. Leashed pets are allowed in motor vehicle camp grounds, roadside picnic areas and along roadsides, mostly as a consideration for those who travel and vacation with their pets.

Regulations

Seasonal Animal Protection Closures

In order to protect the Park's resources, certain areas are closed to access and use. These closures are mostly seasonal, with very few in effect year round. The closures can affect access to some fishing destinations in the Park. Two such fauna deserve special discussion: elk and eagles.

ELK: *(From the National Park Service website)* To prevent disturbance and harassment of elk during the fall mating period and to enhance visitor elk-viewing opportunities, closures in Horseshoe Park, Moraine Park, Upper Beaver Meadows, and the Kawuneeche Valley area are in place from August 30 through October 25, annually. These closures are for travel on foot or horse off established roadways or designated trails from 5:00 p.m. to 7:00 a.m.

EAGLES: *(From the National Park Service website)* Lower Colorado River (between Shadow Mountain Lake and Lake Granby) - Closed mid-November through mid-March. Closures will be lifted or extended as necessary. The Colorado River and a zone 300 yards wide on both sides of the river are closed to human entry from mid-November through mid-March. Hiking on Ranger Meadows Loop trail, outside the closure, is permitted. Approximately 12-15 bald eagles come here each winter to live and hunt for fish along these open sections of the Colorado River. When food is scarce and temperatures are cold, bald eagles waste vital energy fleeing from human disturbance.

While this is not an all-inclusive list of closures, closure notices are posted throughout the Park. Or, stop in at a Park visitor center to receive updated closure information before you set off on a hike or fishing excursion. The penalty for entering a closed area is steep - violators are subject to a fine of $5,000 and/or six months imprisonment.

There are four separate identifiable species of cutthroat trout in the Park (Greenback, Yellowstone, Colorado River and a generic hybridized species) all easily identified with the characteristic vibrant crimson slash under the jaws leading back to the gills.

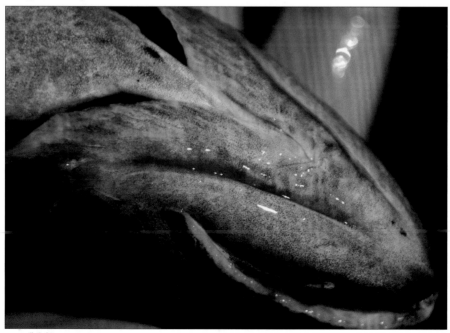

Section II
Hiking in the Park

OPPOSITE: *The trail beyond Fourth Lake is unimproved. Ironically the sign marking the trail needs improvement too.*

Rocky Mountain National Park

Essential Hiking Gear

For day hikes, specialized hiking gear is not necessary. A sturdy pair of walking or athletic shoes are all that is needed for a trek to fishable waters. During the summer, I prefer to wear a durable pair of hiking shorts with plenty of pockets, and wet wade most of the time, hiking in and out of the shoes I wet wade in. During the fringe seasons of spring and fall, I prefer to wear a comfortable pair of convertible travel pants to give a bit of warmth during the chilly days. I might even wear a thin layer of polypropylene underneath for extra warmth when snow is in the forecast. When not wet wading, I wear high-rise Gortex™ lined hiking boots. With them, I can wade in 6-8" of stream water or rock-hop shorelines of lakes to advantageous casting positions, carefully, I might add. Occasionally, I will pack in lightweight waders and sandals or even a pack float tube to fish productive areas of high mountain lakes, especially during colder fringe season days. It should be noted that waders are usually not necessary to reach tantalizing fishing water. Rare is the day you will see a float tuber on a lake. If you do, it just might be me or one of my equally fly-fishing-crazed friends.

I maintain a fanny pack pre-stocked with essentials: an energy bar or two (or a sandwich, a salty snack and a piece of fruit), two liters of water, a Park map (I recommend National Geographic's Trails Illustrated Map #200 - Rocky Mountain National Park), a multi-tool, a working lighter, a mini headlamp, a rain shell, a compass, a notepad and pen, bug spray and a basic assortment of first-aid items such as Band-Aids® and ibuprofen. Except the food, with this pre-stocked fanny pack I can grab-n-go without having to worry that I have forgotten an essential.

For extended trips of two or more days, I'll pack in a tent, sleeping bag, extra clothes, water filter, fuel stove and dehydrated food commensurate with the number of days I'll be in the back country. I find a 4,000 cubic inch pack (60-65 liters) is quite sufficient for a 3-5 day jaunt, including fishing gear. Note that waders and boots are not part of my necessary pack list. I have found that packing waders and boots only adds weight to the pack and usually doesn't yield any extra advantage in accessing fish. With that said, when I do pack waders, I don't pack boots. Instead, I pack Teva sandals or Crocs which make adequate wading shoes to protect the wader feet, not to mention they are light weight, water-friendly and double as fine camp shoes. Be careful however, when wading in shoes that don't have a felt bottom, as they will be slippery on stream bottoms.

Seasons of the Park

The weather in the Park can be unpredictable any time of the year, and you should always be prepared for the worst a season can offer. This means a rain or winter jacket, extra warm clothes (such as polar fleece), plenty of water and some extra energy bars or snacks.

During the high tourist season, many folks not accustomed to high-altitude come into the Park driving through the town of Estes Park noting the temperature is moderate and comfortable. They hit the trail wearing the same clothes they wore driving in; often shorts and a t-shirt. However, as they gain elevation, they get chilly and eventually will experience cooler winds or precipitation. The temperature gets cooler the higher one goes. A rule of thumb to remember is the temperature drops approximately two to three degrees Fahrenheit for every 1,000 feet in altitude gain. So, if it's a comfortable sunny 70F at 7,500 feet in Estes Park, it can be roughly 55F to 60F at 11,500 feet at tree line under the same conditions. Again, prepare accordingly and don't underestimate the power of inclement weather over unprepared hikers.

Seasons and Hazards

SPRING: In the spring, warming weather entices many to hit the trails to shake the 'cabinitis' from the bones. If you look for fishing water during the spring, stick to lower altitude streams that are thawing free of ice cover. Don't waste your time or put yourself in danger by seeking any lakes above 9,000 feet. They will all be frozen until mid-to late June. Rare is the day to find a lake free of ice in May. Daily temperatures can range from below freezing to the mid 50s, however higher temperatures are rare. Expect temperatures in the high 20s to low 40s Fahrenheit.

SUMMER: In early summer (June), the lakes start freeing themselves of their ice cover and can offer some of the most exciting fishing of the season: ice-off fishing. Of course, traipsing around looking for ice-out fishing will have you post-holing waist deep in snow and forging past crowd-beaten snow paths on your own. Be prepared with proper gear and extra food and water. Daily temperatures become more comfortable during this time of year, ranging from the low 40s to the mid 70s Fahrenheit.

Throughout summer, the fishing can be unparalleled and spectacular, especially when dry fly fishing heats up. Be cautious though; the weather during the summer can be just as harsh and unforgiving as in the winter. Daily bouts of rain showers and lightning strikes are common. I call it Dr. Pepper weather because around 10am, 2pm and 4pm every day in the summer, you can expect a rain squall, high winds, lightning and even sleet or hail. Daily temperatures become more consistent in the low 60s to mid 80s. Night time temperatures can still dip down to the mid 40's Fahrenheit, so be prepared for chilly nights if you spend some time in the back country.

FALL: When fall arrives, the crowds recede and the fishing remains spectacular. Fall also brings back the blustery and chilly days, even when the sun is shining. Expect stronger winds, making lake fishing during the fall more of a hit-miss opportunity. It won't be uncommon to experience sleet and hail while hiking in the fall - prepare accordingly. Focusing on streams and rivers is a best bet. Daily temperatures resemble early summer ranges with nightly dips into the mid to low 30's Fahrenheit.

Daily storms are a norm for the Park. Frequently, a mid-day summer squall can roll in without warning packing high winds, driving rain, lightning and hail in a 15 minute span. In this photo of a lightning and hail storm, skies were sunny just a half-hour before.

Rocky Mountain National Park

Focusing on streams and rivers is a best bet. Daily temperatures resemble early summer ranges with nightly dips into the mid to low 30's Fahrenheit.

WINTER: Winter weather in the Park is not too conducive to fishing, although some open water in any of the lower meadows can offer some fishing opportunity, albeit difficult. What is more appealing in the winter months are the photo opportunities with most everything covered in pristine virgin snow cover. Even the most sunny of days can still yield high temperatures in the high teens. As it rains frequently in the spring and summer, it snows equally during the winter. Be cautious of walking or snowshoeing over flowing water as the snow may give way and you'll end up wet and cold, which is extremely dangerous and potentially life-threatening.

Hazards in the Park

LIGHTNING is an ever-present feature of the Park. I call it a feature because it can be as beautifully stunning as it is dangerous. Lightning most often strikes in the afternoon; it can strike at anytime, however. Close-quarters or approaching lightning creates a distinctive 'electric' smell in the air. If you sense or see lightning, go below tree line and away from open low-lying areas such as lakes, gullies and small crevices. It's best to find the nearest dense thicket of trees and find cover within, or better yet to find a valley or canyon and find cover at the bottom. And by all means, don't fish during the threat of nearby lightning strikes. Flinging a fly rod only acts as an attractant.

TICKS can be present from early spring through mid-summer. They are most common east of the Continental Divide. However, most hikers never have problems with ticks. The best way to prevent any ticks from hitching a ride is to wear light-colored long pants and long-sleeved shirts. After a day of hiking, especially if you go off-trail, do a thorough check of your clothes and skin for any small ticks. They will be about 1/8" long and reddish brown.

Lyme disease bacteria are found in Black-legged Ticks, which are specific to white-tailed deer. Currently there are no white-tailed deer in the Park, only mule deer, however as white-tailed deer populations continue to rise, the possibility of introducing the Rocky Mountain Tick into the Park becomes increasingly real. To date, no cases of Lyme disease have been reported in the Park area.

UNDERESTIMATING TRAIL TRAVEL TIME is an unspoken hazard. Each year, many folks not accustomed to hiking in mountainous conditions temporarily find themselves hiking back under the cover of darkness, which can be daunting to say the least - when it gets dark in the Park, it gets *dark and chilly*. While this isn't necessarily a hazard if sticking to a trail, it becomes a hazard if you venture off trail while fishing your way up a stream, for example. As a rule of thumb a hiker in reasonable health can cover one to two miles per hour going uphill and two to three miles per hour going downhill. A seasoned hiker carrying a good pace can average two miles per hour uphill and four miles per hour downhill. Be sure to consider your travel time back when jaunting off in the Park looking for fishable waters.

DEADFALL FROM BEETLE KILL is a burgeoning issue in the Park. The Mountain Pine Beetle develops in Ponderosa, Lodgepole, Scotch and Limber Pine trees. As they mature, they transmit the bluestain fungi to the host tree. Once infected, there is nothing that can effectively be done to save the tree. Infected trees rapidly die and become fodder for wind-blown dead-fall and kindling for forest fires. The Colorado State Forest has prioritized the removal of dead infected trees near roadsides, campsites and trails outside of the Park. However, trees not removed pose an unpredictable hazard in the back-country. Be observant of the area around you - do not pitch a tent or stop for a rest

Health and First Aid

where you suspect an infected tree can be toppled over by a strong gust of wind. And certainly be cautious in using camp stoves near a stand of infected pines. It's worth re-mentioning here - open flame fires are not allowed in the Park.

Removing an Impaled Fishing Hook

It will happen to the best of us at least once in a lifetime; you'll stick yourself with an errant cast or just plain grab a hook the wrong way and presto - it's firmly planted in your finger. Or worse, an over-eager cast drives the fly and hook firmly into your ear. The initial pain is sharp and you are rendered helpless for a few moments until you collect yourself and assess what to do next. Somehow, you have to remove the hook. There are three primary ways to remove a fishing hook from impalement: 1) Retrograde Method, 2) Advance and Cut Method, and 3) String-Pull Method.

However, the absolute best way to help prevent serious injury from hook impalement is to fish with barbless hooks, which should be your standard practice. It's more humane and healthy for fish and it will make it a heckuva lot easier to remove a hook if it gets stuck in you.

Most embedded fishhooks occur in superficial tissue and may be removed streamside without local anesthesia or special skill. Be aware however, that larger hooks, ones that are deeply embedded or in unusual places (ie: nose, ears, eye area or genitalia) are best treated by a qualified emergency physician. A tetanus toxoid injection should be administered if it has been longer than five years since being vaccinated. As with any contaminated wound, any signs of infection such as: redness of the area, swelling, pus drainage or skin that is hot to touch should be treated by a physician.

If possible the wound should be disinfected with an iodine-based, hydrogen peroxide or hexachlorophene solution prior to removal of the fish hook. At a minimum, rinse the wound thoroughly with clean water (bottled water or tap water is best) after removing the hook. If no method for cleaning the wound is available, letting the wound bleed freely for a few moments will aid in removal of bacteria from the puncture wound site. If the hook is impaled in a location other than the face, neck, ears or eyes, you probably have a good chance of helping yourself.

Figure 2 illustrates what to do for a shallow, moderate and deep hook impalement.

Retrograde Fish Hook Removal

This technique works the best with very superficially embedded or barbless hooks. If significant resistance is met while employing this technique, another method should be utilized.

Downward pressure is applied to the shank of the hook while backing the hook out of the point of entry.

Advance and Cut Fish Hook Removal

This tried and true method of hook removal is the one that is most legendary, but is actually quite painful and does cause additional tissue trauma. However, it may be the most practical solution if a very large hook is embedded, particularly if the tip is close to the surface of the skin. It is necessary to have a good multi-tool or wire cutting plier to utilize this technique.

Rotate the shank of the hook away from the barb, forcing the tip through the skin – removed the barb with a wire cutter. The now barbless hook is rotated back out of the path of entry.

Rocky Mountain National Park

String-Pull Fish Hook Removal

The string-pull technique is a highly effective modification of the retrograde technique and is also referred to as the "stream" technique. It is commonly performed in the field and is believed to be the least traumatic because it creates no new wounds and rarely requires anesthesia. A readily available "string" to the angler is the fishing line itself – however, any type of lightweight, sturdy string will suffice.

Loop the string around the bend of the fishhook, holding the free ends tightly or wrapping them around an object like a short stick. Keep the hooked area of tissue flat and stable while depressing the "eye" end of the hook shank. When the angle of the string and the shank of the hook are parallel give a quick yank on the string while keeping shank depressed – it doesn't take a lot of force, so be wary of the hook as it comes free and takes flight.

Altitude Sickness

Altitude sickness (also called Acute Mountain Sickness) encompasses a variety of symptoms ranging from mild to life-threatening, and results from the body's inability to adjust to the physiologic demands and decreased oxygen availability at altitude. Altitude sickness is most common at elevations higher than 8,000 feet above sea level and when the rate of ascent exceeds 1,000 feet per day. Research suggests that up to one in four people which travel to Colorado will develop some form of altitude sickness.

Things that may contribute to development of altitude sickness include ascending too quickly, over-exertion, dehydration, hypothermia, consuming alcohol or other sedatives.

Some of the symptoms of altitude sickness may include fatigue, headache, dizziness, insomnia, shortness of breath during exertion, nausea, decreased appetite, extremity swelling and social withdrawal. Serious symptoms include shortness of breath at rest, gurgling respirations with wet cough and frothy sputum, confusion, decreased coordination and fever.

In general, most symptoms will subside by descending to a lower altitude. Ways to mitigate symptoms include slowing the rate of ascent, keeping well nourished and hydrated, staying warm, and resting frequently. Acetaminophen is generally recommended for mild headache. Remember that although altitude sickness is simple to treat initially, symptoms can quickly worsen and be potentially life-threatening. All serious symptoms should be treated immediately by descending to a lower altitude and seeking medical attention.

Dehydration

Almost 70% of an adult's body weight is made of water and a typical, healthy adult needs to consume between two to three quarts of water each day. Dehydration occurs when there is a deficiency in the body's water supply. This of course, occurs more frequently with exertion, heat, elevation and dry climate – all of which you might experience while searching out that perfect fishing spot in the Rocky Mountains.

Symptoms of dehydration include lightheadedness, headache, rapid heart rate, dry mouth, decreased urine output, weakness, confusion and, in extreme cases, unconsciousness.

The best rule of thumb for remaining well hydrated is "drink before you get thirsty". Thirst indicates that you may already be dehydrated. It is best to be proactive and to plan ahead for your fluid intake needs before you set out on your adventure. For an average day hike, plan generously and bring two to three quarts of water, and a high quality water filter for re-filling your bottles on the move. You may need up to six quarts of water on

Health and First Aid

Figure 2. - Fishing Hook Removal Methods

Three Fishing Hook Removal Methods Compared

Shallow Impalement	Moderate Impalement	Deep Impalement
Retrograde Method	**Advance and Cut Method**	**String-Pull Method**
Use this method for shallow impalements or with barbless hooks	Use this method for moderate impalements where rotating the hook point and barb outward is possible	Use this method for deep impalements where accessing the hook point and barb is not advantageous
Preparation	Preparation	Preparation
Cleanse the area with an alcohol wipe or hand soap and water	Cleanse the area with an alcohol wipe or hand soap and water Access a pair of wire cutters or a multi-tool with wire cutting capability	Cleanse the area with an alcohol wipe or hand soap and water Prepare a 12" section of small sturdy string, nylon thread or fishing monofilament

STEP I

Carefully rotate the hook backwards by pushing down towards the eye of the hook while pulling out on the bend.

STEP I

Carefully rotate the hook forward to expose the hook point and barb.

STEP I

Carefully rotate the hook backwards by pushing down on the shank of the hook while pulling out on the bend of the hook.

STEP 2

Using wire cutters, snip off the hook point behind the barb. If this is not possible, flatten the hook barb with pliers.

STEP 2

Attach a string to the bend of the hook by forming a loop. Position the hook shank parallel to the skin. Firmly grasp the string and pull snug against the hook bend.

STEP 3

Rotate the hook backwards to remove the de-barbed hook bend. Apply sting ointment immediately afterwards.

STEP 3

While applying firm downward pressure on the hook bend, quickly and confidently tug on the string to pull the hook bend out of the skin. Apply sting ointment immediately afterwards.

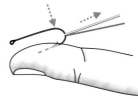

Rocky Mountain National Park

a strenuous day. When filtering water, select clear streams and filter from water that is moving.

Hydration status can be gauged by assessing the color of your urine – the lighter colored the urine, the better hydrated you are. Also be aware of your need to urinate, if you are well hydrated, you should be urinating every 2-3 hours. Commercially made electrolyte drinks may help in replacing valuable electrolytes lost through sweating. Caffeinated and alcoholic beverages and antihistamines should be avoided as these will cause further dehydration.

Frostbite

Frostbite refers to a family of cold-induced injuries, ranging from frost nip (common and generally mild) to deep frostbite that may involve loss of tissue. Frostbite is literally caused by tissue freezing to some degree and is typically accompanied by hypothermia. Frostbite is often seen in alcoholics, smokers, those who are fatigued and/or dehydrated. As the body cools in response to exposure, blood is shunted from the extremities to the central core of the body to protect the vital organs. This leaves areas like fingertips, toes, nose and ear lobes vulnerable to tissue freezing. Symptoms may include numbness, tingling, itching/burning sensation, blue or white discolored skin and hardened or blistered tissue.

At the first sign of frostbite, every effort should be made to increase circulation to the affected areas and to generally get warm. Some techniques that may be effective are applying friction like rubbing fingers and toes, or doing jumping jacks to increase circulation to extremities. Remove any wet clothing, keep affected areas clean and dry, and remove any constrictive clothing and jewelry. Keep well hydrated and drink warm fluid if possible. Ibuprofen may help relieve the pain and decrease swelling to the area. If frostbite is severe and there is a chance that that you might not be able to get and stay warm, don't attempt to re-warm the affected area, as the cycle of freeze-thaw-freeze can cause even greater tissue damage.

Hypothermia

Hypothermia is a potentially life-threatening risk of adventure sports in the Rocky Mountains. Fortunately, it is often preventable with some basic knowledge and preparation. Hypothermia is described as a decrease in the core body temperature to a level at which normal muscular and cerebral functions are impaired. Things that may increase your risk of developing hypothermia are being wet, improperly clothed, fatigued, dehydrated, or intoxicated.

It is important to dress in layers, as Colorado can have a wide range of weather in a very short period of time. In cool temperatures, it is best to "un-layer" as you heat up, preventing your clothing from being soaked with sweat. Evaporative cooling from wet clothes can quickly lead to hypothermia in cool environments.

Symptoms of hypothermia include shivering which can become violent and later stop when exhaustion sets in, decreased motor coordination which can lead to coma and death, slurred speech, decreased cognition, muscle rigidity, or skin discoloration.

Treatment is focused on warming up; increase activity – run in place or do jumping jacks to increase circulation. Get wet clothes off and get dry and sheltered. Build a fire – apply heat (like heated rocks, water bottles or towels) to armpits, groin and head. Stay

OPPOSITE: North Colorado Med Evac helicopter rescue service (1-800-247-5433) has two helicopters in the RMNP area that are available 24 hours a day for extreme emergencies.

Health and First Aid

hydrated and eat carbohydrates or sugar. Share body heat with others and get out of the wind.

Preparedness and Emergency Response

Getting away from it all comes at a risk, and the mountains can be inherently dangerous. Be aware of your resources in the areas where you are hiking – emergency care is available in the mountains, but may be delayed due to lack of communication, remote access and limited manpower.

When extreme emergencies arise and minutes count, the only way to rescue is by helicopter. Anyone can request helicopter transport to a known location or GPS coordinate – the experienced pilots will determine a safe area to land and coordinate with emergency ground crews to bring the most appropriate care to you.

If you are in the back country, calling a rescue service may be difficult due to no cell signal. There are some things you can do to help in advance. Prepare and leave behind a hiking plan with friends or relatives and register at trailhead if available (there's a mandatory registration when you pick up your back country permit). Tell others what trail you'll be taking and how long you expect to be, including when you are expected to return.

In the event you or a hiking partner becomes injured and cannot make it out under self-power, there are several common-sense steps to take before leaving for help. First, ensure the injured is kept warm, dry and sheltered. Wrap them in extra clothing, a sleeping bag or an emergency blanket. In extreme conditions, building a fire near the injured to keep them warm is an option, but comes with additional potential dangers. Typically, this is an option to consider only during the winter. Fires also act as a location beacon. Note: Building fires for emergency response is *the only time* where open flames in the Park are tolerated.

Secondly, ensure they have plenty of water to quench thirst and wash injuries. Ibuprofen helps ease the pain. If the injury is really bad, help them secure a comfortable position without moving them too much. If the injury includes debilitating broken skin or bones, apply general first aid by rinsing and covering the wound areas to help prevent infection. Don't attempt to 'fix' broken bones, you may make things worse.

Thirdly, leave them with a way to signal; a whistle or a mirror are common items. Then go for help. Make sure you know how to get back to the injured, mark the trail if necessary.

Section III
Fishing the Park

OPPOSITE: *High altitude creeks run clear nearly year-round. The super clear water makes trout skittish. Fishing dries well upstream of feeding fish is effective when fishing this type of water.*

Photo: *Chris Bowell*

www.flyfishingrmnp.com   *33*

Rocky Mountain National Park

Essential Fly Fishing Gear

Fishing gear preferences can be as personal and unique as a name. But there are some basics to know about gearing up for the Park. For most applications, a 3-4 weight, 8-foot rod is quite sufficient. Occasionally, I will use a 5-weight, 9-foot rod for windy conditions, especially when fishing lakes, but often this is too much muscle for streams. For smaller stream fishing, an 8 foot rod in 3- to 4-weights will allow you to cast in tight confines. I prefer 4-piece rods which pack and carry nicely on day or extended day hikes. Occasionally, I will traverse a trail with my rod strung and ready to go, however, this tactic falls apart when following a stream through heavy cover. The potential to break a rod increases. So, I generally hike to my fishing destination with my rod packed away and assemble it upon arrival.

A selection of leaders need not be extensive; two basic types are adequate. For stream fishing, a seven to nine foot leader terminating into 5X tippet is quite sufficient. For lake fishing, longer leaders and finer tippet might be required - consider using a nine to eleven foot leaders terminating in 6X for dry flies in sizes 18 through 22. When fishing in lakes with nymphs a 5X tippet is perfectly sufficient. For ultra-finicky trout, before going with a smaller sized tippet consider lengthening the current tippet to provide a bit of "slack" in the leader, which allows the nymph or dry to more naturally move with the currents of the water. This is the basic premise behind George Harvey's slack line leader concept. For more information on leader designs, read *"The Global Fly Fisher's Guide to Hand-Tied Fly Fishing Leaders"*, found at www.globalflyfisher.com/fishbetter/leadercalc/. If you want to try your hand at tying your own leaders, download the accompanying interactive MS-Excel™ spreadsheet tool, *LeaderCalc*, which contains over 120 different leader formulas for all situations.

Since the trout in the Park have a short growing season, they are generally willing to take any decently-presented fly. This means the selection of flies you carry need not be extensive. I carry a few medium-sized 8-compartment fly boxes chock-full of hoppers, ants, para-adams, hare's ears, Tabou Caddis, San Juan worms, damsel nymphs, scuds, Pheasant Tails, egg patterns, stonefly nymphs, drab colored Woolly Buggers and Elk-Hair Caddis. I also carry nippers, 3x-6x tippet, an extra leader or two, floatant and yarn bobber (ok, fly fishers call them strike indicators) or two. This all fits into a small fly fishing pack (a fly fishing purse as my brother refers to it) which can fit in a backpack or fanny pack without taking up too much room. Fifty percent of the time I fish a terrestrial pattern on top or drowned just below the surface, which means I still carry too much.

Lakes, Rivers, Streams and Creeks of RMNP

The Park contains approximately 139 lakes (1,100 acres) and 369 miles of rivers, streams and creeks. *Note: The charts and tables in this book reference 90% of the lakes and streams in the Park, focusing on named bodies of water and significant flowages, not covering seasonal bodies of water or drainages. The lakes and referenced in this book cover nearly 1,000 acres of surface water and all 369 miles of flowing water, respectively.* There are currently 54 lakes (39% in total) in the Park which have known populations of fish. Likewise, there are 111 flowing waters (53% in total) that contain known populations of fish. This amount of water presents the fisher with plenty of opportunity to fish a multitude of water types for the Park's six primary types of trout (brook, brown, rainbow, greenback cutthroat, Yellowstone cutthroat, and Colorado River cutthroat).

The growth season of a trout in the Park is relatively short simply due to sub-freezing temperatures lasting from late September or early October through mid-May or early June

Fly Fishing Gear

each year. This leaves a short period each year of about four months where riparian, stream insect and terrestrial growth is robust enough to promote trout population and size growth. Ironically, while the cold and clear water limits population growth, it does extend the life of lake fish, sometimes to up to 15 years of age.

Volunteer Angler's Reports: Doing Your Part

Since 1984, a volunteer angler creel survey has been conducted to assess angler success, fish population health and the distribution of species. The data is compiled by FWS and analyzed annually. Anglers are asked to pick up a Volunteer Angler Report from any Park entrance station, visitor center or back country office. Despite anglers occasionally mis-identifying fish and even listing fish species caught that are not known to exist in the Park, the creel surveys provide valuable data on species distribution. Here's an open calling for every angler to pick up a creel card and complete it after a day fishing in the Park. In fact, while you are picking one up, pick up a few extra and keep them with you if you are going to fish the Park multiple times in the same year. They are submitted anonymously, so no one will ever know if you catch only 1 fish or 100; and frankly it doesn't matter how many you catch or how big they are. What's important is that you do your simple part in helping restore the fisheries within Rocky Mountain National Park.

Figure 3. - A Volunteer Angler Report, available at any Park visitor center.

Volunteer Angler Report Results 2004 through 2008

Angler reports are only as good as the information provided. At the end of the day, anglers estimate quantities and size to the best of their memory, but the report may not be totally accurate. Despite the inherent inaccuracies of volunteer reports, the data does contribute to the management of the fisheries in the Park by suggesting trends and angler tendencies.

Over a five-year period from 2004 to 2008 nearly 1,700 angler days were logged, reporting just shy of 9,700 fish caught. Eighty percent were cutthroat - the specific species not broken out, although a majority were most likely greenback cutthroat. Thirty-five percent were brook trout and 9% were brown trout. Only 3% reported caught were rainbow trout.

Rocky Mountain National Park

Eighty-nine percent of the angler reports were for waters east of the Continental Divide. However, anglers reported they caught on average four fish per hour on the west side of the Continental Divide versus two per hour on the east. More fishing pressure on the east side by novice anglers could explain the difference. Anglers reported harvesting 247 fish during that five year stretch, a rate of 1 fish every 7 angler days. A catch and release rate of 97.5% is impressive given the generous harvest allowances for brook trout in the Park.

Being Stewards of the Park

As a visitor to the Park, you have two responsibilities; to thoroughly enjoy the Park and to leave it as you found it so it can be enjoyed again and again. This was the premise of Enos Mills' efforts to secure the land as a national park.

LNT (Leave No Trace) doesn't just apply to back country campers. The Park is not immune to clues left behind by previous fishers. Consider picking small bits of trash up and carrying it out with you - which abides by another rule of back country camping, Pack It Out. I often carry a gallon-sized zip-lock plastic bag with me to stow any trash I find. As I exit the trail for the day, I either place it in a trash canister or simply take it home with me to dispose of later.

There are also plenty of ways to lend a hand to the chronically under-funded national park system (to the tune of a $600 million nationwide deficit per recent accounts). Just stop in at any Visitor's Center or back country office to inquire about opportunities for volunteering. You can also contact the Rocky Mountain Nature Association at http://www.rmna.org to inquire about volunteer opportunities on the myriad of Park projects they conduct annually.

Ethics and Courtesy in Fishing

I occasionally run into an unethical or disrespectful fishermen. The most prominent issue I encounter is trash littering trails: trash such as cigarette butts, leader packs, coiled leader material, candy wrappers and drink bottles. I've even found broken reels and rods left behind. There's a really simple solution - if you pack it in, pack it out. It honestly doesn't take any extra effort to pack trash out. There are trash cans at most every trailhead that make it real easy to discard trash as you exit the trail.

Another issue I occasionally see is crowding another fisher. I must admit, however, this has seemed to subside over the past few years. The rule of thumb is to give another fisher plenty of space to fish the area around him including allowing him to fish in solitude as much as possible. Generally on streams and creeks, if you can see another fisher, you are too close. Move on and find another stretch of water that gives you your own solitude and opportunity. For lakes, use prudent judgement to stay out of range of a fellow fisher. Give him or her plenty of casting distance on either side of him and then move down some more. There's plenty of fishing water in the Park to allow every fisher on any given day plenty of solitude.

An issue that sparks controversy amongst the best of anglers is "should one fish for spawning fish?" The premise is that it becomes easier to catch spawning fish. I believe the real issue is whether you should *harvest* fish during spawning season. I do not target spawning fish as a practice, primarily because I believe spawning fish should be left alone in order to create more fish to catch in future years. Take care in avoiding the spawning beds (redds) so as to not disturb them while walking across streams or along lake edges. Brook trout deserve special discussion; if you plan on keeping some brook trout (according to good fisheries management practices), consider harvesting fish during non-spawning

Stewardship, Ethics and Gear Guidelines

seasons. Harvesting other trout species in the Park is not only illegal in most cases, but where allowed, probably not a best practice during spawning season. *See the section entitled "Possession Limits" for more detail on harvest regulations.*

Aquatic Gear Guidelines

Several invasive species and parasites threaten the waters in which trout live. Anglers must take extra precautions to clean gear to protect the waters of the Park.

Whirling disease affects juvenile fish by causing skeletal deformation and neurological damage. Spores are released into the water by infected fish upon their death. Some spores are ingested by small tubificid worms. Juvenile fish are infected by free floating spores through skin or by ingesting the tubificids. It takes only four months for an infected fish to develop new spores to start the cycle all over again.

New Zealand Mud Snails propagate to alarming densities. The mud snail has no natural predators or parasites in the U.S. and is quite adaptable to the harshest of conditions, even living up to 24 hours out of water and up to 50 days on a damp surface (such as felt-bottomed wading boot soles). What's more, they can reproduce asexually, producing over 200 embryos annually. The snails out-compete indigenous water insects for food, eventually displacing the insects which trout feed upon. The snails are deceptively small, less than 2cm in length, blending in with the stream bottom. And, since they are so small they are often overlooked when cleaning gear. Cleaning fishing gear should be an important and essential part of a fisher's regimen.

Figure 4. - The four steps of fishing gear disinfection.

I Clean	2 Wash	3 Sterilize	4 Air Dry
Remove all large debris from boots, waders, nets, etc.	Wash all equipment (and tools used to clean equipment) in tap water containing 10% household bleach. Allow the equipment to soak for 10 minutes.	Freeze gear overnight (the most effective option) *-or-* Soak and agitate the gear in a 1:1 solution of water and Formula 409™ Antibacterial formula for 10 minutes *-or-* Soak and agitate the gear in 120° Fahrenheit water for at least 1 minute (a dishwasher works well)	Allow all equipment to air dry in direct sunlight for at least 4 hours before wearing to your next destination.

High Mountain Lake Fishing

While the following sections are meant to be generally comprehensive in the techniques of fishing high mountain lakes, it does give specific guidance that is applicable to fishing lakes in the Park.

Nearly 70% of fishable lakes in the Park are above 10,000 feet *(For more information, please refer to the Appendix entitled "Lakes over 10,000 feet Which Contain Fish").* To the fly fisher, this means some hiking is involved, so be prepared.

High mountain lakes which fish the best have several common characteristics: they contain some sort of plant growth, are deep enough not to freeze solid, have a shallow littoral zone and deep drop-off and generally are not shaded by the towering confines of

Rocky Mountain National Park

a close-by mountain or rock formation. All of these characteristics are not needed to make a fine lake fishery, but certainly having three or more characteristics helps.

Fortunately, most lakes in the Park which contain fish are prime examples of ideal high mountain fisheries. High mountain lakes in the Park predominately contain brook trout and greenback cutthroat. These two fish behave similarly when searching for food in lakes.

One thing to keep in mind; trout in streams generally stay in one spot and wait for food to come to them, whereas trout in lakes must be highly mobile to seek food. Therefore, the cruising trout is a hungry trout.

Lake Food Types

Lakes are extremely diverse trout food habitats. Trout can find more food in lakes than in streams. Ants, grasshoppers, beetles, small mayflies, caddis flies, midges, mosquitos, scuds, damsels and small minnows among others all can be present in lakes. Trout have much to choose from, so it is the prepared and observant angler that will lure more trout to his fly.

A well-stocked fly box then, would contain several sizes and colors of the aforementioned insects. However, not everyone wishes to carry that much while hiking. There are some flies that are must-haves in any high-mountain lake fly box. Carry ants in sizes 14 through 18, hoppers in size 14, caddis fly dries in sizes 14 through 16, black midge dries in sizes 18 through 22, Adams in sizes 16 through 20, Pheasant Tail nymphs in sizes 16 through 22 and some small minnow imitations in sizes 6 through 10. With this pared-down selection, you can effectively fish any lake in the Park. If you wish to carry a wider selection, consider including midge nymphs and emergers in sizes 20 through 22, beetles in size 12 through 14 and scuds and damselfly nymphs in sizes 12 through 16.

Equipment for Lake Fishing

Wet wading is a popular option during the heat of the summer. Yet, high-altitude lake water remains briskly cold year round, so waders offer insulation from the cold. Wading boots are optional as Tevas, Crocs or wading sandals suffice just fine as light-weight alternatives to lugging around heavy boots.

You *will* experience wind while fishing lakes in the Park, so a longer, heavier lined rod is essential for casting any distance against the wind. An 8-½ foot 5-weight rod is ideal. You'll find yourself wishing you had more if you take a 3- or 4-weight. I usually carry two rods, a 3-weight and a 5-weight; the 3-weight for streams and the 5-weight for lakes.

Full sinking lines are useful from a float tube, but tend to get caught up on underwater logs and boulders when casting from the shore or while wading, so I recommended using a sink-tip line, where the first ten feet or so of the line sinks. It is not needed to get down much below four or five feet from the surface to fish lakes in the Park.

A float tube is a convenient option for fishing more area of a lake. However, typical float tubes, air pumps and fins tend to weigh too much for the casual day hiker/fisher. (There are some ultra light-weight models on the market now, which are under 10 pounds.) Float tubes are allowed on all lakes in the Park and can be a very effective way to reach fish not otherwise reachable from shore, but not necessarily larger fish.

Fishing High Mountain Lakes and Streams

A respectable cruising greenback cutthroat works glass-clear shoreline waters warmed by mid-morning sunshine.

Fishing Tenkara Style

The Park is quickly becoming the epicenter of fishing tenkara-style. Tenkara is the traditional Japanese method of fly-fishing where only a lengthy rod, simple line and fly are used - notice no reel is required. Tenkara is about fly-fishing simplicity and mountain-stream effectiveness. Eleven to fourteen foot long rods allow anglers to fish mountain streams in a way that is nearly impossible with western fly gear. Telescopic rods collapse down to a mere 20 inches. The minimalist equipment needs make tenkara ideal for backpacking in the Park. An eleven foot tenkara rod is perfect for stream fishing while a longer thirteen-foot rod is a good choice for lake fishing. A twelve-foot tenkara rod is a good all-around choice. The fixed length leader can be level mono or fluorocarbon, tapered or furled - your preference. Traditional dry flies or small nymphs are easily fished with a tenkara rod, or one can use the traditional tenkara-style fly, called kebari. Complete information on tenkara can be found at www.tenkarausa.com.

Patterning and Casting to Cruising Fish

As you come upon a lake, resist the temptation to fling the fly right away. Also resist the temptation to crawl upon the highest vantage point nearest the water. While you can see more activity, trout can see you more easily too. Find a protruding log or low-lying rock to stand on. Take 10 minutes to peruse the immediate area at ground level near the shore. A good trick for forcing this behavior is to arrive at the lake with the rod in the tube and the reel in the pack. Putting it together, lining the rod and selecting a fly to tie on gives you time to scan the area for clues. Look for cruising fish near shore. Most likely they will have a general cruising pattern that repeats every few minutes and as long as every ten minutes. A few fish will generally follow each other and in the same pattern, crossing a pod of a few more fish circulating in their own cruising pattern. These shoreline cruisers are opportunistic fish, looking for generally whatever presents itself. However, not every fly will work. Be mindful to present flies that imitate food types in the lake. I have seen on several occasions where stripping a minnow-streamer in a lake where there's no natural reproduction doesn't entice a fish's interest. Those fish are looking for what grows in that lake, which might be callibaetis or midges, for example. Fishing a small Adams or midge nymph would be ten times more productive in this situation.

Rocky Mountain National Park

Sean Miller casts to rising brook trout in a swollen lake outlet. Lake inlet and outlet waters are often very productive waters to fish.

to big? Do you have the right fly? Was your cast less-than-stealthy? Correct the situation and cast to the fish the next time he comes around. I can tell you more often than not, *any* well-presented fly will gain a fish's attention and a take. First look to your cast and your leader as possible turn-offs to cruising fish. Be sure to cast more gently or lengthen the leader to give it more slack. Contrary to "match-the-hatch" fishing, changing the fly is the last thing you should think about when fishing to cruising fish in the Park. On rare occasion, you *will* come across some picky fish that are looking for a certain insect, size and color. These are well fed fish. You'll know when this is the case - a fish or two will act interested in your offering, but turn away at the last moment. If this happens two or three times, then you should consider trying a different size and/or color. A good rule of thumb is to go smaller and darker.

Not all cruising patterns follow the shoreline. Oftentimes, larger cruising fish will come in from the depths, make a swoop in the shallow littoral zone and head back toward the depths. These are prime candidates for a streamer cast out past the shallow zone and left to sink beyond the shelf. Time the fish's pattern and begin stripping the streamer towards shore as the fish is either going to or coming from to the depths. My largest greenback cutthroat in the Park to-date (18") was landed using this method. If the lake supports it

Fishing High Mountain Lakes and Streams

shore as the fish is either going to or coming from to the depths. My largest greenback cutthroat in the Park to-date (18") was landed using this method. If the lake supports it (e.g. - weed growth), a deadly tactic for larger fish is to fish a suspended scud or damsel at the edge of weed growth and a deep drop-off.

Fishing Lake Inlets and Outlets

Water flowing in a lake and out of a lake attract trout for very different reasons. Typically, trout positioned at the mouth of an inlet or outlet stream are staged to eat. They are looking for a meal to be catered right to them via the current. In either case, they both will take a fly. When fishing to trout in an inlet or outlet, use dead-drift stream techniques. Float an attractor dry fly with a small midge or hare's ear 12"-18" under the dry; it's a deadly combination.

Another reason trout may be stacked in an inlet or outlet is to spawn. As discussed earlier, it is advisable to leave spawning fish alone. Find other fish to torment.

What To Do When The Wind Kicks Up

Every afternoon, you'll experience some sort of wind in the Park. Mornings are usually calm and quite conducive to dry fly fishing on mirror-smooth water - a prime reason to get out early. But come midday, anabatic winds form which can create quite a ripple on a lake's surface. Remember this - anabatic winds are your friend. I have witnessed too many times anglers leaving a lake when it gets windy - that's when the fishing gets good! On summer and fall days, anabatic winds are created from the quickly warming lower altitude landscape. Those rising warmer air pockets carry insects en masse, mostly small terrestrials, up to higher altitude lakes. As the wind picks up during the day, small ripples to full-on waves might kick up on a lake. You can't see them, but trout eagerly cruise just under the surface looking for blown-in treats.

FISHING LIGHT WIND. Light wind causes just enough surface distortion which makes spotting fish difficult. While trout may not rise, or at least you can't see them rise, they are cruising and hungry just the same. Fish to them just under the surface. A soft hackle or a drowned ant or beetle is often the ticket. Gary LaFontaine, in *Fly Fishing High Mountain Lakes*, noted that up to 80% of a high-altitude trout diet is comprised of terrestrials. A slow-to-no retrieve is all that is needed for fishing light winds. Let the wind and surface tension of the line do the movement for you. A floating line, by the way, is essential for fishing in this manner.

FISHING STRONG WIND AND WAVES. This is when the dedicated stay! Casting becomes difficult, if not impossible at times. Roll-casting against the wind is futile. The best options are to fish the direct leeward or direct windward ends of the lake. If the winds stay constant, consider yourself lucky. Just when you traverse the shoreline to get to either end of the wind direction, the wind will most likely change.

When fishing the direct leeward end of a lake, its best to have plenty of back cast room to enable a tight double-haul cast into the wind. If you don't have back cast room, or cannot cast comfortably thirty feet outward, consider fishing the windward side of the lake. In strong winds, if you can't get the fly out a good distance, it will only come drifting back in on you quickly, achieving very little in-water time.

There are two very effective techniques for windy conditions: dead drifting and sink-wait-strip. Dead drifting a pair of nymphs under a strike indicator uses the surface wave motion to impart a slight wiggle motion to a brace of flies. Trout cruising a foot or two under the surface find this an attractive meal. The second method is most effective

Rocky Mountain National Park

with larger nymphs and streamers attached to a long leader of eleven or twelve feet, maybe even longer if the lake structure warrants and you feel comfortable casting long leaders into wind. After casting, let the fly sink ten seconds then impart a subtle twitch movement, not much. Wait a few seconds and repeat. If you attract no interest, cast and wait fifteen seconds to get the fly down deeper. Prospect the correct depth in this manner until you feel the exciting take of a cruising bruiser nab your fly. It seems aggressive takes are typically during stronger wind conditions but I cannot document this empirically, it's just a gut hunch from my experience.

Fishing the windward side is certainly much easier, since the wind is going with you towards the opposite shore. The windward side of a lake can also be glass calm with rising fish, whereas the other side of the lake can be painted in whitecaps. Still, fish feed in either situation, so adjusting techniques accordingly is a must.

Lake Wading Techniques

It is very tempting to wade a high mountain lake. Often it isn't necessary, however. With the shallow rim perched over the deep drop-off just out of reach with a cast, it seems reasonable to wade out to fish the drop-off. A majority of food sources grow in the shallow littoral zone, not in the depths beyond. Trout that hang in the depths are not usually feeding trout. With that said, it is still advantageous to wade a lake at times. A few lakes come to mind in Rocky Mountain National Park - Mills Lake, The Loch and Lone Pine Lake. They have long, shallow flats the size of football fields. To access cruising trout in these flats, wading is ideal. Be methodical and patient when wading such expanses. There is no reason to wade in and cause a stir right off the bat. Take a few gentle and stealthy steps, sight search for cruisers. Take a few more steps and do the same. The most effective technique is to wade to an optimum vantage point in the flat so that you can cast in all directions, covering a wide circle. After a few minutes of standing still, you'll notice the cruisers picking up their pattern again and cruising within casting distance. You'll most likely have many doing so that it makes choosing which one to cast towards difficult.

More often than not, lake bottoms in the Park are comprised of soft mud or hard rock at slippery angles. Either presents a wading challenge and an a threat to insect habitat. If the lake supports plant growth, try to avoid walking over it, as they offer immense food-bearing and water cleansing attributes. Extensive damage to plant life can be fatal to a lake.

Similarly, mud bottoms harbor insect life vital to the inhabitants higher up the food chain. Burrowing mayflies, midges, scuds and damselfly nymphs all call mud bottoms home. If the lake bottom is too soft and sucks you in as you wade, back out. Not only are you damaging the eco-system, you also put yourself in danger of not being able to pull a foot out of the mud.

Some lakes in the Park have sharply-angled rock bottoms towards the depths of the lake. Those sharp angles are often covered with slippery slime. If you find yourself wading out on those surfaces, you *will* slide in the direction of the rock which more often than not is directly to the bottom of the deepest part of the lake! Caution noted: don't wade these types of lake bottoms.

Float Tubing Techniques

Another highly effective technique to fishing lake structure is by float tube. Typical float tubing techniques apply - slow motion movement is key. Drifting with the wind or

Fishing High Mountain Lakes and Streams

slowly kicking around while sight fishing to rising fish all around is a dream day on a lake. If you prefer prospecting for larger trout near structure or along the edges of deep drop-offs, float tubing is the way to go. Simply kick parallel to shore in a very slow fashion, dredging a streamer 30 feet behind. Your fly should get down beyond the crest of the drop-off, maybe by a foot or two. Slow drifting a scud or damsel along the outside edges of plant life is also highly effective. For an added chance at a lurking lunker, tie a small nymph such as a hare's ear or prince nymph 18" behind a streamer or wooly bugger. Often, trout will be attracted to the streamer and opt for the "easier to capture" nymph.

Stream Fishing

With over 230 miles of fishable stream water in the Park, there's plenty of flowing water to fling a line and fly. The Park has it all; slow meandering streams teeming with rising brown trout, glides with quick brook trout and pocket water stuffed with hungry greenback cutthroat. As mentioned before, the Park's streams are ideal for tenkara-style fishing.

Most of the streams in the Park are moderate to small in size. There are very few streams that can't be crossed, except during run-off. In fact, most streams are no wider than a rod length and average a foot or two deep. A fishing technique that works on one stream will work on another. And, if you are a dry fly buff the Park is the place for you.

Wading in the Park is personal preference. Some wade wet a majority of the year, even in cold fringe season months. Others wear or pack in waist-high waders. About half the time I wear 9" high Gore-Tex™-lined hiking boots and wade or cross shallow sections

Not only are cased green caddis nature's perfect little architect, they also are an important food source for stream fish. Fish will readily eat the entire caddis with case. These green cased caddis were photographed in the Big Thompson River along Fern Lake Trail.

Rocky Mountain National Park

of streams. Occasionally, I'll get a tad too deep and fill the boots, but on a hot summer day, it's a welcome event.

Stream Food Types

Insect activity is fairly predictable throughout the year. The hatch chart in the Appendix goes into more detail on what to expect for each month of the year. April through October will bring predictable hatches of midges, blue-winged olives, pale-morning duns, little black stones, small yellow stones, caddis, and plenty of terrestrials. If you don't carry hoppers, beetles and ants you'll be missing out on some fine fishing opportunities. The bio-diversity in the Park's streams is expansive. If you are a match-the-hatch type of fisher, you'll have to pack in quite an arsenal of flies to keep up with all that a stream offers. But really, a modest selection of flies is all that is needed: ants, beetles, hoppers, caddis dries, attractor dries like Adams and Wulffs and basic streamers such as a Woolly Bugger is all that is needed to cover all fishing situations you might encounter.

Equipment for Stream Fishing

Unlike lake fishing, stream fishing doesn't warrant long rods and heavy lines. An 8-foot 3 or 4 weight is quite sufficient. For some of the smaller streams a 4- or 5-foot rod can be fun to fish, but that's extreme. The shorter the rod, the less line control (reach) you have. Reach is important for dapping, a highly effective technique described further in this section. Outside of the equipment mentioned in the section entitled "Essential Fly Fishing Gear", not much else is needed.

Reading Streams

The Park has every type of stream situation one could imagine. Pools, glides, riffles, eddies, current seams, tail-outs, flats - all hold catchable fish, if you know how to get to them.

An easy way to read a stream and assess if a section holds feeding trout is to think of a typical house. A house contains rooms, each with a specific function or purpose. Some rooms are for relaxing or sleeping, some for play and others for eating. A stream, broken down in this manner, also has distinct areas for each activity. Figure 5 illustrates the concept. There are four main "rooms" in a trout's house: bedroom, kitchen, dining room and living room. Understanding how to identify and locate each is key to finding and catching more fish.

"Dining Rooms and Kitchens"

Obviously as the name suggests, the Dining Room is the prime target for finding feeding fish. Likewise the Kitchen is, too. However, there is a primary distinction between the two. In a dining room, food is "served" to the fish where there's very little movement required to eat. In a kitchen, the food isn't "served". The trout must search around for food. Hence, a current seam is a dining room to trout, a prime lie in any stream. Look for the intersection of slow and fast currents, often marked by a bubble line, and you've found the best part of any stream; the dining room.

A kitchen is often a wider expanse of a stream of common depth and current flow. As illustrated, they often are found at the end of current seams, as the seam loses flow speed. These are often called glides or slicks. In these areas, trout roam back and forth in a wider pattern nabbing insects as they flow by; like searching through cabinets for just the right snack. Often, the smaller trout inhabit these sections.

Fishing High Mountain Lakes and Streams

"Living Rooms"

Living rooms, often called flats, differ from glides or slicks in that the current in a living room is almost non-existent. The current is often stalled by downfall or a protruding bank. It is here that fish will seek rest from faster current, but still may be enticed to eat. A fish in a flats area of a stream is most likely resting. It is these type of trout close to a bank that you will spook if you rush up on a stream bank eager to fish. I don't seek these types of trout first.

"Bedrooms"

The deepest pools in rivers typically contain fish on the bottom at rest. This is not to say a tasty looking Woolly Bugger swung deep through a pool won't nab a fish or two. Trout, after all, *are* opportunistic. Fishing deep pools is certainly worth it, as some of the largest fish caught come from the deepest lairs, but getting down to fish well tucked behind a boulder seven feet below the surface with unmanageable currents can be a feat in itself. It's best to think of these fish as mostly resting, otherwise they would be in a current seam or glide actively feeding.

Stream Fishing Techniques

How would you approach a stream like in the illustration? Using what you now know about trout "houses", it becomes apparent to fish the dining room (current seams) first, the kitchen (glides) second, the flats (living room) third and deep pools (bedrooms) last.

Figure 5. Classic Mountain Stream Configuration.

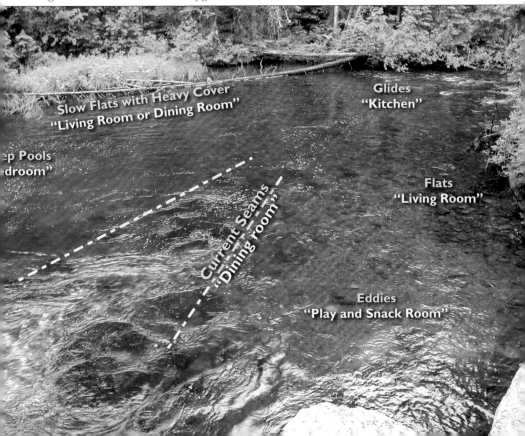

Rocky Mountain National Park

Some may differ and opt to fish the pools first, which certainly can pay off. Ultimately, it's a matter of style and personal preference. I think of it as entering a trout's house, asking myself "where would I find trout feeding"...thus this method works for me.

FISHING CURRENT SEAMS. Fishing current seams is highly productive with either a dry fly or dead-drift nymph or wet fly. An ideal combination for the Park is the classic hopper-dropper technique. A small hopper or large Elk-Hair Caddis trailed by 18" of fine tippet terminating with a nymph of some sort will take trout most of the year. The nymph you choose depends on the time of year and the predominant hatch occurring. An ideal rig would include a Pheasant Tail or Hare's Ear as a dropper. A Tabou Caddis is deadly for a caddis hatch. A high floating terrestrial is also a prime offering for hungry trout.

FISHING GLIDES and SLICKS. Trout in glides and slicks look up, down and all-around for food. They are the most opportunistic feeders in any stream. If you fish dries, ensure the most drag-free drift possible. Trout in glides have more time to inspect your offering. A fly on the surface with any amount of drag will turn fish off pronto. You may catch a smaller trout or two, however. Fishing a dry-dropper where the dropper is a wet fly can be deadly when it is swung at the end of drift. As you swing the fly past and below you, increasingly lift the rod to lift the wet fly up through the drift. Often, the rising fly will imitate an emerging nymph, which trout can't resist. Another effective technique is fishing a drowned ant or beetle.

FISHING FLATS or WATER WITH LITTLE OR NO CURRENT. This is the most challenging stream water to fish for several reasons: there's very little current, the water is typically ultra-clear, a mix of shallow and deep water and fish are most wary. If you see fish holding in this type of water, a longer thinner leader and a stealthy approach is essential. Crawling on your hands and knees is not out of the question. Use nearby trees or large boulders as visual barriers when approaching the trout. Assess the cast required and the back cast room you'll need. Then when you are in position (most often downstream of the fish), loft a gentle cast leading the trout well ahead of where they lie, keeping the fly line out of the line of drift. A reach cast is most effective in this situation. Be patient as the dry fly slowly drifts towards the feeding fish. Typically, a fish will slowly rise to inspect

On an overcast and rainy day, Richard Ross fishes a fast flowing pocket on the Roaring River, staying well back of the target to keep out of sight. In the summer months, wet wading on the Roaring River is the norm.

Fishing High Mountain Lakes and Streams

your offering with a critical eye. If it looks natural and there is no drag on the drift, the fish will rise to take the fly. If your fly is rejected it's most likely not the fly; it's probably micro-drag turning the fish away.

FISHING FAST CURRENT POCKETS and SHELVES. Fast current turns off anglers who don't know how to fish it. If you don't fish faster current and the pockets behind boulders and submerged rocks, you are missing out on a huge opportunity to catch feeding trout. And once you learn the simple techniques of fishing these types of water, it will become your favorite and most exciting way to fish the Park.

Every creek and stream in the Park has sections of fast water with abundant pocket water. They often come in the form of ledges and drop offs, also called stepped pools. These pools may barely offer a foot of drift, but they all demand a cast. Most all of them hold fish. Opportunistic trout use these pockets to hold while they seek food drifting by in the faster currents. While fish holding in pocket water are more difficult to see, the angler is also more difficult to be noticed by the fish. So, it becomes easier to approach pocket water fish within close confines.

Casting is not really needed to reach these fish. The technique known as dapping is much more effective. Using an 8-foot rod and a 4 to 5-foot 5X leader, you can drop a dry fly on the tiniest of pockets without having any line on the water. A shorter leader helps put the fly where you want it during windy days (which is most of the time).

The author makes use of a high vantage point to spot and cast to cruising Yellowstone cutthroat in the Hay-nach Lakes on a beautiful bluebird day.

SPECIAL FISHING REGULATIONS APPLY

Fern Creek, Fern Lake, Odessa Lake, Spruce Lake and Loomis Lake

Greenback cutthroat trout has a conspicuous red color to the gill. The black spots on its light body are large and concentrated toward the tail above the midline. The greenback spawns in spring and early summer.

These waters are part of a program to restore the native greenback cutthroat trout (*Salmo clarki stomias*) to an historic range in Rocky Mountain National Park.

This fish was originally distributed throughout the headwaters of the South Platte and Arkansas Rivers, but is now on the federal threatened species list. It is found only in a few drainages, most of which are within the park and the result of similar restoration programs.

Since the fish stocked in these waters were small, it will take several years for a viable population to be established.

These waters are open to catch and release fishing only. Fishing is allowed only with barbless flies and lures.

Native Greenback Cutthroat Trout must be returned alive to the water as soon as possible.

U.S. Department of the Interior   Rocky Mountain National Park

Section IV
Trout in the Park

OPPOSITE: *Protecting the endangered greenback cutthroat trout is paramount to its recovery in the Park. Signs are posted throughout the Park notifying anglers of the area and species specific regulations.*

www.flyfishingrmnp.com

49

Rocky Mountain National Park

Fisheries Management in RMNP

The Fish and Wildlife Service reports that many of the waters within the Park were originally barren due to the cold temperatures and impenetrable fish barriers restricting population migration. Prior to 1923, fish populations are not clearly documented, if at all, so it's an educated guess as to what waters contained historic populations of trout. greenback cutthroat and Colorado River cutthroat are the only native species to the Park.

Like most waters in Colorado, fish stocking in the Park most likely started during the 1880s and continued until 1968. Rainbow trout, brook trout and "black spotted" trout (the generic term used for cutthroat of any species prior to 1923) were the primary trout types stocked. Interestingly, Cub Lake was stocked with black bass and Emerald Lake was stocked with Atlantic salmon. Today, Cub Lake and Emerald Lake are barren.

Today's fisheries management objectives for the Park have been in place since 1969 and stocking has been abandoned since then. Waters not capable of hosting reproducing populations of fish have been allowed to revert back to a barren state as they were most likely barren before humans intervened.

Of important historical note, Congress and the National Park Service (NPS) authorized national parks to raise their fees in 1996 as part of the Recreation Fee Demonstration Project. This project allows the parks to keep 80% of the entrance fees collected. Some of the money collected in RMNP has been used to fund new native trout restoration work and staff a FWS employee full time within the Park since 1998.

Since 1969, the fisheries management objectives have been three-fold:

1. Protect and restore native fish populations and meet the requirements of the Endangered Species Act of 1973,
2. Complete surveys within the Park to monitor the distribution, condition and abundance of fish and aquatic habitat, and
3. Allow angler use according to NPS policy and within limits necessary to support fish populations and riparian growth.

Brook trout, actually a member of the char family, are the most prolific fish in the Park and without a doubt contain the widest palette of colors making them arguably the most attractive fish in the Park.

Fish Species in the Park

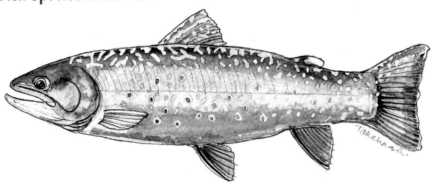

Brook Trout (BKT)

Brook trout are not native to the Park but were introduced in 1872. Since then, they have become the most prolific species in the Park, tolerating a wider range of altitudes than other trout in the Park. Even though they are named brook trout, they are actually part of the Char family. (Char are characterized as having evolved in more northern latitudes and at higher elevations.) Brook trout are found in over 60% of the Park's streams and rivers known to contain fish. They are found in 17 lakes in the Park.

They are identified by the distinctive orange pelvic and anal fins with black and white stripes on the leading edge. The top of a brook trout is typically dark green with lighter green or yellow worm-like tracks. The mid-section is dotted with a mixture of yellow or light-green spots and with distinctive red dots haloed by blue rings. The lower belly is orange-yellow fading into pure white on the bottom. Easily stated, the brook trout is one of the most colorful cold water fish in existence.

Brook trout spawn during the fall. During spawn, coloration on both males and females becomes more intense. Since fall tends to come early in the Park, brook trout begin staging in the inlets of lakes and feeder streams late-August through mid-October. No where else is this more accessible and evident than in the inlet of Sprague Lake. The inlet is conveniently located next to the Sprague Lake trailhead, which attracts plenty of foot traffic. A boardwalk over Boulder Brook gives you a keen vantage point to see the staging males of all sizes vie for prime spawning redds with ready females. The brookies are so focused on their destined job that at times it seems you could reach out and pick them up with your hand (but don't).

Brookies are easily enticed to a fly, especially a dry fly. Brightly colored attractor flies are ideal for most stream fishing conditions. For lakes, a streamer or attractor nymph is just as effective. Many of the lakes in the Park which contain brook trout are over-populated, resulting in stunted-growth fish. They are characterized by heads and mouths that seem abnormally large for the body length and size. The Park's harvest regulations encourage anglers to keep a few fish per day (see *Possession Limits* in Section I). Keep in mind these are the brook trout harvest regulations at the time of this book's printing. Please check for current regulations with any Park office.

Rocky Mountain National Park

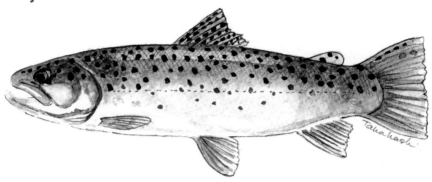

Brown Trout (BNT)

Brown trout are found in only two lakes (Sprague Lake, Mirror Lake) and in 30 creeks and streams. They were introduced in the States during the late 1800's from Germany, hence their less common name of "German Brown". While brown trout are not native to the Rocky Mountains, they represent a naturally thriving and exciting species of trout to catch.

Brown trout are identified by their coloration and spotting. Brown trout may have dull green to bronze-brown backs, yellow to silver sides and yellow to white underbellies. The characteristic spotting is over the entire length of the body, mostly excluding the tail, from just below the lateral line and up. Interspersed with black spots are smaller red spots haloed by white or sometimes bluish rings. The lower fins are most often brassy yellow and tipped with white on the leading edges.

Of all the trout in the Park, they are the most tolerant of a warmer range of water conditions and temperature flucuations, making them ideal for the lower elevation streams and lakes which can heat up during hot summer days. Brown trout are not high altitude tolerant. They prefer lower climes below 9,000 feet, however there are some documented populations at 11,000 feet (Mirror Lake). Brown trout tolerate warmer, less oxygenated water, but prefer moderately cool running stream water (60-65°F).

Brown trout can be maddeningly frustrating at times and quite cooperative on others. If you miss a brown trout's take, chances are it won't be back. You typically get only one chance. The good news is they are typically an aggressive taker, so hooking up is rarely a problem. Brown trout are fond of naturals; hoppers, ants, caddis flies, etc. An attractor dry or colorful streamer is effective, more often than not, lead with a natural-looking presentation. Brown trout are more predatory than other species, so a well-placed natural plays into their 'wiring', looking for easy drift-by prey.

Dick Shinton used a pink San Juan worm to fool this 23" brown trout during spring run-off in Moraine Park.

Fish Species in the Park

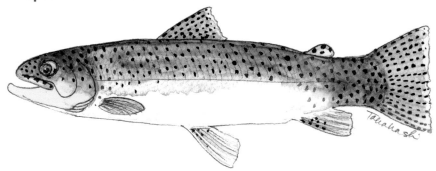

Rainbow Trout (RBT)

Rainbow trout are the least distributed of the four primary angling species in the Park (BKT, BNT, RBT, GBC), being found in only 13 streams and four lakes. Only two locations west of the Divide are known to contain rainbows - Colorado River and Bowen Gulch Drainage. Interestingly, there are no known waters in the Park that contain Colorado River cutthroat or Yellowstone River cutthroat *and* rainbow trout too.

Rainbow trout are native to the streams and lakes of the Rocky Mountains west of the Continental Divide. Their beautiful coloring, acrobatic leaps when caught and delectable taste have lead to its introduction world wide. They are members of the salmon family and like their salmonid cousins, can grow to considerable size. However, in the Park, their growing season is shortened and their 4-6 year life span reduces their size to a modest 12-16". A rainbow trout above 16" in the Park is considered a trophy specimen.

Rainbows prefer clean, cool (55-60°F), well oxygenated water. They are often found in faster water such as riffles or pocket water off the edges off fast water. Rainbows hybridize readily with other species such as cutthroat and often anglers catch 'cuttbows' in the Park - a hybrid mix of usually greenback cutthroat trout and rainbows. Pure rainbows generally are marked with silvery white underbodies, from tan to olive to dark green-blue upper bodies separated by a vibrant pink to red lateral stripe. They are generously spotted with smaller black spots, most often more dense than any other species in the Park. Hybrid cuttbows will exhibit more of a yellow underbody, five to seven blue-green parr marks along the sides and the characteristic cutthroat red slash under the gill plate.

Rainbow trout are generally spring spawners; as early as March and April but can last into August in smaller streams. Rainbows are very opportunistic feeders taking advantage of a wide variety of food sources. Fishing for rainbows is effective with eggs, San Juan worms, standard nymph patterns and meaty Woolly Buggers in olive and crayfish colors. Unlike brown trout, rainbows will often go back after a fly if it missed it the first time. Cast again to the same location.

Glacier Creek produces some of the most colorful rainbows in the Park.

Rocky Mountain National Park

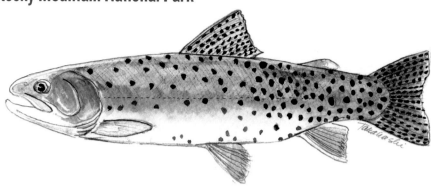

Colorado River Cutthroat Trout (CRC)

Colorado River cutthroat are found on both sides of the Divide, but are primarily a western Park inhabitant. They are found in nine lakes and 17 streams and rivers in the Park. Colorado River cutthroat are not only native to the Park, but to an expansive area covering portions of Wyoming, Idaho, Utah, New Mexico, Arizona and Colorado. However, today the range of distribution covers less than 1% of their historic range.

Colorado River cutthroat are widely variant in color and can often be hard to quickly identify, particularly confused for Yellowstone cutthroat and sometimes greenbacks. Females typically have a silvery yellow back with white, yellow or red bellies, depending on the time of year. Males tend to be more vibrantly colored with darker green backs, yellow lateral lines and dark yellow to red bellies. Their gills are almost all painted with a vibrant pink to red, with the coloration bleeding into a lateral line back to the tail. The spots are generally more sparse and well defined black swatches, being more dense towards the tail.

Like most cutthroat in the Park, they tend to spawn the first few weeks of July. They prefer to spawn in feeder streams or outlets when they migrate out of the depths and comfort of lakes. During spawn, large 18-22" cutthroat are easily spotted in small streams no more than a foot deep.

Like greenback cutthroat, they prefer to cruise lake shorelines during the summer months sipping ants and beetles blown into the water. Colorado River cutthroat are some of the largest fish caught in the Park each year. The elusive larger ones can be enticed at twilight hours on lakes with a streamer or Woolly Bugger. Colorado River cutthroat in streams and rivers are eager to take a nymph or well-drifted dry fly and readily take an egg pattern.

Fish Species in the Park

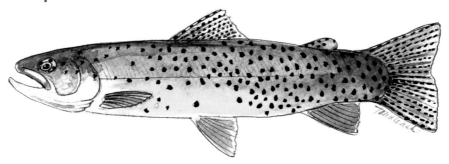

Yellowstone River Cutthroat Trout (YCT)

The Yellowstone cutthroat trout is the rarest trout in the Park, only found in two lakes (Hiayaha, Haynach) and two streams.

The historical range of the Yellowstone River cutthroat is believed to be the Yellowstone River basin, primarily in south central Montana and northwestern Wyoming. Aggressive stocking has expanded this fish into Idaho, Nevada and Colorado. The range today is greater than its original historic distribution. The fish in Rocky Mountain National Park are no exception.

The Yellowstone cutthroat trout has drab brownish, yellowish, or silvery coloration with large black spots concentrated towards the tail. While brighter colors are generally absent, males in spawning colors exhibit a brilliant moss green back and yellow sides and belly. Pinkish to red fins contrast the beautiful butter yellow body. Their drab coloration makes spotting Yellowstone River cutthroat on cloudy days more difficult.

Like other cutthroat in the Park, they are late spring, early-summer spawners and require flowing water to spawn. Lakes that have inlets and outlets are the favorite lairs of Yellowstone River cutthroat during spawn.

As with most cutthroat species, the Yellowstone River cutthroat is less selective than most trout and generally are easier to catch, but don't expect a long-lasting fight. Egg patterns, caddis, PMDs and larger attractor nymphs all work equally well.

OPPOSITE LEFT: The bronze-yellow body and sparse spots are characteristic of Colorado cutthroat and Yellowstone River cutthroat; it's the crimson gill plate and underbody that are key characteristics of a Colorado River cutthroat.

BELOW: Yellowstone River cutthroat have golden butter color and a sparsely dotted midsection. They are the rarest trout in the Park, holding in only two lakes and two streams.

Rocky Mountain National Park

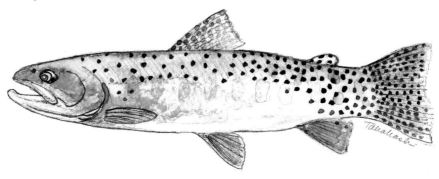

Greenback Cutthroat Trout (GBC)

Greenback cutthroat trout are primarily distributed in the South Platte and Arkansas river drainages in Colorado. Rocky Mountain National Park is part of the South Platte River drainage and is known to be the home of the greenback cutthroat. It is the eastern most species of cutthroat and cannot be found outside Colorado. Because of this unique distinction, it is the Colorado State Fish.

Greenback cutthroat are often hard to distinguish from other cutthroat trout, particularly the CRC. As with all cutthroat, they have the namesake red slashes under the jaw along the throat line. And like the CRC, greenback's have the signature black spots sparsely scattered throughout the body. The spots become increasingly more dense toward the tail. The characteristic for which they got their name, the green backs, is less identifiable than expected. While the green backs are noticeable, CRC have faint degrees of this tinting too, making it difficult to distinguish between the two, particularly when not in spawning colors. Fortunately, there are no known waters in the Park which have both CRC and GRC. Refer to the tables in the Appendix to identify which waters contain which type of fish.

In the Park, greenbacks spawn essentially at ice-off, usually during mid-May through the end of June. A more beautiful trout than a greenback in vibrant crimson spawning colors is hard to find. During spawn, they have a vibrant blood-red belly, extending from under the jaw through to its tail. Nearly the entire lower half of the body is painted with the brilliant crimson color. It is during this time the green backs are noticeably contrasted against the bright red lower half of the body.

Greenback cutthroat thrive best when there are no other fish species competing for food; they aren't a particularly aggressive fish. They become out-competed for food by more aggressive species such as brook trout or Colorado River cutthroat. Surprisingly, there are five waters in the Park which contain both brook trout and greenback.

Greenback Cutthroat Restoration and Recovery: A Success Story

The greenback cutthroat trout has a special place in Rocky Mountain National Park. The near-demise of the fish in the early 20th century was due to its healthy populations and popularity with the locals. Unimaginable quantities of greenbacks were harvested to feed local communities (including Denver) year round to the point where the fish was thought to be extinct by the end of the first quarter of the century.

Fish Species in the Park

Greenback cutthroat historically ranged from the foothills of Colorado's eastern side of the Continental Divide well into the mountains themselves. Drastic declines of greenback populations occurred primarily due to two factors:

- human population explosion and industrial growth of Colorado since the late 1800's, and
- the introduction of non-native species (which hybridize with greenback cutthroat and out-compete the natives)

Prior to the Endangered Species Act of 1973, only two small historic populations of greenback cutthroat were known to exist in Colorado. None were in lakes. It was estimated that fewer than 2,000 fish occupied just over 11 miles of stream. In 1978, Greenbacks were listed as threatened to hasten recovery efforts.

By 2000, pure strains of greenback cutthroat were introduced into 33 locations within the Park. Today, there are 26 lakes and 33 flowing waters that are known to contain greenback cutthroat of pure strain or with some minor hybridization. Catch and release fishing is permitted for all greenback cutthroat waters in the Park, except for Bear Lake, where no fishing is permitted. This is truly a remarkable success story which has unfolded before us in only two decades. Thanks go to those who made it possible.

A male greenback cutthroat trout in spawning colors displays a vibrant red and golden green palette, a beauty unparalleled in any other trout in the Park.

Rocky Mountain National Park

Trout in Lakes

There are 139 recorded lakes in the Park. Only fifty-four of them contain verified populations of fish. As testament to the greenback cutthroat recovery efforts in the Park, 41% of the fish inhabited lakes contain greenback cutthroat (26 lakes). To note: all of the waters containing greenback cutthroat are located east of the Continental Divide in the Park. Brook trout also populate many of the lakes in the Park (17 lakes, 27%).

Lakes west of the Divide contain either brook trout or cutthroat (Colorado River cutthroat, Yellowstone River cutthroat or generic cutthroat). Lakes east of the Divide are more diverse, containing greenback cutthroat, brook trout, rainbow, brown and Yellowstone River cutthroat.

Here's an interesting fact: barren lakes in the Park are at an average altitude of 10,800 feet, while lakes containing fish are at an average elevation a thousand feet lower, at 9,800 feet. That is good news for the hiking fly fisher.

High altitude lakes offer the hiking angler a special reward. Rocky Mountain National Park has 42 lakes over 10,000 feet. More than half contain greenback cutthroat trout. For more information on these lakes, see the Appendix page entitled *Lakes Over 10,000 Feet Containing Fish.*

Table 4. - Trout Distribution in RMNP - Lakes

Lakes - Rocky Mountain National Park

Distribution of Trout Species By Zone (n=139)

Zone	Total lake surface acres	# of lakes barren	# of lakes with fish	TTL Lakes	BKT	BNT	CUT	CRC	GBC	RBT	YCT
East of the Continental Divide											
Central	187	19	7	26			2		5		
East	178	10	13	23	6	1			6	3	1
North Central	17	5	1	6	1	1					
Northeast	141	14	10	24	1			1	9		
Southeast	213	22	9	31	4		1		6	1	
TOTALS	**735**	**69**	**40**	**109**	**12**	**2**	**3**	**1**	**26**	**4**	**1**
					24%	4%	6%	2%	53%	8%	2%
West of the Continental Divide											
Northwest	31	7	2	9	1		1				
Southwest	95	1	7	8	4			4			
West	139	7	5	12				4			1
TOTALS	**265**	**15**	**14**	**29**	**5**		**1**	**8**			**1**
					33%	0%	7%	53%	0%	0%	7%
All Lakes	**1,000**	**85**	**54**	**139**	**17**	**2**	**4**	**9**	**26**	**4**	**2**
					27%	3%	6%	14%	41%	6%	3%

Trout in Lakes and Streams in the Park

Trout in Creeks, Streams and Rivers

The quintessential fly fishing experience in the Park begins with stream fishing. And there's no shortage of stream fishing in the Park. One-hundred eleven of the 208 perennial streams in the Park contain fish. This does not mean however, an entire stream may contain fish. For specific details on what sections of streams contain fish, refer to the Appendix *Creeks, Streams, Rivers and Lakes in Rocky Mountain National Park*. Many streams are broken down into sub-sections for purposes of identifying barren areas versus angling opportunities.

A total of 203 stream miles contain fish, which represents 55% of the stream miles in the Park. There are 115 miles of streams east of the Divide that contain fish and 88 stream miles west of the Divide. Suffice it to say there is plenty of linear water to accommodate even the busiest of days in the dead of summer.

On both sides of the Divide, brook trout dominate the streams, especially at lower to mid-elevations. Brown trout are also prevalent on both sides of the Divide, especially at lower elevations. As with lake populations, greenback cutthroat trout inhabit selected streams east of the Continental Divide; no greenbacks are found in streams west of the Divide.

Table 5. - Trout Distribution in RMNP - Creeks, Streams and Rivers

Creeks, Streams and Rivers - Rocky Mountain National Park
Distribution of Trout Species By Zone (n=208)

Zone	Total Stream Miles	# of Streams barren	# of Streams with fish	Total Stream Systems	BKT	BNT	CUT	CRC	GBC	RBT	YCT
East of the Continental Divide											
Central	25	5	8	13	7	4			5	3	
East	55	16	18	34	12	4	3		6	5	1
North Central	38	5	10	15	9	1	4		1		
Northeast	73	16	20	36	12	7	1	2	12	3	
Southeast	30	13	18	31	10	4	2		9		
TOTALS	221	55	74	129	50	20	10	2	33	11	1
					39%	16%	8%	2%	26%	9%	1%
West of the Continental Divide											
Northwest	87	21	14	35	10	6	2	3		2	
Southwest	26	5	12	17	6	1		5			
West	35	16	11	27	4	3	1	7			1
TOTALS	148	42	37	79	20	10	3	15		2	1
					39%	20%	6%	29%		4%	2%
All Streams	369	97	111	208	70	30	13	17	33	13	2
					39%	17%	7%	10%	19%	7%	1%

"In years to come when I am asleep beneath the pines, thousands of families will find rest and hope in this park."
- Enos Mills

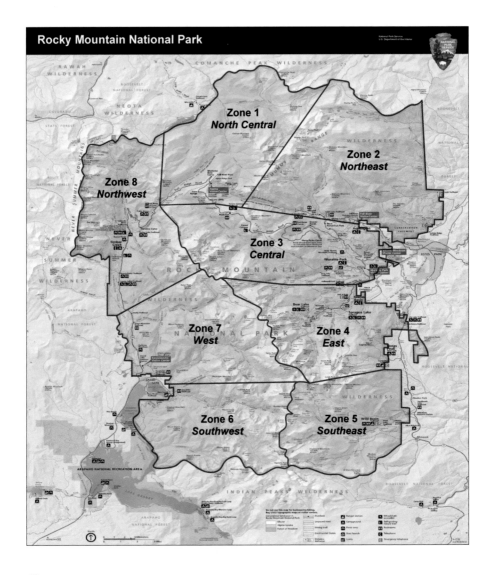

Zone I - North Central

Corral Creek Trail

Cache La Poudre River Trail

Chapin Creek Trail

Mummy Pass Trail

Mirror Lake Trail

Rocky Mountain National Park

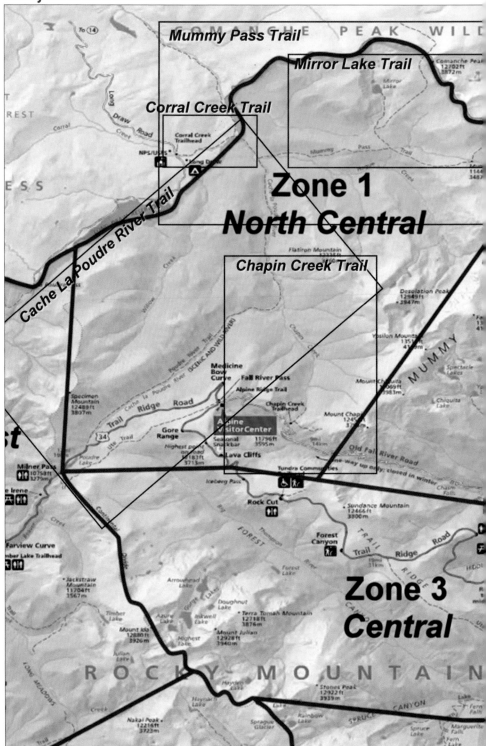

Corral Creek Trail

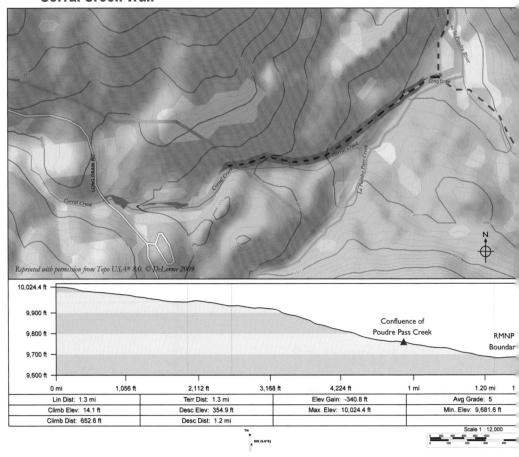

Reprinted with permission from Topo U.S.A® 8.0. © DeLorme 2009

Lin Dist: 1.3 mi	Terr Dist: 1.3 mi	Elev Gain: -340.8 ft	Avg Grade: 5
Climb Elev: 14.1 ft	Desc Elev: 354.9 ft	Max. Elev: 10,024.4 ft	Min. Elev: 9,681.6 ft
Climb Dist: 652.6 ft	Desc Dist: 1.2 mi		

Scale 1 : 12,000

Trailhead: *Corral Creek*   **USGS Quad(s):**   *Chambers Lake*
Comanche Peak

Trail Overview

Corral Creek is a short jaunt of about 1.3 miles (one-way) of easy hiking. The downhill trek in is quick and the uphill climb out is short and gentle. Corral Creek Trail follows the Park boundary (and Corral Creek and La Poudre Pass Creek) by just a few yards to the north. It commences at Corral Creek trailhead and works its way north easterly through the Cache La Poudre Wild and Scenic Area. Just before the Park boundary, the trail meets up with the Big South Trail from the north, which leads to Peterson Lake. Taking the trail spur into the park over the footbridge crossing La Poudre Pass Creek gives you access to two wonderful hikes, Poudre Pass Trail and Mummy Pass Trail.

Corral Creek

Although Corral Creek is outside of the Park boundaries, it deserves mentioning by virtue of passing this creek on the way into the Park property via destinations along the Poudre Pass Trail and Mummy Pass Trail. Cautious brook trout use every available hiding spot to conceal themselves in this very small creek. Getting them to come out and take

Fishing Corral Creek Trail

a fly can be frustrating at times and seductively easy at others.

La Poudre Pass Creek

La Poudre Pass Creek from Long Draw Reservoir to the confluence of the Cache La Poudre River in the Park is a favorite of mine. I often find solitude because of the remoteness of the trailhead, and the river scenery and water clarity are unparalleled. A bonus is being able to hike this section of the trail with a dog while still enjoying the essential beauty of the Park. Once you get to the bridge over this creek, heading south, you are in Park property and pets are not permitted. The entire creek from the Park bridge to the outlet from the east side of Long Draw Reservoir (~two miles) has fishy pockets and pools. The lower third and upper third have less gradient and slower flows than the middle third.

Willow Creek

Willow Creek is on the south side of La Poudre Pass Creek, midway between the Park bridge and Long Draw Reservoir (shown on Cache La Poudre River Trail topographic map on next page). It's a small pocket water and glide stream just slightly smaller than La Poudre Pass Creek. It flows through dense forest, but conveniently follows a narrow clearing much of its course through Specimen Mountain Natural Research Area. From La Poudre Pass Creek, the first four-tenths of a mile has good fishing for small brookies. For the next quarter mile the streamside fishermen paths deteriorate as the gradient becomes steeper and the pines line the stream. Three-quarters of a mile upstream, the creek flows through a long meadow. The upper meadow is rather marshy and loaded with brookies - and full of mosquitos, too.

La Poudre Pass Creek is a clear running stream most of the year - and chock full of fish. A 2- or 3-weight fly rod is a perfect companion for fishing along Corral Creek Trail. Looking East, the left side of the stream is State Land and the right side of the creek is Rocky Mountain National Park. It is well marked.

Cache La Poudre River Trail

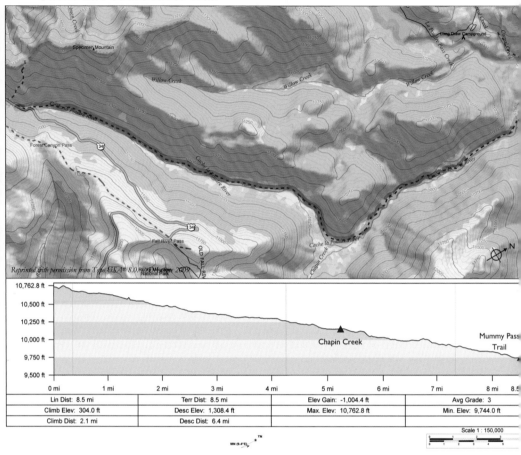

Lin Dist: 8.5 mi	Terr Dist: 8.5 mi	Elev Gain: -1,004.4 ft	Avg Grade: 3
Climb Elev: 304.0 ft	Desc Elev: 1,308.4 ft	Max. Elev: 10,762.8 ft	Min. Elev: 9,744.0 ft
Climb Dist: 2.1 mi	Desc Dist: 6.4 mi		

Trailhead: *Corral Creek* / *Trail Ridge Road*

USGS Quad(s): *Comanche Peak* / *Trail Ridge* / *Fall River Pass*

Trail Overview

Note the orientation of the topographic map above. The most common access to this fun meadow stream fishery is in the small parking lot just north of Poudre Lake. From there, follow the footpath and river downstream for as long as you want to fish - literally - you could fish your way out of the Park to the north if you wanted to travel over ten miles. The river has two looks; a small meandering stream and a small boulder-clad version of the Cache La Poudre River that carves the canyon along Route 14 to Fort Collins, Colorado. Note the trail is also named Poudre River Trail on some topographic maps and trail guides. Poudre Lake is generally barren since it freezes solid in winter, however seasonal fish may enter the lake during high water years.

Cache La Poudre River (the "Poudre")

From the Poudre Lake parking area, the stream is rather small and dominated by small brook trout. As the stream meanders through the valley, it gains water and momentum.

Fishing Cache La Poudre River Trail

It braids and weaves through perennial wet grassy land, so be prepared accordingly. Five miles from Poudre Lake trailhead the river joins Chapin Creek in a large meadow flanked by beautifully forested mountains on all sides including the Desolation Peaks to the east. Springtime fishing can be especially wet going, but nymphing the swollen water with a size 14 BWO nymph or Hare's Ear is especially productive. Fishing a terrestrial pattern in the summer is standard protocol.

Cascade Creek (from Cache La Poudre River) ⤛ ⤛

Although not specifically along the Poudre River or along any trail, this creek deserves mention for its quality brook trout and brown trout fishing. Access is best from the Corral Creek trailhead, following Corral Creek trail to the Poudre River. Follow the Poudre River north for about a half mile to the confluence of Cascade Creek from the east. Going upstream a half a mile brings you to an open meadow much like the Poudre near Trail Ridge Road. The creek meanders nearly three-quarters of a mile and is surrounded by wet grassland most of the year.

ABOVE The Cache La Poudre flows through a wide open meadow near Trail Ridge Road.

BELOW: Mike Kruise gingerly casts to wary cutthroat in the Poudre near Cascade Creek.

Chapin Creek Trail

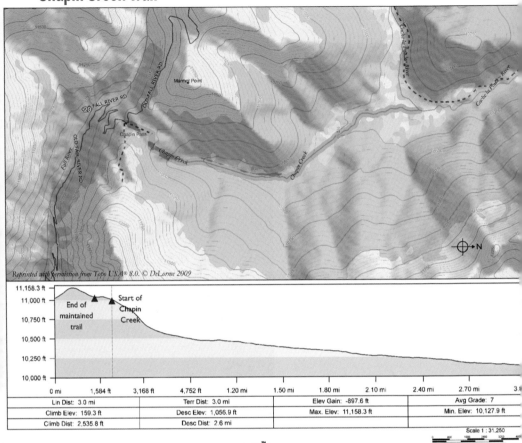

Reprinted with permission from Topo USA® 8.0. © DeLorme 2009

					Avg Grade: 7
Lin Dist: 3.0 mi		Terr Dist: 3.0 mi		Elev Gain: -897.6 ft	
Climb Elev: 159.3 ft		Desc Elev: 1,056.9 ft		Max. Elev: 11,158.3 ft	Min. Elev: 10,127.9 ft
Climb Dist: 2,535.8 ft		Desc Dist: 2.6 mi			

Scale 1 : 31,250

Trailhead: *Chapin Pass*   **USGS Quad(s):**   *Trail Ridge*

Trail Overview

🚶 🚶 - 🚶 🚶 🚶 🚶

Note the orientation of the topographic map above. Access to the Chapin Pass trailhead is via the nostalgic one-way Old Fall River Road. Give yourself plenty of time to get to the trailhead as the vehicle traffic is slow going via the unpaved, wash-boarded and dusty road. Parking at the trailhead can also be at a premium, but because the trail is short, parking spots turn over frequently. The first three-quarters of a mile from the Chapin Pass trailhead is maintained trail - essentially a trail through a 'Sherwood Forest-esque' woods. From the trailhead for the first third of a mile, the trail quickly gains altitude to the crest of the pass. The half-mile trek from the crest is a rather steep downhill jaunt to the start of Chapin Creek. From the edge of the meadow downstream, cross-country travel prevails across wet, marshy drainage. It's best to follow the game trails through the streamside grasses and wiry willows to stay on the highest ground possible. Two miles from the end of the formal Chapin Creek Trail from Chapin Pass, Chapin Creek converges with the Cache La Poudre River. Just before the two rivers merge, a barely distinguishable Chapin Creek Trail resumes to the west and at some mysterious point becomes the Poudre River Trail on most topographic maps. The upper Cache La Poudre River is most easily accessed by Chapin Creek Trail, despite the slow drive on Old Fall River Road, steep climb over the pass and two

Fishing Chapin Creek Trail

mile trek to the confluence. The other option is to hike five miles from the Corral Creek trailhead, which is just over three hours drive-time from the Denver area.

Chapin Creek

Chapin Creek is highly affected by runoff throughout the spring and early summer. In the springtime, expect a beautiful flowing stream that is a dream to fish. In late summer and fall, the flows are at a minimum and the fish are concentrated in deeper runs and micro-pools. During low-water times, fishing is not recommended as it stresses the fish under already stressful conditions – a good rule-of-thumb for any low water conditions in the Park. A good way to judge if Chapin Creek has acceptable flows is to evaluate if the Cache La Poudre in the Poudre Canyon has good flows – as the Cache La Poudre flows, so does Chapin Creek. Brook trout are on the smallish side, but surprisingly plentiful almost all the way up to the headwaters of the creek.

ABOVE: The Chapin Creek valley is wide open and gently slopes to the confluence of the Cache La Poudre River nearly 2.5 miles downstream. Brook trout fishing is good all the way down the valley.

BELOW: Low water levels in fall (such as pictured below) warrants prudent discretion when fishing. Fish are stressed during low water times - fishing for them adds unnecessary stress.

Mummy Pass Trail

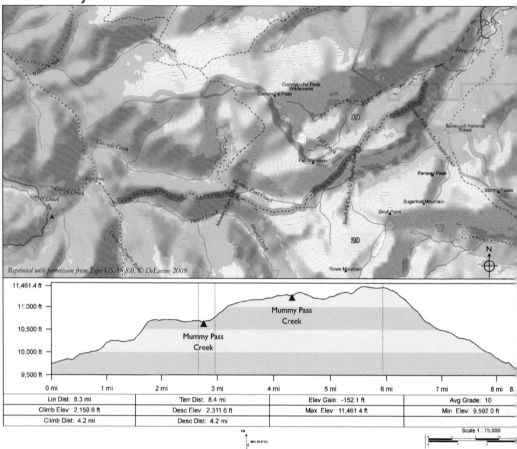

Reprinted with permission from Topo USA® 8.0. © DeLorme 2009

Lin Dist: 8.3 mi	Terr Dist: 8.4 mi	Elev Gain: -152.1 ft	Avg Grade: 10
Climb Elev: 2,159.6 ft	Desc Elev: 2,311.6 ft	Max Elev: 11,461.4 ft	Min. Elev: 9,592.0 ft
Climb Dist: 4.2 mi	Desc Dist: 4.2 mi		

Scale 1 : 75,000

Trailhead: *Corral Creek*   **USGS Quad(Dls):** *Pingree Park*
                                                            Comanche Peak

Trail Overview

The western half of Mummy Pass Trail brings you to the essential fishing destinations along this trail. From the Poudre River Trail, the first third of a mile of Mummy Pass Trail follows Hague Creek before the trail begins to veer north-easterly up the side of a small mountain towards Mummy Pass Creek. Fishing the entire length of Hague Creek through the meadow will take you away from the trail and will require an undesirable steep climb through dense woods and deadfall. Many feeder streams and creeks to Hague Creek may contain fish, but as a general rule of thumb are considered barren, including Hazeline Lake Drainage above 10,068 ft (essentially any water above the Hague Creek meadow area). Hazeline Lake and Desolation Peaks Lake are barren.

Hague Creek

Hague Creek sports two different looks. As Mummy Pass Trail splits from Poudre River Trail, it has the look of the Cache La Poudre River with large boulders and plenty of pocket water. The 'other' Hague Creek is a wildly meandering meadow stream with

Fishing Mummy Pass Trail

deep pools and pebbly runs. The meadow section meanders for well over a mile and requires a stealthy approach to easily spooked fish. Thinner tippets and size 14-16 attractor dries are essential.

Mummy Pass Creek 🐟 🐟

Like Hague Creek, Mummy Pass Creek has two faces as well. The trail conveniently splits the two. To the south of the trail, a small boulder-filled pocket water stream flows down to feed Hague Creek. North of the trail, a really small willow-choked stream meanders through an open meadow. It can be difficult to fish the meadow section due to the tight bends and overhanging willows, especially when the wind rages.

Hazeline Lake Drainage 🐟 🐟

At the upper end of the meadow where Hague Creek meanders, the Hazeline Lake drainage flows from the south. The first few hundred yards are the most fishy water. Beyond that, the stream flows down a steep gradient through dense woods and has marginal populations of fish, if any.

RIGHT: Scott Bley drifts a fly through a small pool on Hague Creek.

BELOW: Mike Kruise lays out a perfect cast to rising brook trout tight along the edges of upper Hague Creek in the meadow.

Mirror Lake Trail

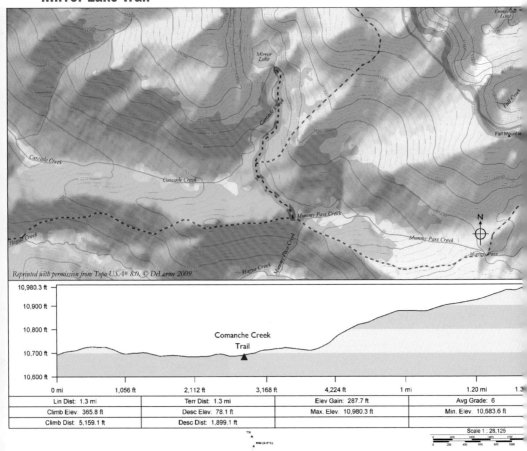

Reprinted with permission from Topo USA® 8.0, © DeLorme 2009

Lin Dist: 1.3 mi	Terr Dist: 1.3 mi	Elev Gain: 287.7 ft	Avg Grade: 6
Climb Elev: 365.8 ft	Desc Elev: 78.1 ft	Max. Elev: 10,980.3 ft	Min. Elev: 10,683.6 ft
Climb Dist: 5,159.1 ft	Desc Dist: 1,899.1 ft		

Scale 1 : 28,125

Trailhead: *Corral Creek*   **USGS Quad(s):**   *Comanche Peak*

Trail Overview

This is one of the most remote trails in the Park. Access to the trail is either from Corral Creek Trail to the west or from Mummy Pass Trail outside the Park to the northeast. Travel time from metropolitan Denver area is over three hours - so simply due to the travel time, you'll find fewer trail mates along the way. The short jaunt of 1.4 miles to Mirror Lake is quite serene as it passes through a tall stand of pines. The trail becomes root-filled and narrow as it is less traveled than others in the area. About a third of the way up you'll begin to hear Cascade Creek rumbling down from Mirror Lake. Above Mirror Lake, Cascade Creek and the smaller unnamed lake are barren.

Cascade Creek (below Mirror Lake)

The upper reaches of this water have the look and feel of a crisp spring creek. Brook trout have plenty of hiding havens in the bountiful flowing moss and underwater stream vegetation. The creek flattens out closer to the beginning of the Mirror Lake Trail and becomes a classic mix of small meadow and tumbling small forested creek fishing. It's

Fishing Mirror Lake Trail

small enough to rock-hop back and forth to access the best casting vantage point. If the brookies aren't looking up, try nymphing a size 14 cress bug or scud in the upper reaches. A San Juan Worm works well in the lower stretches, too.

Mirror Lake 🐟 🐟 11,020 ft

Mirror Lake is surprisingly large and deep. The lake is mostly void of a shallow littoral zone, which is uncharacteristic for a cirque lake of this type. Yet, brook trout thrive in the cold alpine water. While recent Fish and Wildlife Service surveys have revealed brown trout in the lake, they are sparse and generally are not considered to thrive much above 9,000 feet. Due to its placement amongst the Mummy Range peaks, expect wind when you fish this lake and don't be afraid to try a dry fly even in choppy water. Heavily-weighted olive and rust colored Woolly Buggers are effective along the shorelines. Allow them to sink deep before stripping them back in an erratic fashion.

ABOVE: Scott Bley surveys Mirror Lake for cruising brook trout under the wave-rippled water.
BOTTOM: Mike Kruise displays a fine Mirror Lake brook trout which took interest in a Royal Humpy.

"The air is scented with the sweet-smelling sap of the pines, whose branches welcome many feathered visitors from southern climes, an occasional hummingbird whirrs among the shrubs, trout leap in the creeks, insects buzz in the air; all nature is exuberant with life."

- Windham Thomas Wyndham-Quin (a.k.a. The Earl of Dunraven), early settler and land owner of 8,200 acres in and around Estes Park.

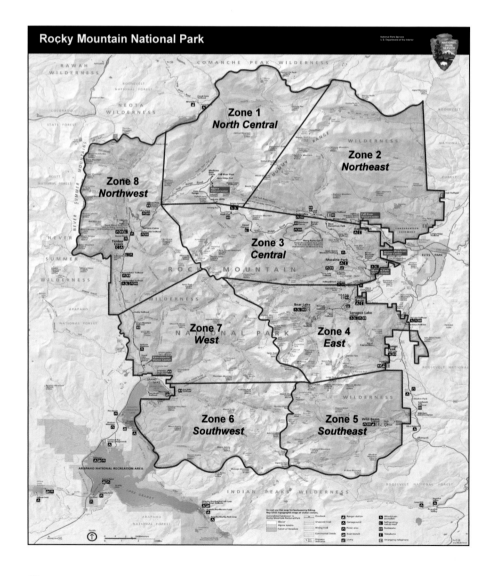

Zone 2 - Northeast

North Fork Trail

North Boundary Trail

Cow Creek Trail

Black Canyon/MacGregor Falls Trail

Horseshoe Park (Fall River)

Horseshoe Park (Hidden Valley Creek)

Lawn Lake Trail

Ypsilon Lake Trail

Rocky Mountain National Park

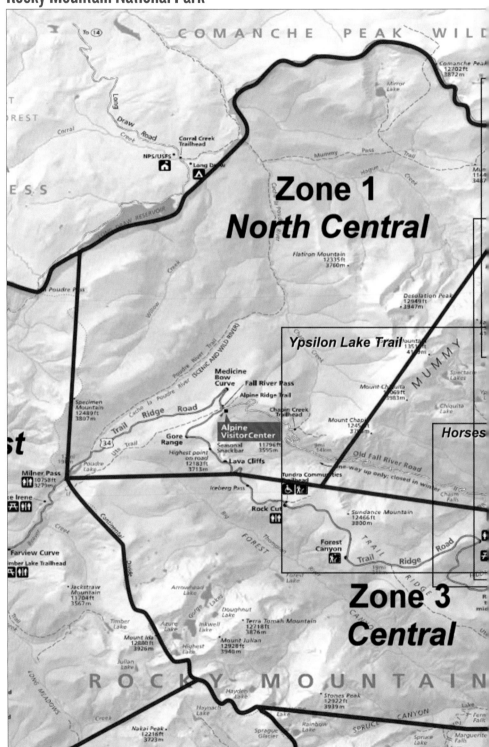

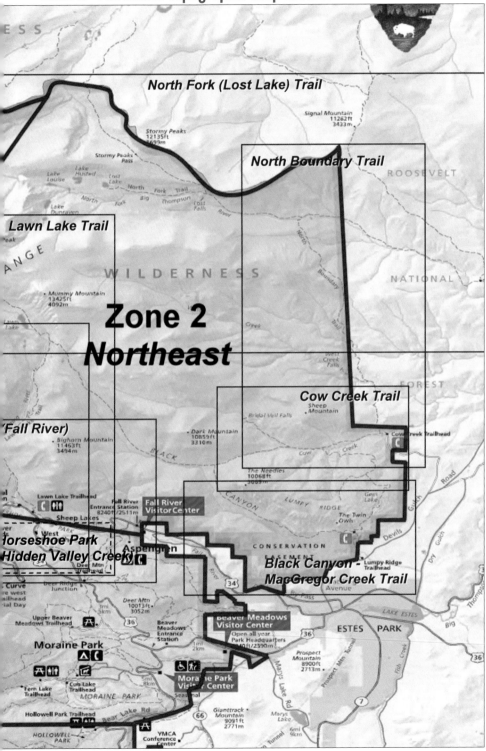

North Fork (Lost Lake) Trail

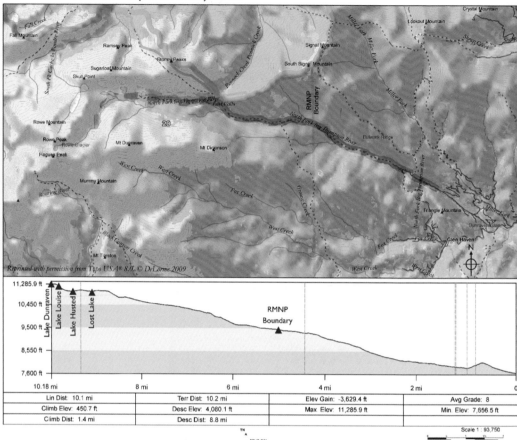

Reprinted with permission from Topo USA® 8.0. © DeLorme 2009

Lin Dist: 10.1 mi	Terr Dist: 10.2 mi	Elev Gain: -3,629.4 ft	Avg Grade: 8
Climb Elev: 450.7 ft	Desc Elev: 4,080.1 ft	Max Elev: 11,285.9 ft	Min. Elev: 7,656.5 ft
Climb Dist: 1.4 mi	Desc Dist: 8.8 mi		

Trailhead: *Dunraven*

USGS Quad(s):   *Glen Haven*
Estes Park
Pingree Park

Trail Overview

🚶 🚶 🚶

Moderate inclines throughout the length take the bite out of this long trail; however, it should not be attempted as a day hike unless you are in good health and very fit. It's a long trek to what is considered one of the Park's best greenback fishing destinations. Prepare accordingly and don't forget plenty of water or a water filter. From the trailhead at the end of Dunraven Glade Road, the first five miles of the trail are outside the Park. This section of the trail is often called Dunraven Trail. The section of trail within the Park is called North Fork Trail or Lost Lake Trail. A few brief steep sections break up a trail that otherwise has a consistently moderate incline. Almost the entire length of the trail is a stone's throw from the North Fork of the Big Thompson. It is all a fisher can do to not frequently stop along the way to fish the North Fork, keeping in mind the real fishing gems are the lakes some ten miles in. These waters are generally considered to be barren: Lake Dunraven and smaller surrounding lakes and the North Fork of the Big Thompson above 11,050 feet.

Fishing North Fork (Lost Lake) Trail

North Fork of the Big Thompson

After the 400 yard climb from the trailhead, the trail drops down to the North Fork and follows it for most of the trail to Lost Lake. The river is a diverse fishery. While brown trout and greenback cutthroat are found in the North Fork to Lost Falls (7.4 miles), it is dominated by brook trout. Greenback cutthroat are rarely found outside the Park boundary at lower elevations. Above Lost Falls, brook trout and greenback cutthroat share the stream. Plenty of vegetation flanks the stream, making terrestrial patterns a good first choice and casting difficult. In spots, the stream is heavily choked with trees, willows and brush. Those are perfect spots to bushwhack and fish a terrestrial.

Lost Lake 10,747 ft

Lost Lake is surrounded by mature pines and is easily accessed around its entire perimeter, offering plenty of casting space. The south shoreline has a quick drop off that attracts cruising greenback cutthroat that will look up for a gently presented Flip-Flop Ant or Griffith's Gnat. Fishing around the drainage can also be highly productive. Camp at Lost Lake if you want to explore Lake Husted, Lake Louise and above.

Lake Husted 10,093 ft

This lake often gets overlooked on the way to or from Lake Louise. Be sure to walk around the U-shaped lake to the north side and fish the deeper shoreline. The southern shore has occasional cruising trout, but the more consistent fishing is on the opposite side. A streamer or Woolly Bugger is a better bet for luring the wary trout your way.

Lake Louise 11,040 ft

Lake Louise is tucked away in a cirque with a deep bowl middle and a shallow shelf on the outlet side of the lake. There aren't many trees at the lake's altitude but there is a grove

The silvery paleness and sparse large spots resemble a female Yellowstone River cutthroat, but the pinkish gill plates and dark greenish hue on the head and upper back indicate this is a female Greenback (Lake Husted).

Fishing North Fork (Lost Lake) Trail

of stunted trees and krummholz to make north shore access a bit difficult. Walk around to the west side and scramble around the large boulders to gain a higher perspective to spot cruising greenback cutthroat. Fish the drainage for some aggressive greenback cutthroat if you can handle bushwhacking and hungry mosquitos.

Lake Dunraven 🐟 11,367 ft

While Lake Dunraven itself is barren, the two smallish and unnamed lakes below Lake Dunraven contain greenback cutthroat. A cautionary note: It's a rather steep hike with no formal trail, but it's short - 300 foot elevation gain over 0.43 miles. Going above these lakes to Lake Dunraven is pointless for the fisher but worth it if fishing is off and you wish to take a few scenic photos of Lake Husted and Lost Lake. The entire area is open and off-trail travel is relatively easy.

Kollin Evens (L) and the author walk the shoreline of Lake Husted looking for cruising greenback cutthroat trout. The far rocky shoreline can be difficult to navigate but offers a better vantage point to spot trout.

Lake Louise has a marshy outlet where the occasional cruising greenback cutthroat is easily spotted.

The author used a small heavily-weighted olive-brown muddler minnow to fool this beautiful male greenback cutthroat on Lake Louise.

North Boundary Trail

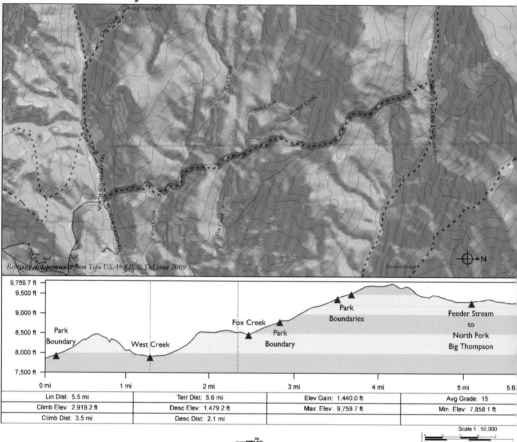

Trailhead: *Cow Creek*　　　**USGS Quad(s):** *Estes Park*

Trail Overview

🚶 🚶 🚶 🚶 🚶

Note the orientation of the topographic map above. While it's a short 1.3 mile hike to West Creek, there's an altitude gain of nearly 800 feet in just 0.6 of a mile from the trailhead. The descent to West Creek is 800 feet, wiping out the altitude gain. There's barely a flat portion on the trail to West Creek. The trail is not easy to negotiate with exposed roots, loose rock, sand, loose gravel and small boulders. Beyond West Creek, the North Boundary Trail crosses many small seasonal feeder creeks and streams which may contain fish, but are generally considered barren, including: West Creek above 8,925 feet, Fox Creek and Grouse Creek.

West Creek (below West Creek Falls) 🐟 🐟 (above the falls to 8,925 ft) 🐟

Once at West Creek, it's worth hiking the half mile upstream to picturesque West Creek Falls. The falls plunge over slick rock to a crystalline pool below and then more worn granite below. The stream is well covered, making casting difficult in spots. Shorter rods and bow-and-arrow casts are useful for this creek. The creek has plenty of downed logs and small hiding places for larger brookies, which dominate the stream.

West Creek just below West Creek Falls is part of West Creek Natural Research Area, where natural entropy is left to rule. The creek and surrounding land is quite wild and untouched, just as it was before the area was settled.

Cow Creek Trail

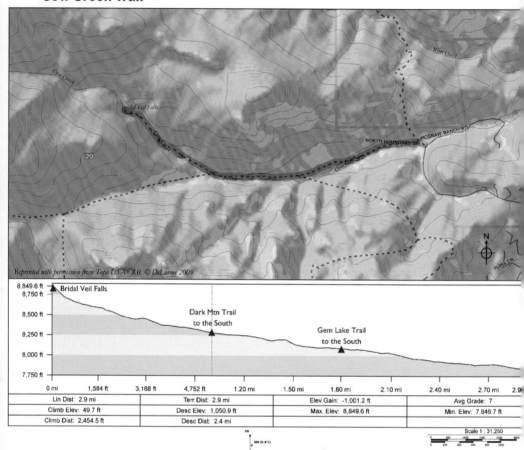

Reprinted with permission from Topo USA® 8.0. © DeLorme 2009

Lin Dist: 2.9 mi	Terr Dist: 2.9 mi	Elev Gain: -1,001.2 ft	Avg Grade: 7
Climb Elev: 49.7 ft	Desc Elev: 1,050.9 ft	Max. Elev: 8,849.6 ft	Min. Elev: 7,846.7 ft
Climb Dist: 2,454.5 ft	Desc Dist: 2.4 mi		

Trailhead: *Cow Creek*

USGS Quad(s): *Estes Park*
Glen Haven

Trail Overview

This is one of the more leisurely strolls in the Park. Day hikers make the trail busy, but most do not come to fish Cow Creek. The creek contains mostly smaller fish and the water runs thin during late summer. There is parking for about 10-12 vehicles just a few paces from historic McGraw Ranch, where the trailhead begins. The trail begins following a two-track from the ranch across a long open meadow, roughly following Cow Creek. The trail leaves the two-track and ascends up the side of a slow sloping hillside, taking you away from Cow Creek for about three quarters of a mile. Where Gem Lake Trail meets with Cow Creek Trail, you'll see Cow Creek again. From here to Bridal Veil Falls, small stream fishing prevails for brook trout and brown trout.

Cow Creek

If you are short on time, Cow Creek can be a fun half-day adventure. Its close proximity to Estes Park makes this an attractive destination, but plan on securing a parking spot early as this is also a popular destination for day hikers and families with little ones. A

Fishing Cow Creek Trail

small weight rod such as a 1, 2 or 3-weight rod from seven feet to eight feet is ideal. I have even fished this locale with a micro rod of four feet because of the tight canopy that encompasses much of the creek. Cow Creek is a perfect wet-wading creek as it rarely gets more than a few feet wide, ten feet wide at the most, and is rather shallow much of the summer. In the springtime pay attention to run-off in the area, which will throw this system out of commission for fishers. Fishing above Bridal Veil Falls will yield no fish. Below the falls, plenty of small brook trout and brown trout can be found.

RIGHT: The last tier of Bridal Veil Falls is a great place to cool down after the short hike to the falls. From here downstream, brookies and browns can be found.

BELOW: Cow Creek Trail and North Boundary Trail begin at the Cow Creek trailhead, located just behind the historic McGraw Ranch facility. The ranch was homesteaded in 1873 and contains 42 buildings. The house in the background was built in 1896 and serves as a historic museum today.

Black Canyon - MacGregor Falls Trail

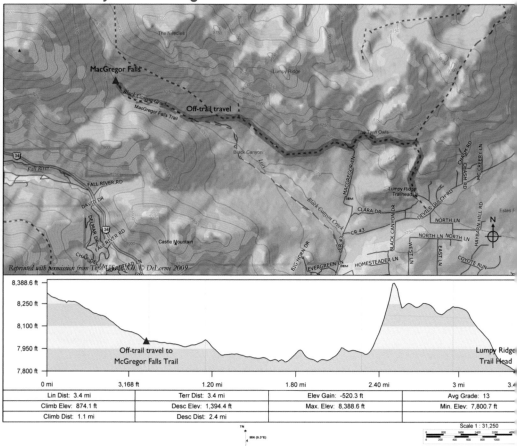

Reprinted with permission from TopMLHWDER.0 © DeLorme 2009

Lin Dist: 3.4 mi	Terr Dist: 3.4 mi	Elev Gain: -520.3 ft	Avg Grade: 13
Climb Elev: 874.1 ft	Desc Elev: 1,394.4 ft	Max. Elev: 8,388.6 ft	Min. Elev: 7,800.7 ft
Climb Dist: 1.1 mi	Desc Dist: 2.4 mi		

Scale 1 : 31,250

Trailhead: *Lumpy Ridge* **USGS Quad(s):** *Estes Park*

Trail Overview

🥾 - 🥾 🥾

   Black Canyon Trail is the perfect trail to take the family hiking and get in some fishing too. The trail slope is modest throughout - don't let the steepness of the first few hundred yards scare you. For the first mile and a quarter, the well-groomed and smooth trail winds in and out of private land of the MacGregor Ranch. Be careful not to trespass; stay on the marked trails. On older topographic maps, two trailheads are marked for MacGregor Ranch and Gem Lake. They are both no longer in existence and have been combined into the new Lumpy Ridge trailhead. Lumpy Ridge trailhead has plenty of parking, but can get full in a hurry due to the popularity of Lumpy Ridge for rock climbing and the close proximity to Estes Park.

   Getting to MacGregor Falls Trail can be tricky. Since the construction of Lumpy Ridge trailhead, there is no direct access to the trail along marked trail ways. It was formerly accessed via the MacGregor Ranch trailhead. The best way to access MacGregor Falls Trail is to follow Black Canyon Trail through the wide open meadow until you reach the mouth of the canyon at the end of the meadow. In a tall stand of aged pines, you'll reach a Park Service entrance gate with a sign noting you are about to enter into Park

Fishing Black Canyon - MacGregor Falls Trail

land. Go through the gate staying on Park land and immediately traverse off trail to the left (south) just a few hundred feet to Black Canyon Creek and the MacGregor Falls trail. The trail does not lead back to Lumpy Ridge trailhead as it formerly did when the MacGregor Ranch trailhead was in operation. For all practical purposes, the trail ends downstream at the City of Estes Park water facility buildings next to the creek. To go upstream, follow the trail northwesterly for about a three-quarters of a mile to MacGregor Falls, which is the upper end of fish-inhabited water on the creek.

Black Canyon Trail connects with Cow Creek Trail, which in turn leads to Lawn Lake Trail 6.5 miles upstream. Black Canyon Creek above MacGregor Falls contains no fish.

Black Canyon Creek (below MacGregor Falls)

Like the neighboring Cow Creek, Black Canyon Creek is small but mighty. Plenty of micro plunge pools and very small runs provide ample habitat for small stream brook trout. Don't expect large brookies - an eight inch fish is a beauty. In the spring, this creek drains a large amount of acreage and can become swollen in a hurry. It is then, when the waters are highest, trout migrate upstream to settle into the many pools. By mid-summer, the creek is back in a fishable state. Since the water is small, the trout are easily spooked. Stalk to holding fish carefully and get as low as possible. A small rod helps casting in and around the tight cover. Black Canyon Creek has healthy hatches of BWOs, PMDs and caddisflies.

LEFT: Black Canyon Creek is no wider than a rod's length but contains plenty of habitat for small brook trout, which do a great job of finding every hiding spot available.

RIGHT: Black Canyon Trail from Lumpy Ridge trailhead offers a scenic day hike for families and those less capable of a more strenuous trek.

Horseshoe Park (Fall River)

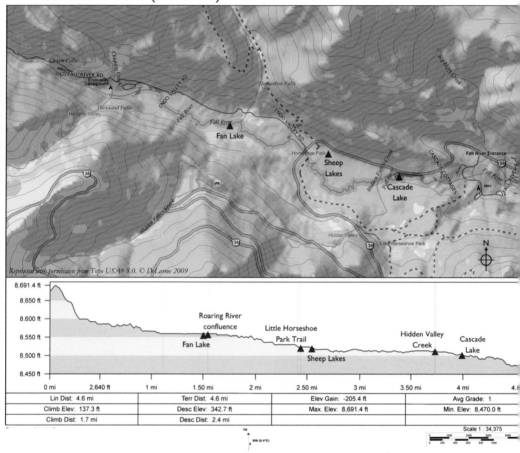

Reprinted with permission from Topo USA® 8.0. © DeLorme 2009

Lin Dist: 4.6 mi	Terr Dist: 4.6 mi	Elev Gain: -205.4 ft	Avg Grade: 1
Climb Elev: 137.3 ft	Desc Elev: 342.7 ft	Max. Elev: 8,691.4 ft	Min. Elev: 8,470.0 ft
Climb Dist: 1.7 mi	Desc Dist: 2.4 mi		

Trailhead:	*Multiple roadside access points*	**USGS Quad(s):**	*Estes Park Trail Ridge*

Trail Overview

Note on the topographic map above: Fall River is highlighted, not a trail. Horseshoe Park proper extends from the western point of Endovalley campground eastward through Horseshoe Park to Aspenglen campground on the eastern end of the valley. Essentially, there is no formal hiking required as most of the stream can be accessed via roadside pull-offs. Access the river by the Fall River Entrance station to the Park and via Endovalley Road, which leads to the one-way Old Fall River Road. Several streams that feed the Fall River through Horseshoe Park may have seasonal populations of fish but are generally considered barren, including Sundance Creek above Thousand Falls, Chiquita Creek, Fall River (above 9,500 ft), Hidden Valley Creek West Branch and Sheep Lakes.

Fall River (9,500 ft down to Chasm Falls)

For about a mile and a quarter above Chasm Falls, the Fall River contains sparse populations of trout. The best way to access the water is to follow Old Fall River Road to Chasm Falls and find a pull-out parking space at the falls or just beyond. Venture just

Fishing Horseshoe Park (Fall River)

a few yards off the road to the stream and fish upstream with a size 14 Elk Hair Caddis.

Fall River (Chasm Falls to Fan Lake)

For approximately two miles below Chasm Falls, brook trout readily take a dry fly. It's best to fish the stream from Endovalley Campground to Chasm Falls upstream with a dry fly. The stream gets small and densely covered with trees, both overhead and from deadfall. From Endovalley Campground down to the Fan Lake, classic meandering meadow stream conditions prevail.

Fall River (Fan Lake to Sheep Lakes)

While recent surveys suggest you can catch a grand slam in this section of stream, it is dominated by browns and brookies. Rainbows are uncommon and greenback cutthroat are more rare. There are plenty of sweeping bends with deep pools and odd currents to hold tough-to-get-to trout. Nymphing a small mayfly imitation, Prince Nymph or a San Juan Worm is not a bad option during high flows or off-color water. Fishing a caddis dry or hopper close to the bank is a good bet during the summer.

Fall River (below Sheep Lakes)

This is the most popular section of the stream as it ribbons through wide-open meadow; there is easily double the stream miles for every mile of linear travel in this meadow. A few sections of this stretch are fenced to prevent wildlife grazing near the stream as riparian growth is rejuvenated. There are people gates at selected corners to allow fishermen access. The stream flows crystal clear in the summer and the trout are extremely wary. This is a great stream for a small hopper.

Sundance Creek (below Thousand Falls)

The creek is extremely small and fishing can be hit-or-miss during low water years. Sundance fishes best closest to Fall River and is limited to about a thousand feet upstream to Thousand Falls.

The Fall River in Horseshoe Park is wide open and gin clear. Fish find solace in the undercut banks as seen on the left hand side of this river photo. Surprisingly, the undercuts often extend three to five feet under the bank.

Horseshoe Park (Hidden Valley Creek)

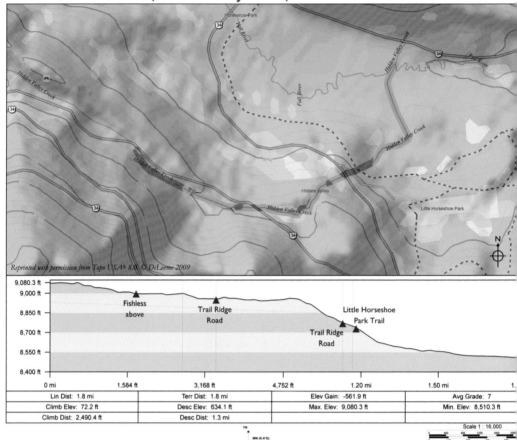

Reprinted with permission from Topo USA® 8.0, © DeLorme 2009

Lin Dist: 1.8 mi	Terr Dist: 1.8 mi	Elev Gain: -561.9 ft	Avg Grade: 7
Climb Elev: 72.2 ft	Desc Elev: 634.1 ft	Max. Elev: 9,080.3 ft	Min. Elev: 8,510.3 ft
Climb Dist: 2,490.4 ft	Desc Dist: 1.3 mi		

Scale 1 : 16,000

Trailhead:	*Multiple trail and roadside access points*	USGS Quad(s):	*Estes Park Trail Ridge*

Trail Overview

 ♿ 🚶

Note on the map above that Hidden Valley Creek is highlighted, not a trail. As you enter the Park from the east side and begin your trek up Trail Ridge Road, you'll notice a gem of a little stream following and crossing under the road. Plenty of roadside parking pull-outs will give you access to walk the wooded and brush-lined creek. Look for a wood-planked walkway on Trail Ridge Road leading you in the midst of a beaver pond area where there is handicapped fishing access.

Hidden Valley Creek (9,000 ft to 9,200 ft) 🐟 🐟 🐟

This stretch of the creek has a tad more gradient than the lower section. While you'll mostly find brook trout, in late summer you'll catch a brown trout or two. Greenback cutthroat also inhabit this stretch sparingly, but they are few and far between. It's easy to make a half-day event of fishing this stretch, especially if fish are actively rising in the beaver ponds area around the boardwalk. Fish all the expected spots that might hold fish;

Fishing Horseshoe Park (Hidden Valley Creek)

they are usually there. This is a small stream so small rods and light lines is all that are necessary. A 6 or 7-foot, 2 to 3 weight rod is quite fun on this stretch. Most of the stream has dense cover, so working upstream or downstream while wet wading is best. During high water times in the spring, this creek gets quite full. It's a lower altitude stream that drains quite a bit of surface land. During run-off, waders are needed and fishing a streamer or San Juan Worm is most effective. The area is a favorite of wildlife such as elk and bear, so keep an eye out for them and maintain a wide berth. If you stay alert, you'll have no problems fishing this roadside section of stream.

Hidden Valley Creek (Fall River to 9,000) ➤● ➤●

Just north of the intersection of Trail Ridge Road and US Highway 36 is a small turn-out that provides access to the creek as it tumbles down into Horseshoe Park. It meets up with the Fall River which offers more fine meadow fishing. The section of the creek just above and below US Highway 34 has the steepest gradient of the entire creek. Pocket water fishing with a short controlled line is the norm here. Brookies dominate this higher section. Lower downstream as the creek flows through Horseshoe Park, brown trout become more prevalent.

The lower section which flows into the Fall River is small pocket water compared to the Fall River, but holds fish nonetheless. It flows through a neat stand of pine before opening up to the Fall River. Look to the south for picturesque views across the Park.

During high water in the spring and early summer, nymphing is the best tactic for this stream. Try a Steve's Baetis or a Yoosta-B Emerger below a San Juan Worm.

LEFT: Hidden Valley Creek just below the beaver ponds has some nice runs and riffles which are mostly inhabited by brook trout. The creek is barely a rod length wide throughout.

RIGHT: High up on the creek and north of US Highway 34 where the creek flows into Horseshoe Park, the creek is choked with overgrowth making casting more difficult.

Lawn Lake Trail

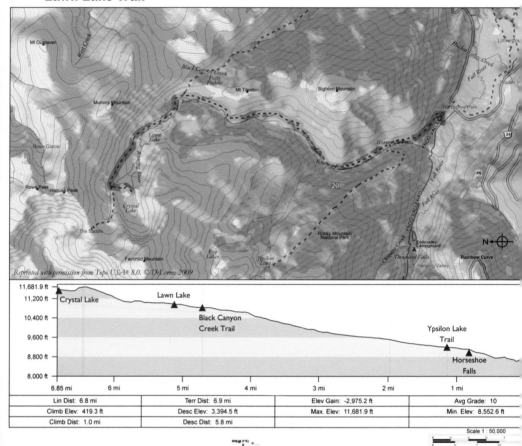

Reprinted with permission from Topo USA® 8.0, © DeLorme 2009

Lin Dist: 6.8 mi	Terr Dist: 6.9 mi	Elev Gain: -2,975.2 ft	Avg Grade: 10
Climb Elev: 419.3 ft	Desc Elev: 3,394.5 ft	Max. Elev: 11,681.9 ft	Min. Elev: 8,552.6 ft
Climb Dist: 1.0 mi	Desc Dist: 5.8 mi		

Trailhead: *Lawn Lake*   **USGS Quad(s):**   *Estes Park*
Trail Ridge

Trail Overview

🚶🚶🚶 - 🚶🚶🚶🚶

Note the orientation of the topographic map above. This steadily sloping trail starts out with a steep incline to an overlook on the Roaring River. From here you can see the result of the twenty-nine million gallon Lawn Lake dam breakage on July 15, 1982. The scouring of the river channel and the spreading of the 42-acre alluvial fan shows the immense power of flowing water. From here, a sandy trail follows the Roaring River through a steady uphill trek of switchbacks and straight inclines to Lawn Lake. It's a mighty day trip better suited for an overnighter at Lawn Lake. Little Crystal Lake is barren.

Roaring River 🐟 🐟 🐟 🐟

    The river is mostly inhabited by greenback cutthroat and rainbow trout, and even a hybrid of the two. This is a classic pocket water fishery, with eager trout hiding behind most every boulder and in any pocket of any size. The best way to fish this river is to wade upstream, dapping an attractor dry allowing no line other than a few inches of the leader to touch the water. Fishing this water tenkara-style is ideal. Focus behind boulders

Fishing Lawn Lake Trail

(L) The Roaring River is a wide open stream perfect for pocket water fishing to eager greenback cutthroat.
(R) Crystal Lake is the highest lake in the Park containing fish, at 11,528 feet.

boulders and on the edge of any slack water. When rising fish are sparse, attach a dropper nymph about 6-10 inches below the dry. The standard Hare's Ear or Pheasant Tail in size 16 works well. Keep your leaders short as the wind most always howls down the river corridor from Fairchild Mountain.

Lawn Lake 〜 11,007 ft

The lake is always a consistent fishery offering the classic cruising fish scenario along the entire shoreline. Early morning and late evening are best on this water. Don't forget to try your luck at the outlet of the lake as well. This lake benefits from strong anabatic winds, so be sure to take ants and beetles in sizes 14 to 18.

Crystal Lake (a.k.a. Big Crystal Lake) 〜 11,528 ft

Bypassing the enticing, but barren Little Crystal Lake brings you to gorgeous Big Crystal Lake. This lake harbors large greenback cutthroat, but numbers are thin compared to other lakes. You won't see numbers of trout actively cruising the rocky shoreline like in Lawn Lake. This lake is best fished with streamers, Woolly Buggers, nymphs and soft hackles. Sight fishing is the best approach in this super clear, deep lake. Don't be disappointed if you don't see or catch fish, as the lake is very temperamental. If the fish are hungry, you'll be rewarded with some of the largest greenback cutthroat in the Park.

On a perfectly still morning, Lawn Lake reflects The Saddle in the background. To get a perspective of size, can you spot the two anglers in the middle of the photograph?

Ypsilon Lake Trail

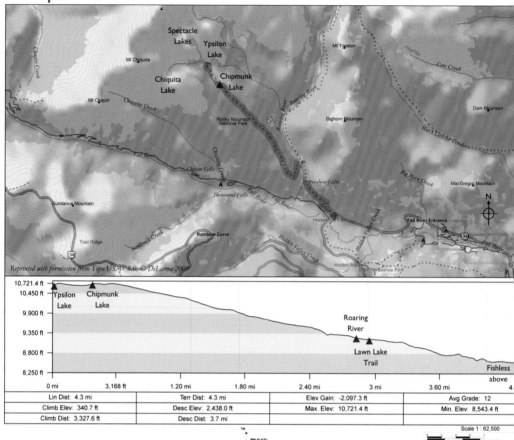

Reprinted with permission from Topo USA® 8.0, © DeLorme 2009

Lin Dist: 4.3 mi	Terr Dist: 4.3 mi	Elev Gain: -2,097.3 ft	Avg Grade: 12
Climb Elev: 340.7 ft	Desc Elev: 2,438.0 ft	Max. Elev: 10,721.4 ft	Min. Elev: 8,543.4 ft
Climb Dist: 3,327.6 ft	Desc Dist: 3.7 mi		

Trailhead: *Lawn Lake*   **USGS Quad(s):** *Trail Ridge*

Trail Overview

🚶🚶🚶 - 🚶🚶🚶🚶

The trail to Ypsilon Lake is consistently steep throughout, letting up when you reach barren Chipmunk Lake. The reward is one of the most serene and aromatic hikes through a picturesque stand of tall pines. It's one of the best places in the Park to truly hear silence. Unfortunately, the trees won't be around long as many are plagued by the pine beetle. The Roaring River is discussed in the Lawn Lake Trail section. Chiquita Lake, Spectacle Lakes, Upper Fay Lakes and Ypsilon Creek above Ypsilon Lake are barren.

Ypsilon Lake 🐟 10,547 ft

Like many lakes above 10,000 feet, Ypsilon Lake is an on/off proposition. Don't be disappointed if you arrive at the lake to see no fish cruising. These are finicky fish that expect the right conditions. The lake sits in a bowl which is benefactor of anabatic winds, so during the heat of the summer, fish an ant, beetle or Griffith's Gnat pattern to cruising fish. Longer and lighter tippet is usually required on this lake, but be warned the winds are fierce as the air warms during the day. As early morning and late evening winds settle, the sight fishing gets that much easier.

Fishing Ypsilon Lake Trail

Ypsilon Creek (from the lake down) 🐟

While brushy and tough going, the outlet holds smaller greenback cutthroat which are less finicky. It's better not to fish the creek from the lake downstream, but to fish the creek from Lawn Lake trail upstream.

Lower Fay Lakes (aka Caddis Lake) and Drainage 🐟 🐟 10,757 ft

A rigorous off-trail hike NNE from Ypsilon Lake through dense woods will take you to a small clearing revealing Caddis Lake. While recent surveys suggest fish are up this far on the drainage, it shouldn't be high on your list of places to fish. The area contains small fish, difficult navigation due to blow-down and muddy/swampy terrain. Fishing from the Roaring River up to the confluence of Ypsilon and Fay Lakes drainage is your best bet for an off-trail fishing adventure. Expect hybrid cutthroat over pure strain greenbacks.

UPPER LEFT: The inlet to Ypsilon Lake is a good spot to find actively feeding cutthroat.
UPPER RIGHT: The outlet of Ypsilon Lake is choked with dead fall, attracting cruising fish in late summer.
LOWER LEFT: The shallow southern shoreline warms rapidly during the day - look for cruisers here.
LOWER RIGHT: The Lawn Lake flood of 1982 scoured the Roaring River bed, as clearly seen here.

"The national parks are an American idea...the one thing we have not imported. They came about because earnest men and women became violently excited at the possibility of these great assets passing from the public control."
- Stephen Mather - President and Owner of the Borax Company and pioneer of the federal agency The National Park Service.

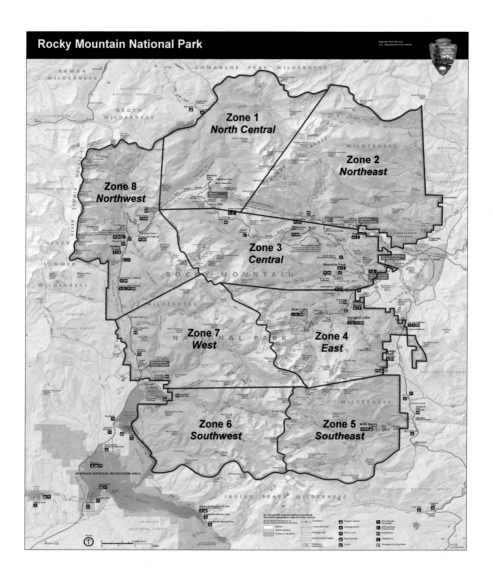

Zone 3 - Central

Moraine Park

Fern Lake Trail (including Forest Canyon)

Gorge Lakes

Rocky Mountain National Park

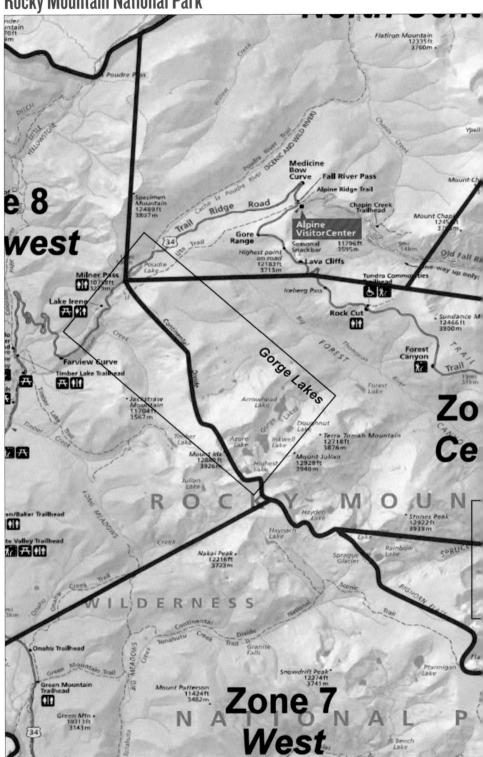

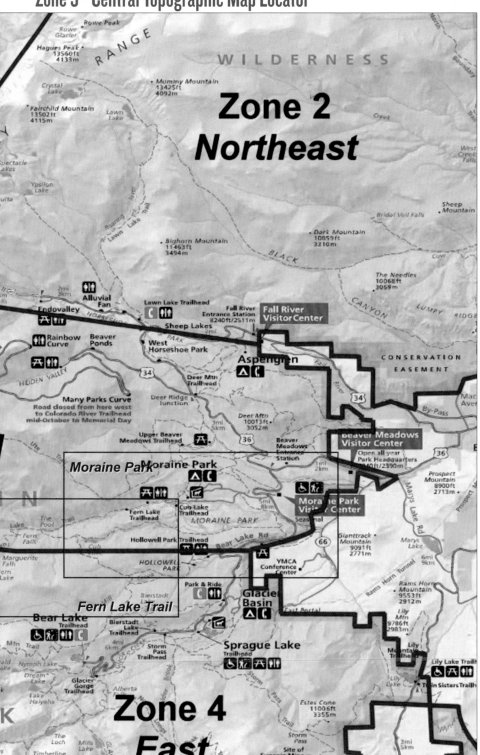

Moraine Park

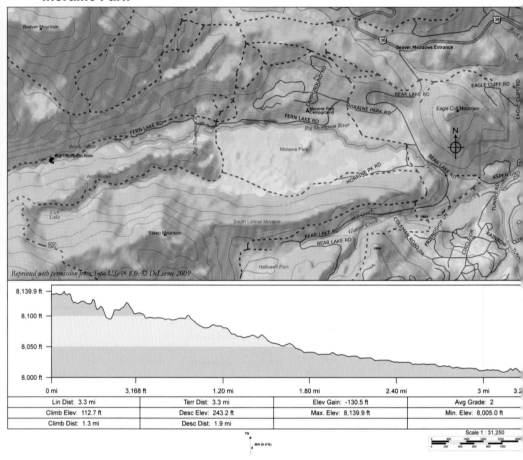

Reprinted with permission from Topo USA® 8.0. © DeLorme 2009

Lin Dist: 3.3 mi	Terr Dist: 3.3 mi	Elev Gain: -130.5 ft	Avg Grade: 2
Climb Elev: 112.7 ft	Desc Elev: 243.2 ft	Max. Elev: 8,139.9 ft	Min. Elev: 8,005.0 ft
Climb Dist: 1.3 mi	Desc Dist: 1.9 mi		

Trailhead: Fern Lake and Cub Lake TH access road

USGS Quad(s): Longs Peak McHenry's Peak

Trail Overview

While there is no formal trail that follows the river in Moraine Park, informal foot paths follow the banks of the winding Big Thompson River. There is limited handicap accessible fishing in a few spots near pull-off parking. Crossing the entire valley takes you to a very braided Cub Creek. In the southern-middle of the park, you'll notice subtle remnants of a turn-of-the-century resort which sported a golf course and a lodge. Roaring River is discussed in the Lawn Lake Trail section.

Big Thompson River (the "Big T")

The Big Thompson River in Moraine Park is a rare location in which you can catch a Grand Slam without moving to other waters. However, greenback cutthroat are rare and probably hybridized. The river snakes for over three miles through the valley offering plenty of fishing opportunities that can consume a whole day. Hoppers, ants and caddis are the flies of choice during the summer and early fall months. Fishing a caddis nymph or emerger can also be productive. There's not a lot of cover, so walk slowly with a soft foot and plan your casts accordingly. Don't cast unless you see a fish or at least fishy

Fishing Moraine Park

water. Fish in the Big T spook easily.

Easy access and plenty of drive-by sightseers will be your companion in the moraine where they look for the Park's popular symbol, the elk. Moraine Park is a popular destination for viewing the Park's many herds of elk. In the spring and fall, be careful as you fish the valley, keeping a look-out for cow elk protecting their calves.

Cub Creek ▸● ▸●

Cub Creek is the name for a branch of the Big T. Contrary to popular opinion, it does not flow from Cub Lake. Cub Creek is a braided stream that has many paths throughout the south-middle of the valley. It's a fun creek that fishes the best during the hot summer days when the flows are steady and lower than spring levels. Fish it going upstream walking the shoreline or in the water, casting to the banks. Casting a hopper or L.A. Ant pattern near any bank with overhanging vegetation will most always entice a strike from a brook trout or brown trout. The fish aren't necessarily big but plentiful and don't really mind a fly which is slapped on the water. It makes for the perfect place youngsters can learn fly fishing and catch fish at the same time.

Brook trout in Cub Creek lay in only inches of water, making them easily accessible when fishing upstream.

Mill Creek ▸● ▸●

While not formally in Moraine Park, it is in the adjacent valley to the south and can be accessed via South Lateral Moraine Trail (Cub Lake Trail). Mill Creek is a fine small tributary of Glacier Creek that follows Bear Lake Road coming from the west at Hollowell Park. It has the look and feel of a smaller Glacier Creek and even fishes similarly. This is a popular location for some of the Park's many black bears. The upper reaches are barren.

A golden September sunset in Moraine Park. Hundreds, if not a thousand elk, come down to the moraine in the evenings to graze and prepare for rut.

Fern Lake Trail

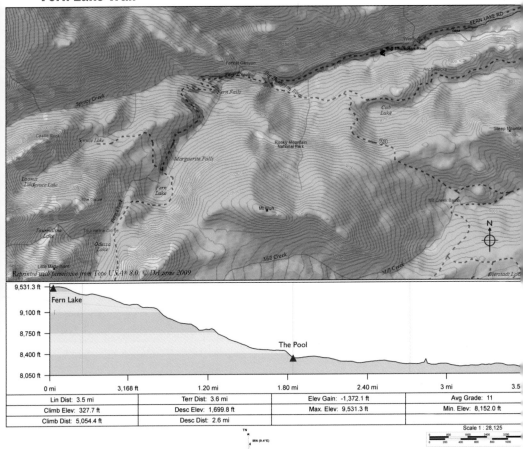

Reprinted with permission from Topo USA 8.0, © DeLorme 2009

Lin Dist: 3.5 mi	Terr Dist: 3.6 mi	Elev Gain: -1,372.1 ft	Avg Grade: 11
Climb Elev: 327.7 ft	Desc Elev: 1,699.8 ft	Max. Elev: 9,531.3 ft	Min. Elev: 8,152.0 ft
Climb Dist: 5,054.4 ft	Desc Dist: 2.6 mi		

Scale 1 : 28,125

Trailhead: *Fern Lake* **USGS Quad(s):** *McHenry's Peak*

Trail Overview

The first 1.8 miles of the trail is deceivingly flat and easily traversed. It lulls the unsuspecting and unprepared into thinking the rest of the hike is similar. After 'The Pool', the off-trail hiking gets a bit steeper. Hiking from the trailhead to Fern Lake is about 4.2 miles one way. From Fern Lake, you can plan additional excursions to Spruce and Loomis Lakes or Odessa Lake. From Fern Lake, it's approximately another mile to Odessa and eight tenths of a mile to Spruce. Loomis Lake is another six tenths of a mile from Spruce, with a significant off-trail altitude gain of 565 feet. These waters found on or near the trail are considered barren: Cub Lake, lower and upper Spruce Creek, Marigold Pond, Marigold Lake, Two Rivers Lake, Primrose Pond, Round Pond, and Lake Helene.

Big Thompson River (the "Big T")

The "Big T", in local vernacular, follows the trail for much of the way up to The Pool. In the summer, wet wading the river along the trail is popular among fly anglers. Expect to catch mostly brookies and brown trout, but an occasional cutthroat or rainbow may come to hand. The further up the trail you go, the more dense the streamside growth.

Fishing Fern Lake Trail

During summer flows, wade upstream and cast a size 12 or 14 Elk Hair Caddis or Royal Wulff to every possible holding spot for a fun day of dry fly fishing. Moose are starting to show up in the lower and mid sections of the stream. This is a fascinating development as moose are generally considered to inhabit the west side of the divide. From The Pool upstream is serious off-trail travel.

Big Thompson River (in Forest Canyon) ➤

If you are looking for a rugged off-trail fishing adventure without hours of scrambling to get there, this is the section for you. An easy 1.8 mile hike along Fern Lake Trail to The Pool brings you to the start of some fun off-trail fishing. The stream becomes smaller only a quarter mile upstream. Spruce Creek and Fern Creek add to the stream flows below. The river has plenty of deadfall, tight cover and boulders that require scrambling to obtain the best casting advantage, but it is also these obstructions that offer great holding places for fish. Short, tight and accurate casts are a necessity for fishing this wild section of the Big Thompson River. The steepest part of the river is just above The Pool for about a mile, then the gradient tames for another mile to the confluence of the seasonal water from Lost Brook - this area is called Raspberry Park.

Another way to fish Forest Canyon is from the west side of the Park. Follow the Poudre Lake Trail from Milner Pass for just over a mile to the junction of Ute Trail. Take Ute Trail through the pine forest to the pass and travel off trail to the east down to the headwaters of the Big Thompson River. Follow the river into Forest Canyon. Good fishing starts about a mile from the trail. This isn't a walk in the park, though. Forest Canyon is heavily wooded with significant wetland all around. Deadfall and boulders make this area is very difficult to traverse quickly. Expect to get wet and to fight off plenty of mosquitos during the summer months.

Spruce Creek (middle) ➤

Three hundred yards to the north of Spruce Lake is this fast flowing creek. The creek has heavy overgrowth and plenty of streamside boulders which make following the creek slow going. The best way to get there is to follow the outlet out of Spruce Lake, which brings you to the stream, but it is definitely rugged travel. The better fishing is well upstream (six tenths of a mile), but requires even more rugged travel to get there. Suffice it to say there are easier ways to catch brook trout in the Park.

Spruce Lake ➤ 9,646 ft

Spruce Lake is a little gem of a lake which fishes consistently for greenback cutthroat. Don't expect large-sized fish here, but they sure are colorful. The lake has a large littoral zone harboring plenty of cruising Greenbacks. Be sure to check the inlet and outlet of the lake for more good fishing action. Following the outlet downstream for a few hundred yards brings you to more good Greenback fishing with smaller more aggressive stream fish. The fish don't always look up so hang a small Pheasant Tail, San Juan Worm, egg or midge nymph six inches below a dry fly for an effective combination for this stream.

Loomis Lake ➤ 10,247 ft

Accessing Loomis Lake is only for the fit and experienced, but the reward is less-pressured and larger fish than Spruce. Loomis is 700 yards uphill, gaining 600 feet in altitude. Following an unimproved trail on the north side of the creek, you'll pass barren Primrose Pond to Loomis Lake. Fishing the outlet is always a good bet, especially if it's windy in the cirque, which makes fishing Loomis difficult.

Fishing Fern Lake Trail

Fern Lake 🐟 9,547 ft

Fern Lake is a popular day hike destination; don't be surprised to see close to a few hundred day hikers or more come to the lake in any single summer day. The eastern shore seems to garner the most fishing traffic, although all shore lines fish equally well. The lake is particularly well shielded from the howling winds that can rip through the area. The Greenbacks are well seasoned on this lake and won't just rise to any fly. I have found smaller and darker your fly is, the better. Fishing small midges or Griffith's Gnats is a good bet under the well shaded shoreline. Ant patterns work well too.

Odessa Lake 🐟 10,023 ft

Odessa sits in beautiful surroundings with The Gable and Little Matterhorn as backdrops. If you make the hike to Fern, the extra three-quarter mile hike up to Odessa is worth it. Odessa has a large, flat littoral zone where Greenbacks cruise for dinner; look for them closer to the middle drop off area and not towards the southern end of the lake. The outlet is usually choked with dead fall which provides good cover for feeding fish, but makes for difficult access to them.

ABOVE: Gil Bangert and Ed LeViness survey Fern Creek between Odessa Lake and Fern Lake for holding greenback cutthroat. BELOW: During an early morning midge hatch, Martin Joergensen scans Fern Lake for cruising and rising greenbacks.

Fishing Fern Lake Trail

Martin Joergensen fishes a small run on the Big Thompson mid-way up from the trailhead to "The Pool".

Loomis and Spruce Lakes have some of the Park's most colorful greenback cutthroat.

Gorge Lakes

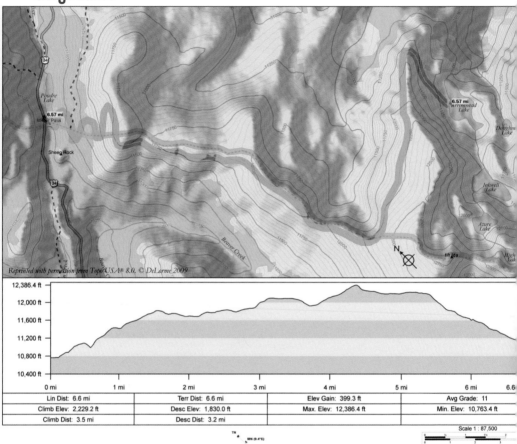

Reprinted with permission from Topo USA® 8.0, © DeLorme 2009

Lin Dist: 6.6 mi	Terr Dist: 6.6 mi	Elev Gain: 399.3 ft	Avg Grade: 11
Climb Elev: 2,229.2 ft	Desc Elev: 1,830.0 ft	Max. Elev: 12,386.4 ft	Min. Elev: 10,763.4 ft
Climb Dist: 3.5 mi	Desc Dist: 3.2 mi		

Scale 1 : 87,500

Trailhead: *Milner Pass*   **USGS Quad(s):**   *Fall River Pass*
Grand Lake

Trail Overview

The Gorge Lakes rank as one of the most inaccessible and remote places in the Park. From Milner Pass, the trail ascends one thousand feet in under a mile, making your heart race from the start. For the next three miles or so, the trail gradually ascends another eight-hundred feet to a distinctive ridge line from Mount Ida, which separates a series of unnamed shallow ponds in a valley to the north west of the Gorge Lakes and the Gorge Lakes themselves. From the Continental Divide Trail, follow the ridge line to the northeast just before reaching the summit of Mount Ida. Following the ridge line to the northeast for about a mile and a half brings you to an overlook of Arrowhead Lake which makes for a safe descent along steep terrain and rock. The descent to Arrowhead Lake is deceiving - it looks only a few hundred feet below the ridge line, but is actually four tenths of a mile away and 850 feet down.

Note: The hike demands top stamina and physical condition; don't attempt the hike if you are not experienced in back-country, off-trail travel or have known medical issues which may be aggravated by a demanding hike with significant altitude gain and loss. Half of the hike is off-trail, so basic navigation skills are also a necessity - be sure to carry a map and compass at a minimum. A GPS unit is

Fishing the Gorge Lakes

recommended. *Caution being pinned on the divide due to rapidly developing summer afternoon thunderstorms. Several waters in the Gorge Lakes area are considered barren: Azure Lake, Highest Lake, Inkwell Lake, Hayden Lake, Hayden Creek, Hourglass Lake, Irene Lake, Julian Lake, Lonesome Lake and Rainbow Lake. Forest Lake and Doughnut Lake have recent reports of fish populations.*

Arrowhead Lake 11,158 ft

For the seasoned back-country adventure-seeker, Arrowhead Lake yields rewards unparalleled in the Park. The scenery is outstanding and the remote location almost ensures a solemn day on the lake. Larger than average greenback cutthroat patrol the lake's edge looking for anything that floats and looks remotely like food. The wind always blows down from nearby Mount Ida, so small terrestrials fall victim and are knocked off the banks into the water. During the still twilight hours, look for cruisers sipping midges all around the lake. More often than not, however, the fish aren't too picky and anything that looks like real food will attract a lazy rise and take. The fish just don't seem to be in a hurry, ever.

Rock Lake and Little Rock Lake 10,307 ft

From the outlet of Arrowhead Lake, a beautiful stream flows down to Rock Lake - not all of it is fishable. After dropping 450 feet in just a third of a mile, there's a confluence with the stream coming from Doughnut Lake. Below the confluence, the stream flattens out and becomes fishable for average-sized brook trout. Above the confluence the gradient is too steep and acts as a natural barrier separating the greenback cutthroat from Arrowhead and the brook trout of the Rock Lakes. The only back country campsite in the area is just below Little Rock Lake. However there is a cross-country zone below Love Lake and to the west of the Rock Lakes that allows leave-no-trace camping; a permit is required. The brook trout feed like the greenbacks in Arrowhead Lake - they aren't too selective and any decently-presented fly, whether it be a dry fly, nymph, wet fly or streamer, will work equally well.

A typical Arrowhead Lake greenback cutthroat is larger than most greenbacks in the Park.. Despite this male greenback being caught in the early fall, it still displays the bright crimson red body characteristic of spawning time.

Fishing the Gorge Lakes

ABOVE: Kerry Evens walks the shoreline of Arrowhead Lake in search of cruising greenback cutthroat. Notice the steep incline to the ridge line above; it is the best way to and from the lake despite it being nearly a 45-degree grade with an altitude difference of 850 feet over four tenths of a mile.

BELOW: This panoramic shot looking northeast over the Arrowhead Lake area is comprised of 6 individual photos. The small lake to the left is Love Lake. Rock Lake and Little Rock Lake is just out of sight at the base of the rock slide below Arrowhead Lake.

Fishing the Gorge Lakes

ABOVE: A bird's eye view of Arrowhead Lake inlet waters show the shallow grade which contains plenty of insect habitat for trout. The shallow shorelines drop off quickly to the cold depths towards the opposite end of the lake.

"If any normal person under fifty cannot enjoy being in a storm in the wilds, he ought to reform at once."
    - Enos Mills

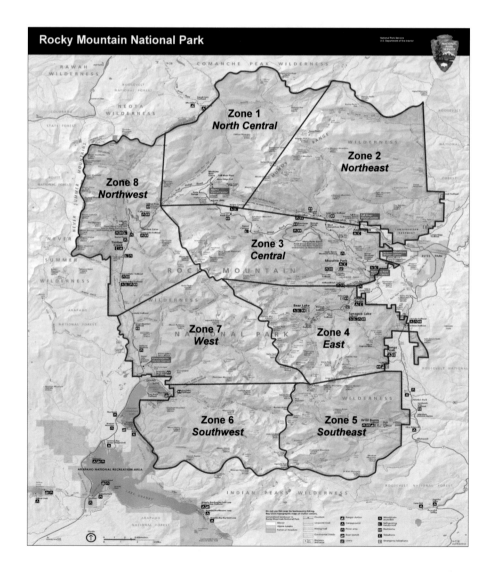

Zone 4 - East

Lily Lake Trail

Sprague Lake Nature Trail

Wind River Trail

Glacier Creek and Glacier Gorge Trails

Loch Vale Trail

Sky Pond Trail

Lake Haiyaha, Dream Lake, Emerald Lake Trails

Chasm Lake Trail

Rocky Mountain National Park

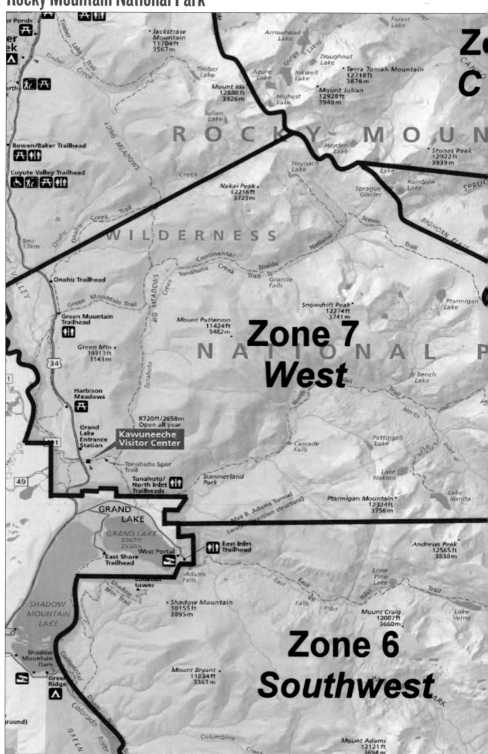

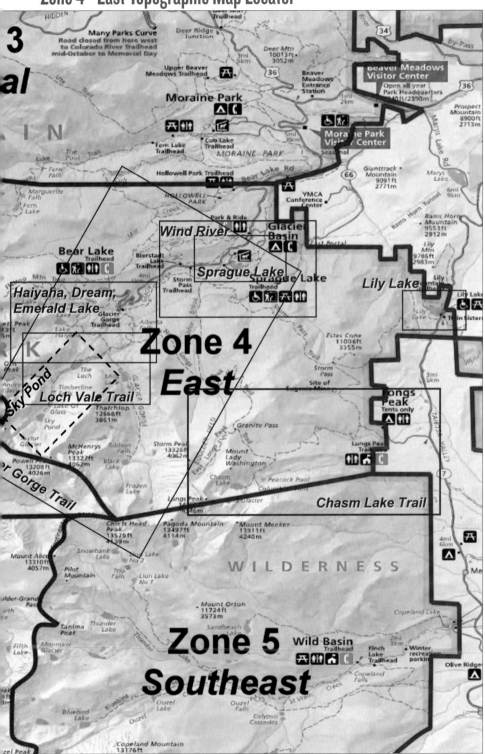

Lily Lake

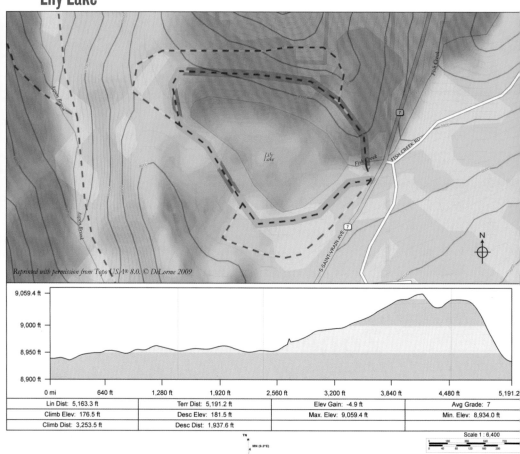

Lin Dist: 5,163.3 ft	Terr Dist: 5,191.2 ft	Elev Gain: -4.9 ft	Avg Grade: 7
Climb Elev: 176.5 ft	Desc Elev: 181.5 ft	Max. Elev: 9,059.4 ft	Min. Elev: 8,934.0 ft
Climb Dist: 3,253.5 ft	Desc Dist: 1,937.6 ft		

Fishing Lily Lake

Trailhead: *Roadside access from Colorado Highway 7* **USGS Quad(s):** *Longs Peak*

Trail Overview

 ♿ ⛹

Gorgeous views of Mount Meeker and Longs Peak are the backdrops to Lily Lake, especially at sunrise or sunset. The lake gets plenty of visitors, mostly just to walk the flat mile around the lake. The lake is popular with float tubers as well. Windy days make for tough fishing as the lake sits in an exposed area. Fish Creek, which flows from Lily Lake and is the official start of the creek, is generally considered to be barren but may contain seasonal runs of greenback cutthroat. Nearby Aspen Brook is also barren.

Lily Lake   🐟   8,933 ft

Please note that current regulations state that fishing is closed on the east shoreline from May through June annually, open July 1 through April 30 annually due to protecting spawning fish. Despite Lily Lake being part of the Park, it is open to all visitors without entering the Park. Almost all of the lake shore trail is within in casting range of the shoreline making this an ideal fishery for any fly-fisher. Wading is also quite easy all along the shoreline and the lake is especially popular with float tubers. Due to its popularity and easy access, expect sizable crowds at times - not all come to fish, but expect an excited onlooker or two if you hook up on a fish. The lake is designated as an accessible lake for those with special access requirements.

The rich aquatic plant life supports a healthy population of scuds and damselflies, which should be a clue to what you might want to fish in this lake. At any given time of the fishing season (when there's no ice on the lake) midges, BWOs and smaller PMDs hatch as well. Since the lake receives plenty of pressure, take a moment to assess what the fish might be keying on before selecting a fly. Fish a dry and a dropper to help figure out what they might take.

The panoramic view of Lily Lake below shows it is a very accessible fishery nearly all the way around the lake. Notice the rich underwater plant life which can be seen on the surface in areas. This is prime habitat for scuds and damselfly nymphs. There are few other lakes in the Park that have such diverse aquatic habitat as Lily Lake.

Sprague Lake

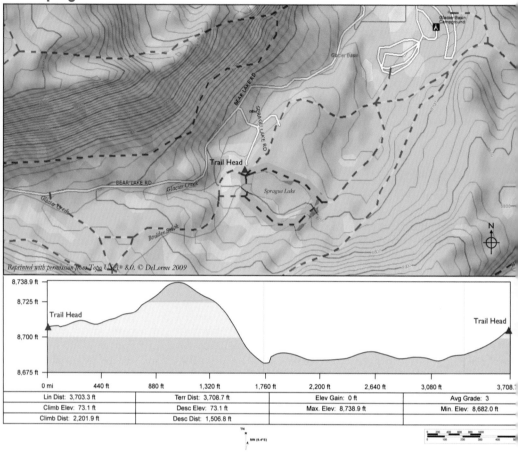

Reprinted with permission from Topo USA® 8.0. © DeLorme 2009

Lin Dist: 3,703.3 ft	Terr Dist: 3,708.7 ft	Elev Gain: 0 ft	Avg Grade: 3
Climb Elev: 73.1 ft	Desc Elev: 73.1 ft	Max. Elev: 8,738.9 ft	Min. Elev: 8,682.0 ft
Climb Dist: 2,201.9 ft	Desc Dist: 1,506.8 ft		

Trailhead: *Sprague Lake*   **USGS Quad(s):** *Longs Peak*

Trail Overview

 ♿ 🚶

    Sprague Lake Nature Trail is a flat loop of only ¾ of a mile (despite what the map and profile shows above), offering good fishing and great views of Hallet Peak and Flattop Mountain. It receives plenty of use by walkers, artists and fishermen. Sprague Lake is the only lake in the Park that is man-made. Abner Sprague dammed Boulder Brook to create a fishing pond for guests of his resort lodge in Glacier Basin which operated from 1910 through 1940.

Sprague Lake 🔵 🔵 🔵 8,688 ft

    The trail around Sprague Lake is well manicured to enable handicap accessibility, including access to two back country camp sites. Expect fishers to try their luck with the brookies that stack up in the slack water that forms just as Boulder Brook enters the lake, which is essentially an aquarium for viewing. Also expect plenty of anglers line the shore or even wade out a few yards casting to browns, brookies or the occasional rainbow. It is the only lake in the Park which supports three species of trout. The lake is relatively

Fishing Sprague Lake

shallow and in low water seasons can nearly be waded across. There are a few deeper areas throughout which are prime areas to cast a streamer.

Boulder Brook (a few hundred yards upstream of Sprague Lake) 🐟 🐟

Boulder Brook feeds Sprague Lake from the southwest. It is a quaint little stream above the marshy area and beaver dams just to the southwest of lake. While past stream fish surveys found modest populations of browns and brookies just a few hundred yards above the lake, recent beaver activity all but prevents fish from migrating upstream. From Sprague Lake, Boulder Brook Trail follows the brook upstream but quickly gives way to significant incline, making the stream impassible by fish.

LEFT: Boulder Brook has small runs and pools near Sprague Lake and steep stair-stepped plunges higher up.
RIGHT: Anglers wade out from shore in Sprague Lake.
BELOW: Whitley and Betsy Porter hike around Sprague Lake enjoying views of Otis Peak and Hallet Peak.

Wind River

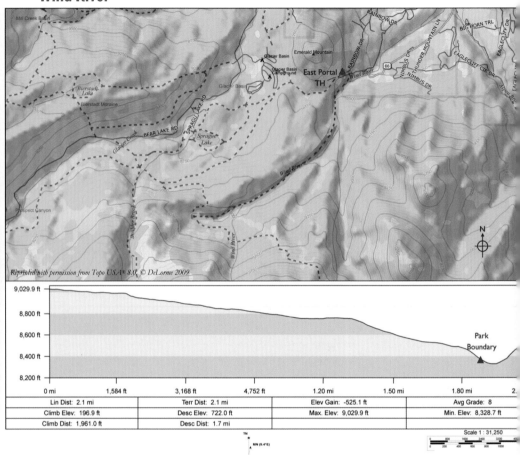

Lin Dist: 2.1 mi	Terr Dist: 2.1 mi	Elev Gain: -525.1 ft	Avg Grade: 8
Climb Elev: 196.9 ft	Desc Elev: 722.0 ft	Max. Elev: 9,029.9 ft	Min. Elev: 8,328.7 ft
Climb Dist: 1,961.0 ft	Desc Dist: 1.7 mi		

Scale 1 : 31,250

Trailhead: *East Portal*   **USGS Quad(s):**   *Longs Peak*

Trail Overview

Wind River Trail is a great day hike or few hour destination point for the traveler with little time to spare. Within minutes of the trailhead, the trail takes you by plenty of small stream fishing opportunity. The trail profile is deceiving as the first mile or so of the stream has the easiest fishing. There is no need to go any further than a mile or so in, as the last eight tenths of a mile of the stream is generally considered barren.

Wind River

Wind River is more of a creek than a river. It meanders through sparse woods and lush micro meadows. Dapping most any dry fly from a short 5X leader is the best method for this stream. Since the stream is small, the fish are commensurate in size. A six-inch brook trout is a nice catch, with an eight-incher being a reward. Walk softly as heavy feet will have these skittish fish running for cover. Low summertime flows can push fish into deeper bends and undercuts where a small slightly weighted streamer works best.

Fishing Wind River

UPPER LEFT: *Kollin Evens teases a few brookies holding in a small riffle.*

UPPER RIGHT: *Kerry Evens daps a dry fly in a heavily covered meadow channel.*

LOWER: *Kollin Evens holds a nice Wind River brookie caught on a high floating Royal Humpy.*

Glacier Creek and Glacier Gorge Trails

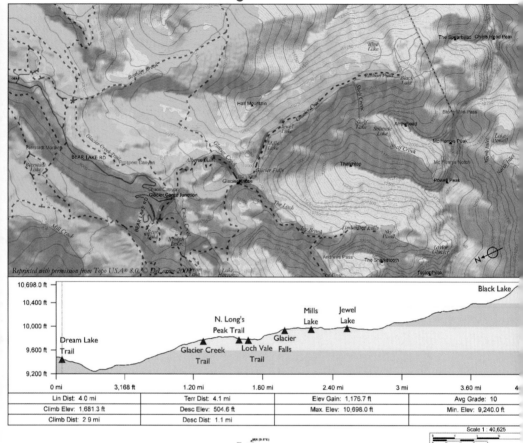

Trailhead: *Glacier Gorge*   **USGS Quad(s):** *McHenry's Peak*

Trail Overview

🚶 - 🚶 🚶 🚶

Note the orientation of the topographic map above. Glacier Creek Trail follows Bear Lake Road. Glacier Gorge trail is highlighted. Plenty of fishing water from the trailhead to Black Lake helps break this nine mile round-trip hike into bite-sized chunks for a great day hike and fishing outing. Expect plenty of trail traffic, but most do not hike this trail to fish. After the trail turns from a nicely manicured path to a more rugged back-country trail, crowds thin out.

This trail, referred to as the Ansel Adams Trail because of its picturesque photo opportunities, is the second most traveled trail in the Park. For the first mile, several winding switchbacks help ease the 500+ foot elevation gain. Drinking plenty of water and taking a rest or two is helpful. The trail traffic thins after Alberta Falls, one of the most visited falls in the Park. The trail meets up with Loch Vale Trail in another four-tenths of a mile. Another half mile and 200 feet in elevation gain reveals photogenic Mills Lake. From Mills Lake and adjacent Jewel Lake, the trail traverses marshy land on a well maintained and elevated trail, following closely Glacier Creek to the west. From the three mile mark to Black Lake, the trail again becomes steeper with the last third of a mile being the steepest portion anywhere on the trail. Note: Bear Lake is closed to fishing.

Fishing Glacier Creek and Glacier Gorge Trails

Glacier Creek (Prospect Canyon to Glacier Falls)

The lower section of this stream gets plenty of pressure since it is nearly drive-by fishing; however, it fishes well for brookies and rainbows. (Not shown on map - follows Bear Lake Road) Consider taking a walk up to Mills Lake for what is considered one of the most beautiful views in the Park; the walk gives plenty of opportunity for good fishing for rainbows and brookies along the way.

Glacier Creek (Glacier Falls to 10,100 ft, just above Jewel Lake)

Look for faster flowing and well-oxygenated water to locate the rainbows. The numerous pools below Mills Lake are good bets for rainbows. Brookies are plentiful throughout this entire section of Glacier Creek. Don't be surprised if you are photographed casting for fish by shutterbugs who share the trail.

Glacier Creek (10,100 ft to 10,200 ft, halfway to Black Lake)

The brookies aren't too selective and will readily take a well-presented dry fly, however they will scatter with heavy feet and a haphazard cast. Rainbows can be seasonal in this stretch. Catching a Colorado River cutthroat is a big bonus as they are present but more scarce. The water runs shallow during the summer months making the fish more skittish, yet very catchable since they are easily spotted. There is plenty of drainage coming in from the east and west of the creek year-round, making stream traversing marshy and wet.

Joe Johnson works a leaping rainbow out of a beautiful plunge pool on Glacier Creek.

Glacier Creek (10,200 ft to Black Lake)

The higher gradient of this section of Glacier Creek all but prevents the rainbows from Mills Lake and Jewel Lake from migrating upstream; however, the brookies from Black Lake have made their way down Ribbon Falls flowing from Black Lake. Spend some time exploring this section if you like small pocket water fishing.

Mills Lake   9,952 ft

Hiking up to Mills Lake reveals a lengthy shallow shelf spilling into a deadfall choked section of Glacier Creek. There's fun dapping-style fishing for an occasional larger rainbow in and around the deadfall during higher water times of the season. Of course, use common sense and caution when scrambling on slippery deadfall. The lake itself has plenty of cruising rainbows that will look up for an ant or

Fishing Glacier Creek and Gorge Trails

off the shelf edge. Walking out on the large exposed rock shelf about midway on the lake's east side will help you get an unobstructed double-haul cast past the shelf into the deeper water. Wading out is an option too, but some photo bugs get annoyed at having a wading fisher spoil the shot.

Jewel Lake 🐟 9,946 ft

Nearly adjacent to Mills Lake, Jewel Lake is smaller and shallower. It is connected to Mills Lake by a small section of Glacier Creek, worth exploring for rainbows and brookies. The same techniques used on Mills Lake apply here as well. Concentrate on the Glacier Creek drainages into and out of the lake.

Black Lake 🐟 10,634 ft

For the hiking fisherman in reasonable health and condition, the hike to Black Lake is not only rewarding for the hike itself but also for casting to larger shore-cruising brook trout. There are plenty of large boulders on the west side of the lake to stand upon, sight fish and cast. The lake has plenty of natural reproduction, so a small brook trout streamer imitation is a good bet when trout aren't rising. This lake is a popular watering hole for bighorn sheep and elk. An early morning hike into this lake before the crowds will give the best opportunity to see wildlife. Don't forget to look up and spin around, taking a moment to gather in spectacular views of Longs Peak, Keyboard of The Winds, Arrowhead, Stone Man Pass, The Spearhead and Chief's Head Peak. No where else in the Park will you be surrounded by peaks of this elevation, all 12,500 feet and higher. Of concern to the fisher: Blue Lake, Green Lake and Frozen Lake are all higher elevation feeders to Black Lake, but are barren.

Black Lake has the classic shelf and deep drop off of highly productive fishing lakes. Cruising brook trout search for a variety of floating insects, and will readily take a small Woolly Bugger or streamer as well.

The trail alongside Mills Lake is often called the Ansel Adams trail, due to its stunning beauty and incredible photographic opportunities.

A bull elk grazes in a braided section of Glacier Creek above Jewel Lake.

Loch Vale Trail

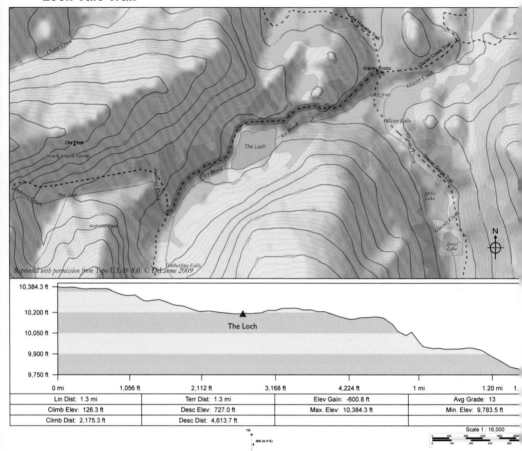

Reprinted with permission from Topo USA® 8.0. © DeLorme 2009

Lin Dist: 1.3 mi	Terr Dist: 1.3 mi	Elev Gain: -600.8 ft	Avg Grade: 13
Climb Elev: 126.3 ft	Desc Elev: 727.0 ft	Max. Elev: 10,384.3 ft	Min. Elev: 9,783.5 ft
Climb Dist: 2,175.3 ft	Desc Dist: 4,613.7 ft		

Scale 1 : 16,000

Trailhead: *Bear Lake or Glacier Gorge*

USGS Quad(s): *McHenry's Peak*

Trail Overview

🚶 🚶 - 🚶 🚶 🚶

From Glacier Gorge trailhead, follow the well-traveled Glacier Creek Trail to a confusing junction of four trails: Lake Haiyaha Trail, Loch Vale Trail, Glacier Creek Trail and North Longs Peak Trail. Along the way you'll walk with many to Alberta Falls where the crowds and maintained trails wane away. Follow Loch Vale Trail to the lake. Much of the trail is exposed to sun and weather so be prepared with sunscreen and a rain jacket if poor weather sets in.

The Loch 🐟 🐟 10,184 ft

This lake has to be one of the most fun to fish in the Park. The fish are always eager as they cruise the tree-laden shoreline looking for food. Because the fishing can be consistently good, it's a good lake for the novice. Much of the shoreline can be waded. In the spring waders are nice to have when the water is cooler, otherwise wet wading can be a nice relief to the hot summer days. The lake receives plenty of year-round drainage from the adjacent land. Because of this the soggy drainage is perfect homestead for

Fishing Loch Vale Trail

mosquitos. Heed this warning - bring bug spray. If you don't, you'll pay the price.

The lake has extremely healthy bug populations far exceeding most other lakes in the Park. Expect to see on any given day ants, midges, caddis and mayflies floating in the surface film. You'll often notice trout rising to almost nothing at all. They're taking small midges. If you want some extremely small dry fly fishing fun, pack a few small gray midge emergers and dries in sizes 22-24. Richard's Gnat is a highly effective fly for this lake.

Educated greenback cutthroat in The Loch rise to insects right at your feet, undisturbed by your presence. Getting them to take an artificial fly is another story.

Icy Brook

Icy Brook enters The Loch at the southwest corner. This is a beautifully braided section of stream along a busy trail. If you hook a fish, expect an onlooker or two. You'll typically see some nice-sized greenback cutthroat feeding mid-stream in the gin clear water. If they are not interested in a dry fly, drift a small midge nymph or Hare's Ear about 10"-12" below the surface. Small tippet sizes, a quiet approach and gentle casts are a must here. Expect mostly greenback cutthroat closer to The Loch, with brook trout higher upstream. More on Icy Brook can be found in the *Sky Pond Trail* section.

The Loch ranks as one of the most beautiful spots in the Park. Its extended shallow littoral zone is frequented by many cruising greenback cutthroat. Look for the many cutaway coves protected by the wind to find rising trout.

Sky Pond Trail

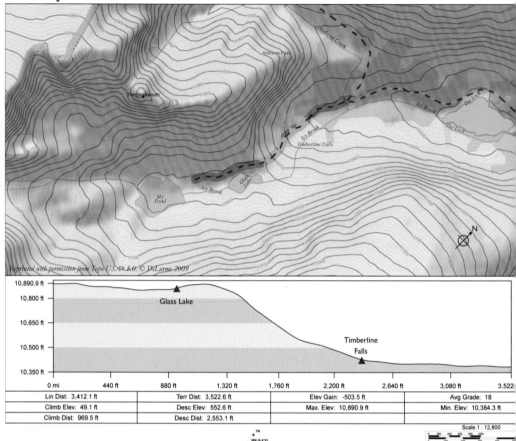

Lin Dist: 3,412.1 ft	Terr Dist: 3,522.6 ft	Elev Gain: -503.5 ft	Avg Grade: 18
Climb Elev: 49.1 ft	Desc Elev: 552.6 ft	Max. Elev: 10,890.9 ft	Min. Elev: 10,384.3 ft
Climb Dist: 969.5 ft	Desc Dist: 2,553.1 ft		

Scale 1 : 12,800

Trailhead: *Bear Lake or Glacier Gorge*　　**USGS Quad(s):** *McHenry's Peak*

Trail Overview

Sky Pond Trail is a short trail spur of the Loch Vale Trail. The shortest distance to Sky Pond is to take the Glacier Creek Trail from Glacier Gorge trailhead to the Loch Vale Trail. Walking around The Loch (which is difficult to do without stopping to fish) and following the trail south along Icy Brook will bring you to Sky Pond Trail. From The Loch, Sky Pond trail to Glass Lake is essentially like walking up a staircase; it can get steep in spots. The quarter mile hike from Glass Lake to Sky Pond is easy. Andrews Creek and Icy Brook above Sky Pond are both considered barren.

Icy Brook

This section of Icy Brook, between The Loch and Glass Lake ranks as one of the most scenic stretches of stream water in the Park. It has very clear water protected by beautiful stands of tall pines. Midway between Glass Lake and The Loch, the stream offers a wide variety of long glides, smooth bends, plunge pools and riffles. Fish in this section of creek routinely sip dries on the surface. However, I have found they prefer smaller flies such

Fishing Sky Pond Trail

as size 18-22 midge dries, small Griffith's Gnats, size 16-18 Elk Hair Caddis and size 18-20 Parachute Adams. If they aren't looking up, try nymphing a small midge or pheasant tail a foot below the surface to fish you've spotted feeding. Thinner tippets are also required - 5X or smaller. More on Icy Brook can be found in the Loch Vale section.

Glass Lake 🐟 🐟 10,827 ft

This lake must be misnamed; I have never been to Glass Lake where it has been calm as glass (it is also referred to as Lake of Glass by some) The wind seems to always howl between Thatchtop Mountain and The Sharkstooth spires and commensurate weather usually follows. Glass Lake is less protected than Sky Pond, so if the wind is a bit much for you here, go on up to Sky Pond where there are some natural wind blocks in the shallow cove areas. The trek up to Glass Lake has you manually 'four-wheeling' as you climb up alongside and within Timberline Falls. Brookies dominate the water, but an occasional Greenback can be found.

Sky Pond 🐟 10,887 ft

The easy trek to Sky Pond from Glass Lake traverses rock slabs and loose boulders. If you make it to Glass Lake, it's a disservice to yourself not to continue on to Sky Pond. The view back down the valley to Glass Lake and the The Loch is spectacular. I have found Sky Pond to contain some of the largest brook trout in the Park. Find a section of the shore protected by the wind and look for rising fish. Cast a size size 12-14 attractor dry. If no risers are seen, tie on a size 6-8 Woolly Bugger and cast along structure where the brook trout tend to hide.

LEFT: Icy Brook between The Loch and Glass Lake is one of the most beautiful streams in the Park. In the midsection, gently flowing emerald water and plenty of submerged boulders offer perfect habitat for trout.

RIGHT: Sky Pond has some of the Park's largest brook trout. Don't forget to fish the lake's outlet rocks .

Lake Haiyaha, Dream Lake, Emerald Lake Trails

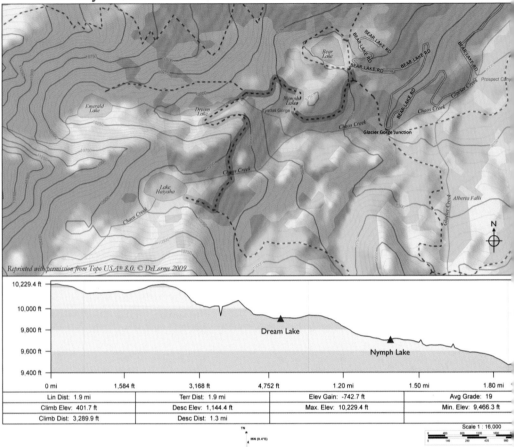

Reprinted with permission from Topo USA® 8.0. © DeLorme 2009

Lin Dist: 1.9 mi	Terr Dist: 1.9 mi	Elev Gain: -742.7 ft	Avg Grade: 19
Climb Elev: 401.7 ft	Desc Elev: 1,144.4 ft	Max. Elev: 10,229.4 ft	Min. Elev: 9,466.3 ft
Climb Dist: 3,289.9 ft	Desc Dist: 1.3 mi		

Scale 1 : 16,000

Trailhead: Bear Lake or Glacier Gorge

USGS Quad(s): McHenry's Peak

Trail Overview

🧍🧍🧍 - 🧍🧍🧍🧍🧍

It's only fitting that Lake Haiyaha lies in a canyon named Chaos. A renegade glacier carved the canyon out long ago, leaving unusually large boulders strewn about, a situation unlike any other canyon in the Park. In fact, Haiyaha is a Native Indian word loosely interpreted as 'large rocks'. The trail is a spur of Dream Lake Trail which begins at the Bear Lake trailhead. It continues on to Loch Vale Trail to the southeast. The interconnected trails that support hikes to lakes Haiyaha, Nymph, Dream and Emerald is arguably the most used trail system in the Park. Expect to hike with plenty other visitors to these destinations. These waters are considered barren: Upper Chaos Creek and Nymph Lake.

Lake Haiyaha   10,227 ft

The lake is only one of two lakes in the Park that have Yellowstone cutthroat. This lake is a very finicky lake to fish. At times, it will be teeming with rising fish rather easy to catch. At other times, the fish won't give your fly any attention. Rarely does the wind not blow in this canyon, so position yourself on the side of the lake that is the calmest.

Fishing Lake Haiyaha, Dream Lake, Emerald Lake Trails

Attractor dry flies such as the Go-To-Hell Variant or Royal Wulff are choice patterns.

Chaos Creek

Just below Lake Haiyaha, Yellowstone cutthroat hide between the rocks and boulders. Since the creek is small, a short leader is best. Dap a fly around the small pockets that surround the boulders to catch average sized fish. Small greenback cutthroat can be found further down where the outlet of Dream Lake joins Chaos Creek. Some Yellowstone cutthroat travel upstream above Lake Haiyaha, but not far.

Dream Lake   9,916 ft

It's an easy hike to Dream Lake, but expect plenty of hiking partners from the Bear Lake trailhead. The long, skinny lake is a popular destination for photographers, especially as the sun rises, in order to catch the purple-orange glow that resonates off Hallet Peak onto the still waters. The shores get plenty of traffic and the fish tend to be oblivious to the onlookers, but also are more wary of a fly. Try using a small midge such as Richard's Gnat or Mike's CDC Puff.

Tyndall Creek

Tyndall Creek flows in and out of Dream Lake. Small caddis dries are the norm to use in the summer. During off-color or high water times, nymph a Steve's Baetis or Tabou Caddis on the edge of slower runs and behind boulders.

Emerald Lake   10,117 ft

Hardly can a lake become more splendid than Emerald Lake. You'll see and hear a beautiful waterfall flowing from the saddle to the west. The lake is less impacted by wind since it is tightly nestled under the watchful pose of Hallet Peak and Flattop Mountain. Emerald Lake is roughly the size of Bear Lake and much deeper. For the few fish that are in the lake, small black flies such as ants and midges tend to produce better than larger attractor flies.

Sean Miller finds a rare still day on Lake Haiyaha is the perfect time to cast a small midge to cruising Yellowstone cutthroat. Long leaders and small tippets help ease the wariness of the trout.

Chasm Lake Trail (Peacock Pool)

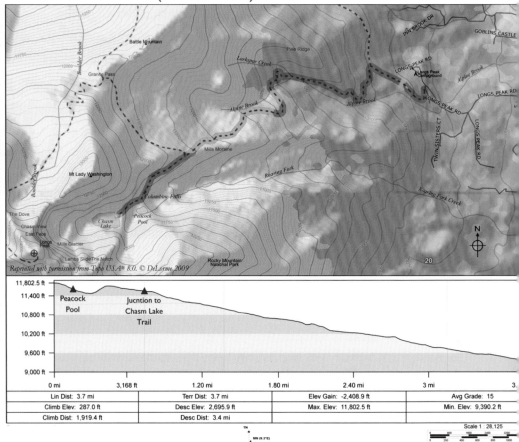

Reprinted with permission from Topo USA® 8.0. © DeLorme 2009

Lin Dist: 3.7 mi	Terr Dist: 3.7 mi	Elev Gain: -2,408.9 ft	Avg Grade: 15
Climb Elev: 287.0 ft	Desc Elev: 2,695.9 ft	Max. Elev: 11,802.5 ft	Min. Elev: 9,390.2 ft
Climb Dist: 1,919.4 ft	Desc Dist: 3.4 mi		

Scale 1 : 28,125

Trailhead: *Longs Peak*   **USGS Quad(s):**   *Longs Peak*

Trail Overview

🚶🚶🚶 - 🚶🚶🚶🚶

The trail to Peacock Pool starts at Longs Peak trailhead. This is one of the most visited trails in the Park due to Longs Peak summit seekers. In the summertime afternoon hours, you'll pass weary hikers coming down from reaching the 14,259' Longs Peak - give them the right-of-way, they deserve it. East Longs Peak Trail from the trailhead is a dogged schlep uphill, gaining 2,250 feet over 3.5 miles. Once you reach Peacock Pool, you'll need to scramble down a few hundred feet of loose boulders. It can be fun to scramble down, but be careful. The Roaring Fork above Peacock Pool, Chasm Lake and Alpine Brook are considered barren.

Peacock Pool   11,309 ft

If you venture high above Peacock Pool, you'll see why it is named as such. On sunny days, the shallow littoral zone edges and deep bowl in the middle yield an array of wonderful colors ranging from copper-bronze to emerald-blue – just like a peacock tail feather. The lake is even shaped like a peacock eye feather. This lake has a perfect shape

Fishing Chasm Lake Trail

and structure to support trout, much like Black Lake on Glacier Creek Trail. Look for cruising brook trout along the shallow edges, particularly along the western and eastern shores. Small terrestrial patterns work well here.

Roaring Fork

The stream below Peacock Pool rapidly drops down a few hundred feet to a thin flat shelf. The travel is rough going and the fish are more sparse. Mosquitos are thick so be prepared. About a half mile below Peacock Pool is an unnamed shallow pond that has a few brookies in it as well. Fish can be found above and below the pond. Below the pond, the stream braids, then starts a rapid descent to the densely wooded slopes north of Meeker Park.

RIGHT: The author fishes the Roaring Fork below Peacock Pool.

BELOW: Peacock Pool is majestically guarded by Longs Peak.

"Fly fishing is the excuse, getting there is the real reward. If I can see all the world's stars and hear what silence really sounds like, then I've hiked far enough."
- Steven B. Schweitzer

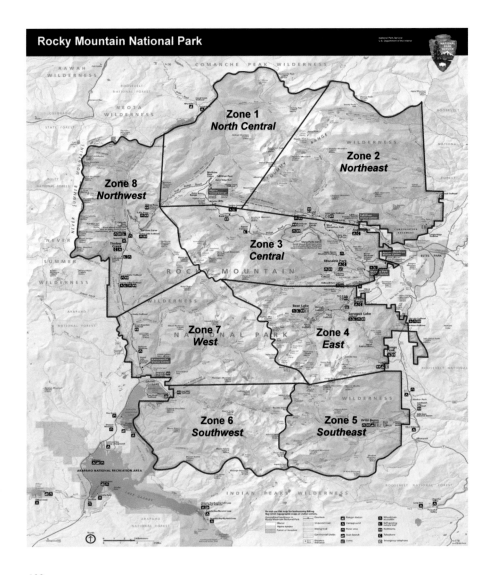

Zone 5 - Southeast

Sandbeach Lake Trail

Wild Basin Trail

Thunder Lake Trail

Finch Lake Trail, Pear Lake Trail

Bluebird Lake Trail

Rocky Mountain National Park

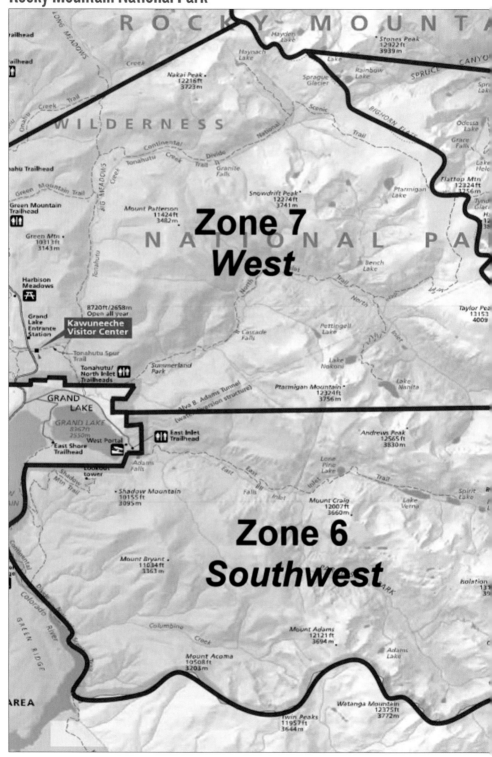

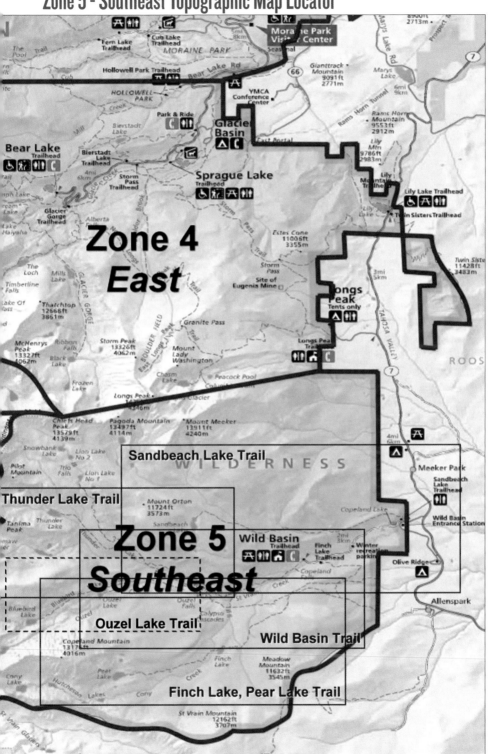

Sandbeach Lake Trail

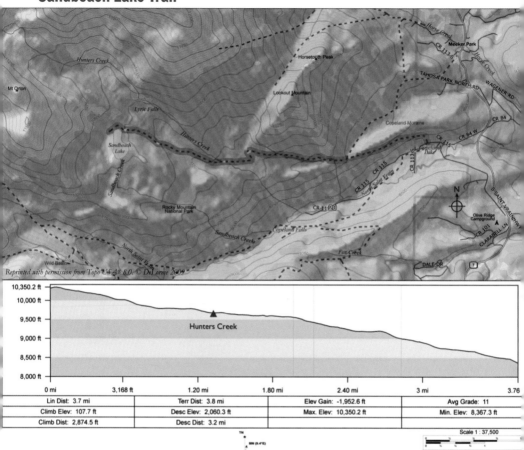

Reprinted with permission from Topo US 4® 8.0. © DeLorme 2009.

Lin Dist: 3.7 mi		Terr Dist: 3.8 mi		Elev Gain: -1,952.6 ft		Avg Grade: 11
Climb Elev: 107.7 ft		Desc Elev: 2,060.3 ft		Max. Elev: 10,350.2 ft		Min. Elev: 8,367.3 ft
Climb Dist: 2,874.5 ft		Desc Dist: 3.2 mi				

An October snow squall over Mt. Meeker darkens the skies and brings high winds with blowing snow over Sandbeach Lake as Liz Yaeger looks on. Late season fishing on high altitude lakes such as Sandbeach require a good cast against strong winds with heavily weighted flies.

Fishing Sandbeach Lake Trail

Trailhead *Sandbeach Lake* **USGS Quad(s):** *Allenspark*

Trail Overview

🚶🚶🚶 - 🚶🚶🚶🚶

Sandbeach Lake is a perfect day hike. The lake has plenty of picnic spots along the expansive sandy north and east beaches. The 4.5 mile hike from the trailhead is a continuous uphill trek through beautiful tall pines and gangly aspen. It's not particularly steep in any one spot, but the continuous altitude gain makes for a nice day hike workout. The portion of Hunter's Creek above the Wild Basin trailhead contains a population of greenback cutthroat; however, there is no fishing above the ranger station as posted (note: Hunter's Creek regulations may change in future years). Kepplinger Lake (not on topographic map), the headwater of Hunter's Creek, and Camper's Creek are also barren.

Copeland Lake 🐟 🐟 8,326 ft

Copeland Lake is one of the few drive-by lakes in the Park. The park access road to Wild Basin and Sandbeach Lake Trailheads circumnavigate the lake. It's worth noting the small valley in which Copeland Lake lies is barely over a mile long and it warrants exploring all the small ponds and braided river sections of the North St. Vrain River. You'll find almost exclusively brook trout in these waters. The area around the lake and in the meadow is quite wet and soggy; be prepared with hip waders at least.

Sandbeach Lake 🐟 10,307 ft

This beautiful bean-shaped lake is nestled adjacent to mammoth Mt. Meeker and has always been one of the Park's classic greenback fisheries. In early summer, plan on an early morning hike to greet the sun and rising trout during the morning midge hatch. This lake has a diverse insect habitat so don't be afraid to drift a scud or damselfly several feet deep during the heat of the day - a larger hopper or caddis fly can act as an indicator fly.

Sandbeach Creek 🐟

For an energetic day hike and rewarding fishing opportunity, access Sandbeach Creek via the southern end of Sandbeach Lake, then fish the creek down to Wild Basin Trail just before Copeland Falls. The stream is small, boulder strewn and littered with plenty of deadfall. Traversing the stream path is tedious and slow work. Low flows in the fall make for some difficult fish finding. The greenbacks will eagerly take a caddis dry or Adams.

Wild Basin Trail

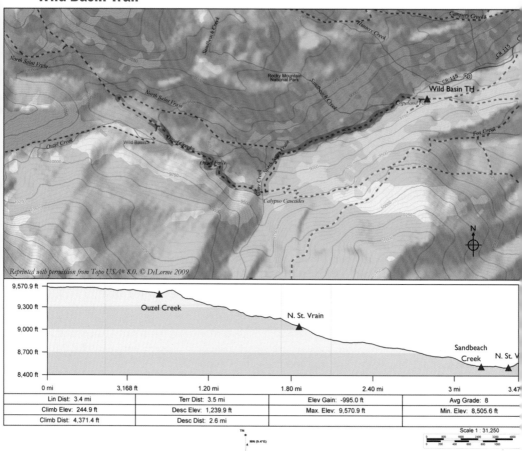

Reprinted with permission from Topo USA® 8.0. © DeLorme 2009.

Lin Dist: 3.4 mi	Terr Dist: 3.5 mi	Elev Gain: -995.0 ft	Avg Grade: 8
Climb Elev: 244.9 ft	Desc Elev: 1,239.9 ft	Max. Elev: 9,570.9 ft	Min. Elev: 8,505.6 ft
Climb Dist: 4,371.4 ft	Desc Dist: 2.6 mi		

Scale 1 : 31,250

Trailhead: *Wild Basin*   **USGS Quad(s):**   *Allenspark*

Trail Overview

Wild Basin Trail takes the hiking fisher to several small streams for an easy day hike to all. Just minutes into the hike, the trail crosses Sandbeach Creek and then follows the North St. Vrain closely for about 1.4 miles. Wild Basin Trail takes a sharp turn to the south about 1.5 miles from the trailhead, at the junction of the Campsite Shortcut Trail. It then turns northwesterly, following Ouzel Creek for a short time. The trail is wide and well-maintained for the first mile, then becomes thinned and more rock-strewn as it gains altitude modestly and steadily throughout. While it follows the North St. Vrain, it is flanked by tall pines and aspen, making a beautiful stroll in the autumn as the aspen leaves turn yellow.

Sandbeach Creek

Sandbeach Creek begins a steep climb for about eight tenths of a mile from the trail. The section mentioned here references the first quarter of a mile, which is the easiest off-trail fishing to be had in this stretch. The forest is dense around the stream amid rock clearings as it loosely parallels the North St. Vrain. Fishing for Greenbacks is marginal in

Fishing Wild Basin Trail

this section, but the off-trail exploration is exceptional.

North St. Vrain

This is the mainstay fishing destination on this trail. The further up the creek you travel, the more brook trout and an occasional hybrid cutthroat can be found. Brown trout dominate the first mile of stream beyond the trailhead. Much above 8,800 feet in altitude (after the first mile and a quarter), brown trout become sparse. The North St. Vrain is the quintessential Rocky Mountain National Park stream. It contains gentle cascades, plunge pools, boulders and tail-outs throughout. Plenty of deadfall also provide eddies and pools to hide larger trout. While this stream fishes well using the full life-cycle of caddis, depending on the season, small yellow sallies (stoneflies) are also plentiful. This is a perfect day hike or afternoon fishing destination for those short on time in the Park.

Cony Creek (N. St. Vrain to Calypso Cascades)

A short stretch of this creek follows the trail and is heavily influenced by the brookie population in the North St. Vrain. Cony Creek even has the look and feel of the North St. Vrain as well. While it can be fun to catch a few brookies in this section, Cony Creek further up towards Pear Lake and Hutcheson Lakes is considerably more productive with greenback cutthroat. Calypso Cascades separates the Greenbacks above and the brookies thriving below.

Ouzel Creek (N. St. Vrain to Ouzel Falls)

This is a short, steep section of the creek with limited populations of fish simply because of the incline of the terrain. The water swiftly flows over boulders and deadfall from Ouzel Falls to the North St. Vrain; it's unfishable until well after run-off.

The North St. Vrain is a feature-packed stream that will appeal to all types of fly fishers. Despite being only yards from a popular trail, its wild and undisturbed nature is classic RMNP fishing water.

Thunder Lake Trail

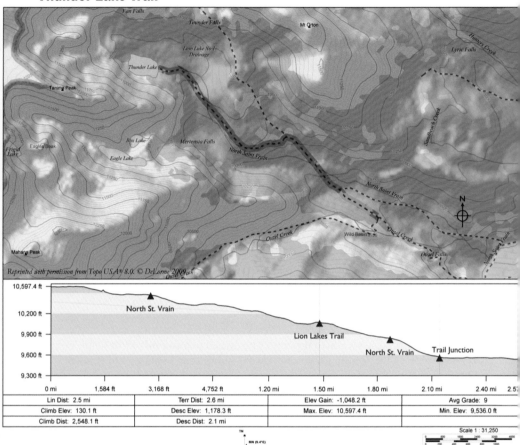

Reprinted with permission from Topo USA® 8.0. © DeLorme 2009

Trailhead: *Wild Basin*   **USGS Quad(s):** *Allenspark*
Isolation Peak

Trail Overview

🧍🧍🧍 - 🧍🧍🧍🧍

Reaching Thunder Lake requires an aggressive day hike of 6.7 miles one-way from the trailhead. Be sure to use the short-cut trail connecting Wild Basin Trail to Thunder Lake Trail. If you plan on fishing Box Lake and its drainage, consider making this an overnight trip. The three miles or so from the Wild Basin trailhead is an easy day hike; then the altitude gain begins, rising nearly 1,800 feet over the next four miles. These waters are considered barren: Falcon Lake, Eagle Lake, Snowbank Lake, Lion Lake No. 1, Lion Lake No. 2, Castle Lakes, Twin Lakes, Lake of Many Winds and drainage, Indigo Pond and drainage.

North St. Vrain (from Falcon Lake down) 🐟 🐟 🐟

There's no need to go all the way to Falcon Lake as the steep incline to the lake is barren. Just follow the trail around the northern side of Thunder Lake to fish the inlet for a half mile. You'll cross two inlets to Thunder Lake, the southern one coming from

Fishing Thunder Lake Trail

Lake of Many Winds (this lake's name could actually describe many of the lakes in the Park!) The stream is characterized by dense wood cover and stair-stepped pools, which make for easy dry fly fishing. While brown trout and cutthroat have been sampled in these waters, it is mostly dominated by brook trout. Surprisingly, not too many greenback cutthroat inhabit the mid- and lower reaches of this stream.

Lion Lakes Drainage (below Thunder Falls) 🐟

Just before you arrive at Thunder Lake, you'll cross two streams, the first being the drainage from Lion Lakes. Loaded with brookies, you could spend all day following this small drainage upstream catching fish after fish on dry flies. The drainage meanders through some marshy open areas flanked by tall stands of mature evergreens. The entire area looks very "moosey" and attracts plenty of wildlife including deer, elk, bear and moose.

The second drainage you'll encounter has no official name and comes from no formal lake. This drainage originates from the cirque of Mount Alice and is indistinguishable from the Lion Lakes drainage, fishing just as well.

Box Lake 🐟 10,767 ft

A rather rigorous off-trail trek brings you to Box Lake, a small lake over-loaded with brook trout. Do not attempt to approach the lake straight from Thunder Lake. Instead, fish your way down the North Saint Vrain to the outlet of Box Lake. Follow the outlet past Mertensia Falls to Box Lake. The lake is at 10,767 feet and is in the shadows of Tanima Peak and Mahana Peak, keeping it from icing off until very late in the spring. This makes the fish very hungry most of the open water season. Any fly, any tactic will catch you plenty of fish.

Box Lake Drainage (to North St. Vrain) 🐟

While short in distance and smallish in size, the Box Lake drainage is a fun brook trout fishery. The drainage cuts deep channels a few feet wide in marshy land. Stealthy approaches casting an attractor dry on a short leader with entice strikes from beautifully dark brook trout. The brookies tend to be darker in color due to the rich food content and seasonal tannic water color.

Thunder Lake 🐟 🐟 🐟 10,574 ft

The trail's namesake is one of the finest greenback cutthroat fisheries in the Park. And it's one of the most scenic, too. The two inlets on the western end of the lake, both fish well with dry flies. Moreso than in other feeder streams in the Park, the Greenbacks tend to be more selective to specific flies. Griffith's Gnats will work one day and not the next. Switch between a Para Adams, Ant, Humpy, Caddis or Royal Wulff until you find a fly that brings a strike. Stick with medium small flies in the 14-18 size range. If they are really picky, a size 20 Para Adams or ant pattern can be the ticket. Thunder Lake's outlet fishes particularly well right at ice-out as the fish start eating anything in sight.

Fishing the lake itself is most productive with the standard suite of dry flies cast well ahead of patterned and cruising fish. If they aren't looking up, slow stripping or twitching a general nymph pattern or a soft hackle a few feet below the surface can be the ticket. And of course, fishing an olive, black or brown Woolly Bugger is effective too.

On rainy or inclement days, taking a rest at the covered porch of the patrol cabin is a welcome break.

Fishing Thunder Lake Trail

ABOVE: The outlet of Thunder Lake fishes best just after ice-out.

BELOW: North Saint Vrain Creek on the way up to Thunder Lake has plenty of pools and pockets to float a dry fly over hungry brookies and browns.

Fishing Thunder Lake Trail

ABOVE: The unnamed drainage from Lion Lakes cuts through marshy bog and tall stands of pines. Don't forget the bug dope to keep the mosquitos away.

Lower LEFT: Box Lake drainage is small, but is full of brookies.
Lower RIGHT: Sean Miller explores the upper reaches of North Saint Vrain Creek.

Finch Lake Trail, Pear Lake Trail

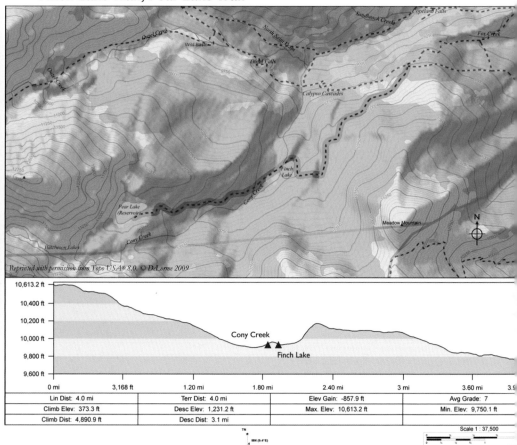

Reprinted with permission from Topo USA® 8.0. © DeLorme 2009

Lin Dist: 4.0 mi	Terr Dist: 4.0 mi	Elev Gain: -857.9 ft	Avg Grade: 7
Climb Elev: 373.3 ft	Desc Elev: 1,231.2 ft	Max. Elev: 10,613.2 ft	Min. Elev: 9,750.1 ft
Climb Dist: 4,890.9 ft	Desc Dist: 3.1 mi		

Trailhead: *Wild Basin*   **USGS Quad(s):** *Allenspark Isolation Peak*

Trail Overview

The easiest way to get to Pear Lake Trail is via the Allenspark trailhead taking Allenspark Trail to Finch Lake Trail. Finch Lake Trail then takes you to Pear Lake Trail. Finch Lake and Pear Lake Trail are essentially the same trail. Finch Lake Trail past barren Finch Lake is called Pear Lake Trail. The three trails combined span 5.6 miles from trailhead to Pear Lake over a moderate incline of 1,750 feet. These waters are considered barren: Finch Lake and drainage and Frigid Lake. Cony Lake is considered barren by most sources, but recently has been discovered to contain some fish.

Pear Lake (Reservoir) ➤ 10,587 ft

Pear Lake was once a reservoir in the early 1900's, being dammed to serve water to the immediate Front Range of Colorado. The dam was removed in 1988 leaving a noticeable scar along the boulders and cliff sides around Pear Lake. Most topographic maps still refer to Pear Lake as Pear Reservoir. During the day, the sun pounds the water pushing the fish deeper. But before the sun rises and after the sun is blocked by Mount Copeland,

Fishing Finch Lake, Pear Lake Trail

the fish look up for any tasty morsel blown in by afternoon winds. If you plan an overnight stay at one of the lake's two nearby campsites, venture to the Hutcheson Lakes during the day and come back to Pear Lake at sunset to continue good fishing. A size 20 Griffith's Gnat or a size 18 Para-Ant is a good choice. A small dark streamer is also a good choice around the lake outlet.

Pear Creek 🐟

Pear Creek is like any other creek in the Park. Fish will seek the pools, pockets and deep bank cuts, although this stream runs rather straight and has a fast drop to it past Pear Creek campsite to the confluence of Cony Creek. The first hundred yards of the stream fishes the best, working a size 14 attractor dry or caddis in the slack water areas.

Cony Creek 🐟

Cort Langworthy casts to rising fish on Middle Hutcheson Lake.

Cony Creek has its official start at Cony Lake and runs through each of the Hutcheson Lakes and Pear Lake before running south of Pear Lake Trail to Finch Lake. It then crosses the trail to the north to feed the North St. Vrain. The sections of the creek between the Hutcheson Lakes and from the intersection of Pear Creek and Cony Creek down to Finch Lake are prime dry fly fisheries in the summer.

Lower Hutcheson Lake 🐟 10,589 ft

There's a mostly unmarked faint foot trail heading up the incline from the southwest corner of Pear Lake. Follow it through a nicely wooded incline for about three-quarters of a mile. All of a sudden, you'll come to a small rise overlooking Lower Hutcheson Lake at 10,859 feet. You'll notice two inlet streams, both of which fish well upstream to Middle Hutcheson Lake.

Middle Hutcheson Lake 🐟 11,067 ft

Most folks who venture this far up rarely go past Middle Hutcheson, 11,067 feet. And for good reason - there is so much good fishing between this lake and Lower Hutcheson to keep the hiking angler busy all day. This lake is only a quarter mile upstream from Lower Hutcheson and easily missed. Most attractor dries and streamers work well. The growing season is short at this elevation, so the fish are noticeably more eager than greenback cutthroat at lower altitudes.

Upper Hutcheson Lake 🐟 11,490 ft

If you decide to venture the extra mile or so to Upper Hutcheson, you'll be amazed at the size of the lake and with the spectacular fishing. The hike up goes through some braided and ponded marshy sections, which can fish well, and should not be skipped.

Fishing Finch Lake Trail, Pear Lake Trail

ABOVE: The inlet to Lower Hutcheson Lake is prime habitat for greenback cutthroat.

LEFT: Neil Sudaisar fishes Cony Creek for colorful greenback cutthroat.

OPPOSITE PAGE: Cony Creek from Upper and Middle Hutcheson Lakes holds greenback cutthroat in the tiniest of pockets.

The entire Hutcheson Lakes area has good populations of Bighorn Sheep. Walk quietly and keep a sharp eye when walking from lake to lake...you just may see them grazing in the lush grassy areas or moving along a rocky slope.

Fishing Finch Lake Trail, Pear Lake Trail

Bluebird Lake and Ouzel Lake Trails

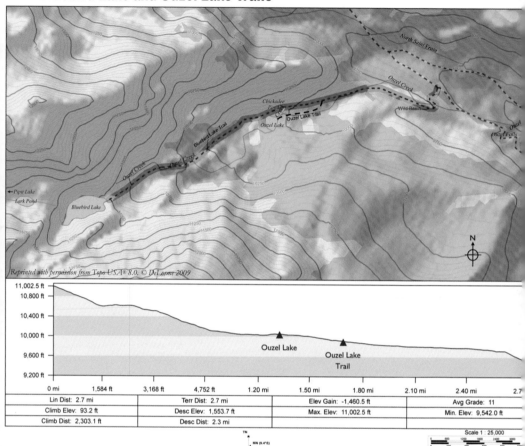

Reprinted with permission from Topo USA® 8.0, © DeLorme 2009

Lin Dist: 2.7 mi	Terr Dist: 2.7 mi	Elev Gain: -1,460.5 ft	Avg Grade: 11
Climb Elev: 93.2 ft	Desc Elev: 1,553.7 ft	Max. Elev: 11,002.5 ft	Min. Elev: 9,542.0 ft
Climb Dist: 2,303.1 ft	Desc Dist: 2.3 mi		

Scale 1 : 25,000

Trailhead: *Wild Basin*   **USGS Quad(s):** *Allenspark, Isolation Peak*

Trail Overview

🚶🚶 - 🚶🚶🚶

The entire hike to Ouzel Lake, which is the furthest practical fishing destination on this series of trails, is a moderately easy 4.9 miles one-way over a well-maintained pathway. The falls and lakes are popular day hike destinations. The most convenient access to Bluebird Lake Trail and Ouzel Lake Trail is from the Wild Basin trail head. Only 1.75 miles from the trailhead, Wild Basin Trail meets Bluebird Lake Trail at picturesque Calypso Cascades. From there, follow Bluebird Lake Trail past Ouzel Falls to the Ouzel Lake Trail. Ouzel Lake is only four tenths of a mile from the trail junction. These waters are considered barren: Bluebird Lake, Chickadee Pond, Isolation Lake, Lark Pond, Pipit Lake, Junco Lake and drainage (not on map; SW of Bluebird Lake) and Ouzel Creek above 10,600 feet.

Ouzel Creek (Ouzel Falls to Ouzel Lake) 🐟 🐟

From the junction of Wild Basin Trail with Bluebird Lake Trail, another eight tenths of a mile of several sweeping switchbacks leads to stately Ouzel Falls. You can follow the trail onward to Ouzel Lake Trail or take an unmarked fisherman's trail which gives access

Fishing Bluebird Lake and Ouzel Lake Trails

to Ouzel Creek just above the falls. Follow the trail upward to a large rock outcropping overlooking the valley, just past the falls. The fisherman's trail can be found directly behind the large rock outcropping. It steeply leads upward above the falls and is faint at best in most areas. Shortly after the trail leads to the head of the falls, faint fishermen footpaths and game trails take over.

Much of the lower section is dominated by brook trout. Since this section of the creek flows through a former burn area, there is not much cover to comfort the trout. Hence, they are skittish and will flee for cover with one errant cast or the flash of a shiny rod. Keep low and make your casts count and you'll be rewarded with some really colorful trout. Most of the greenback cutthroat are found within a hundred yards downstream from Ouzel Lake, although some occasionally are further downstream.

Ouzel Lake 🐟 🐟 10,107 ft

Of the four lakes in the Park which contain brookies and greenback cutthroat, Ouzel Lake is the most prolific with sizable populations of both. The lake is surprisingly shallow to have holdover fish, but a few deep channels keep fish through the winter. The shoreline is marshy throughout. Casting to cruising greenbacks might require wading. The brook trout are particularly spooky and will scatter before you get a chance to cast to them; it's a real reward to catch a brookie in this lake. Note the several feeder creeks around the perimeter of the lake which contain fish throughout the season.

Ouzel Creek (Ouzel Lake to 10,600 ft) 🐟

Ouzel Lake is at 10,107 feet. Only five hundred feet higher, just shy of Upper Ouzel Creek campground, is the upper limit of greenback cutthroat in Ouzel Creek. For all practical purposes, most greenbacks will be within a few hundred yards upstream of the lake.

LEFT: One of the most picturesque scenes in the Park - Ouzel Creek as it flows out of Ouzel Lake.

RIGHT: Josh Rickard hooks into a greenback cutthroat on the southwest corner of the lake. Ouzel Creek dumps into the lake just a few yards to his right.

"The new agency should manage the Parks for the enjoyment of the American people, and at the same time keep them unimpaired for the enjoyment of future generations."
- Stephen Mather - President and Owner of the Borax Company and pioneer of the federal agency The National Park Service.

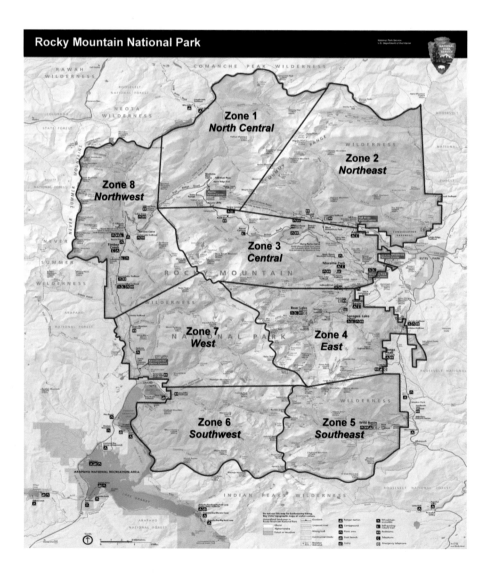

Zone 6 - Southwest

East Inlet Trail

Outlet Trail

Rocky Mountain National Park

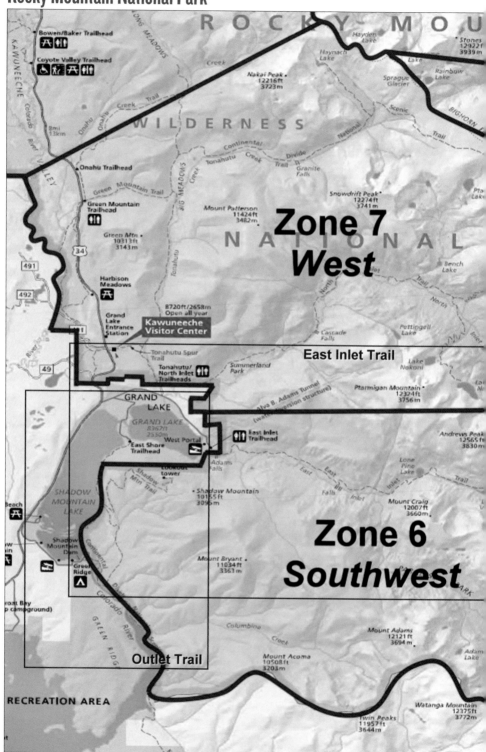

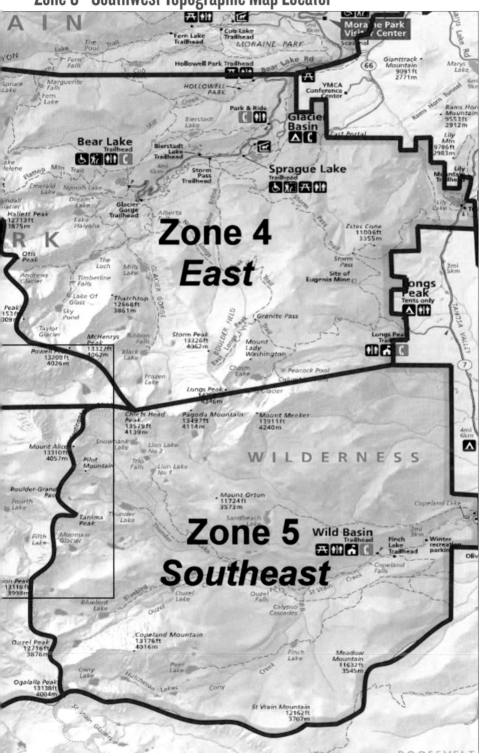

East Inlet Trail

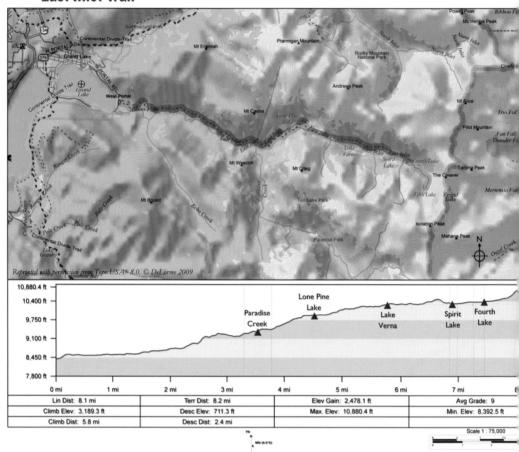

Lin Dist: 8.1 mi	Terr Dist: 8.2 mi	Elev Gain: 2,478.1 ft	Avg Grade: 9
Climb Elev: 3,189.3 ft	Desc Elev: 711.3 ft	Max. Elev: 10,880.4 ft	Min. Elev: 8,392.5 ft
Climb Dist: 5.8 mi	Desc Dist: 2.4 mi		

Scale 1 : 75,000

Trailhead:	*East Inlet*	**USGS Quad(s):**	*Shadow Mountain*
			Isolation Peak

Trail Overview

Don't be deceived by the moderately easy hike for the first few miles of this trail. From 2.5 miles in, the trail gains significant altitude to all fishing destinations throughout. For the first two miles, the trail gradually climbs along East Inlet Creek, offering plenty of opportunity to fish near the trail. Only a third of a mile from the trailhead is picturesque Adams Falls, which is a big draw; much of the trail traffic drops off from here. From Cat's Lair campsite to Lone Pine Lake, the trail breaks into a steep climb of roughly 1,000 foot elevation gain over two miles. For the next 3.5 miles to just before Fifth Lake, the altitude gain is relatively flat, only gaining approximately 500 feet. The last six tenths of a mile to Fifth Lake gains 400 feet in altitude. This trail offers the fly fisher ample opportunity to fish streams and lakes for eager brookies. Paradise Creek, just beyond Cat's Lair campsite, offers some incredible fishing for both brookies and Colorado River cutthroat, at the expense, however, of a steep hike following the creek on unimproved trails at best - and don't forget the bug dope.

Fishing East Inlet Trail

East Inlet Creek ⥲

Only a quarter mile from the trailhead brings you within 100 yards of East Inlet Creek. There's plenty of fishing for more than three miles, although the best fishing is in the first two miles. This is a fun stream to fish with a dry fly during the summer. Be stealthy as the brookies will scatter if you are too obvious or heavy-footed. Expect other fly fishers and curious on-lookers to be with you.

Echo Creek ⥲

Echo Creek comes in at the south end of East Meadow from its start some three miles upstream. It's a rather steep hike up for the first mile. The next mile offers small stream fishing for brook trout. The last mile is steep and small, not offering the best fishing opportunities. This should not be your first fishing choice along the East Inlet system.

Paradise Creek ⥲ ⥲

This is a demanding yet fun and highly rewarding destination for the dedicated hiker. It can be done in one day or camp at Cat's Lair or Gray Jay group camp on East Inlet Trail for a multi-day adventure. Follow East Inlet Creek to Paradise Park Trail (just over four miles from the trailhead, just before Lone Pine Lake). Soon, the trail peters out giving way to very difficult off-trail travel between Mt. Westcott and Mt. Craig. You can fish Paradise Creek for about a mile and

East Inlet Creek from the East inlet Trail - one of the most photographed vistas in the Park.

third (with approximately 450 feet of elevation gain) for brook trout. Following the river from Cat's Lair campsite takes you on a steep incline of 420 feet of elevation gain in only 0.4 miles, not really a recommended route, but an option. As you travel south, be sure to follow Paradise Creek to the left (flowing from the east), veering towards the rocky crags of Ten Lakes Park. Above the steep gradient incline lies a mile and a quarter of low gradient stream and meadow that provide ideal habitat for some really nice Colorado River cutthroat that rarely see a fly. The steep cascade of Paradise Creek separates the brookies and cutthroat.

Ten Lake Park Lake ⥲ 11,076 ft

This area is thought to be undisturbed since the glaciers came through. The price to pay for seeing this undisturbed beauty is a rough hike. Follow the instructions to Paradise Creek, then as you reach the first small meadow with a braided Paradise Creek, head east over the rock crags to the shelf where Ten Lakes Park sits. Give yourself all day and don't fish Paradise Creek first - I've made it half-way up the crags only having to turn around to make it out by dark. Oh, and don't forget the bug dope.

Fishing East Inlet Trail

Adams Lake 🐟 11,217 ft

Adams Lake is one of, if not the most, remote back-country lake in the Park. There is no short or easy way to get there. Follow Paradise Creek instructions above and continue to follow the creek for six miles through very difficult terrain loaded with deadfall and wet meadows. Another route is the Roaring Fork Trail just outside of the Park on the east side of Lake Granby. The nine mile trail is intensely steep (grade 20+) and requires just shy of three miles of off-trail travel. There are much easier destinations in the Park for Colorado River cutthroat.

Lone Pine Lake 🐟 9,891 ft

Lone Pine Lake has the classic fish producing shape with a deep middle and shallow shelf edges. Cast a streamer in this lake for hard-hitting brookies of average size. This lake is typically the uppermost water reached by fishing day hikers. The muddy shelf on the south side of the lake contain plenty of cruising fish.

Lake Verna, Spirit Lake 🐟 10,187 ft, 10,297 ft

On the hike from Lone Pine to Lake Verna, you quickly rise above Lone Pine Lake for a spectacular vista. Spirit Lake and Lake Verna both have healthy populations of brookies. Be sure to fish the connector stream from Spirit Lake and Lake Verna for fun small stream brookie action, particularly on an attractor dry fly such as a Royal Wulff.

Fourth Lake 🐟 10,397 ft

The pocketed meadows around Fourth Lake are moose country and their signs will be everywhere. Hike quietly and you'll increase your chances of seeing these majestic high country inhabitants. Fourth Lake fishes similarly to Lake Verna and Spirit Lake. If the fish aren't rising, try a small naturally-colored streamer such as an olive Woolly Bugger.

Fifth Lake 🐟 10,867 ft

The diminutive size of the stream from Fifth lake may fool you, but don't skip this water until you carefully peruse the deepest holding areas for Colorado cutthroat, especially during spawning time – the latter half of June and first half of July. The lake fishes more consistently with streamers than any other type of fly, but can be a finicky lake. Like the Paradise Creek valley, this area is a spectacular wide open valley.

Chris Bowell displays a beautiful Fifth Lake male Colorado River cutthroat in spawning colors.

The open meadow hike from Fourth Lake to Fifth Lake has beauty surpassed by few other spots in the Park. Peaks named The Cleaver are in the background.
Photo: Chris Bowell

Outlet Trail

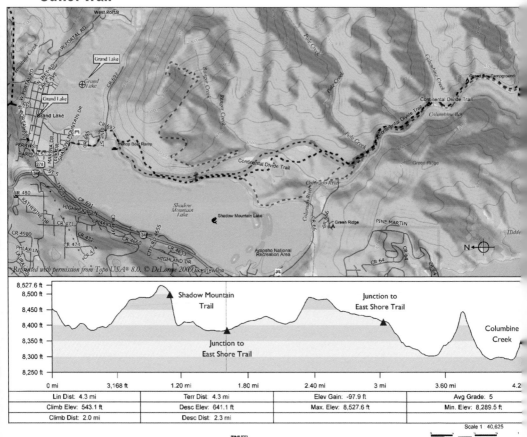

Lin Dist: 4.3 mi	Terr Dist: 4.3 mi	Elev Gain: -97.9 ft	Avg Grade: 5
Climb Elev: 543.1 ft	Desc Elev: 641.1 ft	Max. Elev: 8,527.6 ft	Min. Elev: 8,289.5 ft
Climb Dist: 2.0 mi	Desc Dist: 2.3 mi		

Trailhead: *East Inlet*   **USGS Quad(s):**   *Shadow Mountain*

Trail Overview

Note the orientation of the topographic map above. An easy, short day hike takes you along the east shore of Shadow Mountain Reservoir and the out-flowing Colorado River. Despite the ominous look of the trail profile above, the trail traverses only 227 feet in altitude from the lowest point of the trail to the highest. Midway through the hike, the official trail takes the high road and veers off into the woods presenting a perfect opportunity to spot moose. Following the shoreline takes you on East Shore Trail. Both trails reconnect below the foot bridge crossing along the Colorado River outlet of Shadow Mountain Reservoir. Pale Creek may contain seasonal fish but is generally considered barren.

Colorado River (below Shadow Mountain Dam)

This section of the Colorado River has the look of the big classic freestone water like the flow several hundred miles downstream, particularly during run-off or when excess water is being released from Shadow Mountain Reservoir. In the heat of the summer, fishing becomes more difficult as low flows create few areas fish can hold in and

Fishing Outlet Trail

subsequently the fish head downstream to Lake Granby.

During higher flows of the spring and early summer, the water becomes a fine fishery for sizeable rainbows and browns, many of which come up from Lake Granby. Nymphing is best with stoneflies and green caddis larvae patterns. Swinging a Woolly Bugger or streamer downstream is also a very effective technique. During this time of the year, expect a crowd.

Columbine Creek (Colorado River to 9,000 ft) 🐟

Columbine Creek can best be described as a small feeder creek bubbling through dense cover. The brook trout population is sparse in spots and the fish are on the small side, concentrated in stream bends and the occasional small pool. There's a foot trail that follows the stream although it is not maintained and barely noticeable in places.

Columbine Creek (9,000 ft to 9,200 ft) 🐟

Following the creek for about a mile and three-quarters reveals an open marshy area where a modest population of Colorado River cutthroat live in a meandering stream…and mosquitos thrive. If you've never fished for Colorado River cutthroat in the Park, this location shouldn't be your first choice simply due to the effort required for smallish trout. For the adventurous, though, this day hike into remote southwest Rocky Mountain National Park is a perfect choice.

The outlet of Shadow Mountain Reservoir, part of the Colorado River, is a favorite springtime and run-off fishing destination on the western side of the Park.

"In any moment of decision, the best thing you can do is the right thing, the next best thing is the wrong thing and the worst thing you can do is nothing."
 - Theodore Roosevelt

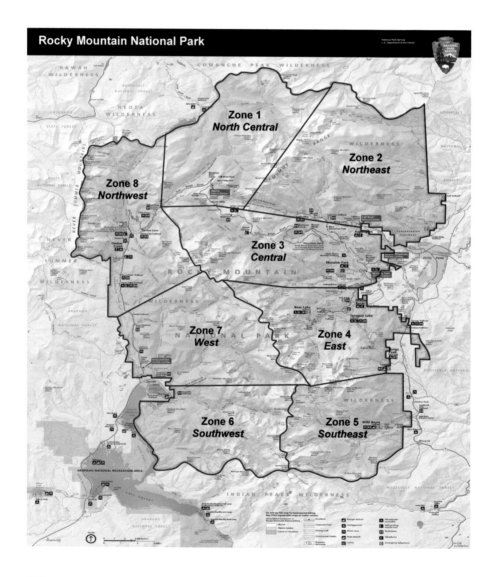

Zone 7 - West

North Inlet Trail

Lake Nanita Trail

Tonahutu Creek and Haynach Lakes Trail

Rocky Mountain National Park

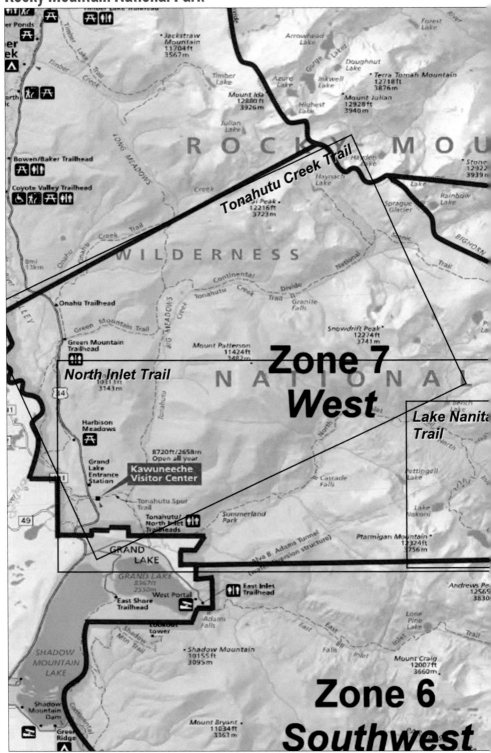

North Inlet Trail

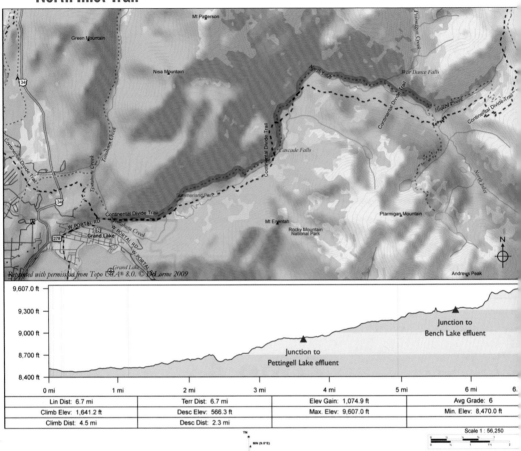

Reprinted with permission from Topo USA® 8.0. © DeLorme 2009

Lin Dist: 6.7 mi	Terr Dist: 6.7 mi	Elev Gain: 1,074.9 ft	Avg Grade: 6
Climb Elev: 1,641.2 ft	Desc Elev: 566.3 ft	Max. Elev: 9,607.0 ft	Min. Elev: 8,470.0 ft
Climb Dist: 4.5 mi	Desc Dist: 2.3 mi		

Scale 1 : 56,250

Trailhead: *Tonahutu/North Inlet*   **USGS Quad(s):**   *Grand Lake*
McHenry's Peak

Trail Overview

🧍🧍 - 🧍🧍🧍

North Inlet Trail is a gem of a trail and fishery from the very start. After a short three-quarter mile hike from the trailhead, the river meets the trail on the right. It's all one can do not to stop and fish the gorgeous flat stream water. For the next mile and a quarter, the trail heads to the north while the stream flows a few hundred yards to the south. This section is called Summerland Park. For the first three miles from the trailhead the trail is relatively flat, gaining only a few hundred feet of altitude as it closely follows North Inlet Creek to Cascade Falls. For the next 2.8 miles to the junction of Ptarmigan Creek (Bench Lake outlet) gives you plenty of streamside fishing opportunity. The next mile takes you to the junction of Lake Nanita Trail. From here, the trail gets decisively steeper and veers north of any fishing water.

These waters are considered barren: Hallet Creek, North Inlet Creek from the Continental Divide Trail to Lake Powell, Lake Powell, Pettingell Lake drainage, Ptarmigan Lake, Snow Drift Lake, Snow Drift Lake drainage above 10,400 ft. While Bench Lake and Ptarmigan Creek drainage above War Dance Falls are not barren (Colorado River cutthroat), current regulations close them to fishing.

Fishing North Inlet Trail

North Inlet Creek (Summerland Park area) ⟩⟩ ⟩⟩ ⟩⟩

Only minutes into the hike along the scenic North Inlet Trail, you'll approach a smooth stretch of North Inlet Creek. The stream is 20-30 feet wide and appears slow flowing due to the smooth surface appearance, although the flow is faster than you think. From the trailside water, the stream lazily meanders through very "moosey" Summerland Park. Fish in this area are very schooled, requiring sneaky approaches and delicate casts. In the spring during run-off, fish a nymph rig as dry fly rises are sparse. During the summer months, casting a size 14 Elk Hair Caddis, tan/yellow PMD, or yellow hopper close to the banks will yield a few nice fish. The occasional Colorado River cutthroat is caught in this section. The larger brookies and browns tend to cooperate nicely early in the morning and right at dusk.

North Inlet Creek (above Cascade Falls) ⟩⟩ ⟩⟩

This section has the bulk of the stream fishing water along the trail. While the entire trail can give you opportunities to see moose, there is always evidence of them wandering the stream banks along this stretch, looking for their favorite food: willows. Without a doubt this is one of my favorite spots in the Park, not only for the fishing, but for the scenery and the wildlife spotting opportunities. I routinely run into more moose on this trail than any other.

North Inlet Creek above Cascade Falls is a prototypical dry fly stream any fly fisher would drool to fish. For nearly 4 miles, the creek is a non-stop rerun of falls, pools, riffles, glides, etc. Behind every boulder lies a trout looking up. During the spring run-off, this river can be difficult to fish, however focusing a nymphing rig (size 14 Hare's Ear or Pheasant Tail) behind boulders is a good bet. Once run-off subsides and the water turns clear, dry fly fishing for brookies and Colorado River cutthroat can be epic. Matching the hatch is not usually necessary as any well placed dry fly will attract splashy interest. If the trout seem picky, focus on size 16 BWOs in the spring, size 12-14 PMDs in early to mid-summer and Elk Hair Caddis from mid summer into fall. Expect more brookies lower in this section while Colorado River cutthroat are more prevalent, even to exclusivity, the higher up you go.

North Inlet Creek (Lake Nanita Trail to Continental Divide Trail) ⟩⟩

This short section of creek is scattered with large boulders and steeper gradients. Using similar techniques discussed above, focus on areas behind the boulders and in the slack water. This section also has plenty of streamside willows, so keep your eyes out for quietly feeding moose, especially at dusk.

Pettingell Lake ⟩⟩ 10,517 ft

A discrete warning: this is not a fishing location for most folks, unless, of course, you are a back country off-trail junkie. There's so much fishing opportunity along the maintained North Inlet Creek trail that it makes this off trail trek only for the dedicated. Instead of trying to follow Pettingell Lake drainage up 1,600 feet of elevation over 1.3 miles of scrambling and deadfall hopping, consider the easier 1.3 mile off-trail route over the saddle just North of barren Lake Nokoni. The north shore is well wooded while the west and south shores are more open and rock strewn. Wait until snow is well cleared (early July), which makes the trek easier.

Fishing North Inlet Trail

Ptarmigan Creek (from trail to War Dance Falls) ➤

This four tenths of a mile hike up rather steep terrain follows the creek, which is a miniature North Inlet Creek in features. Dry fly fishing the pockets and micro-pools will give you plenty of action with smaller Colorado River cutthroat. The fish aren't the only attraction, however; War Dance Falls has to be one of the most beautiful falls in the Park.

Fishing North Inlet Trail

ABOVE: Chad LaChance casts a dry fly to rising brookies and Colorado River cutthroat on North Inlet Creek. Wet wading during the summer months is the preferred wading method on most Park waters.

OPPOSITE TOP: *North Inlet Creek near the junction of Lake Nanita Trail.*

OPPOSITE LOWER LEFT: *A brightly colored Colorado River cutthroat fooled by a Royal Humpy.*

OPPOSITE LOWER RIGHT: *Big Pool is deep, clear and full of larger cutthroat, but it is also a popular swimming location for hikers.*

BELOW: *North Inlet Creek in the Summerland Park area is a rather wide and crystal clear stream demanding a stealthy approach and delicately precise casts to avoid putting down wary trout.*

Lake Nanita Trail

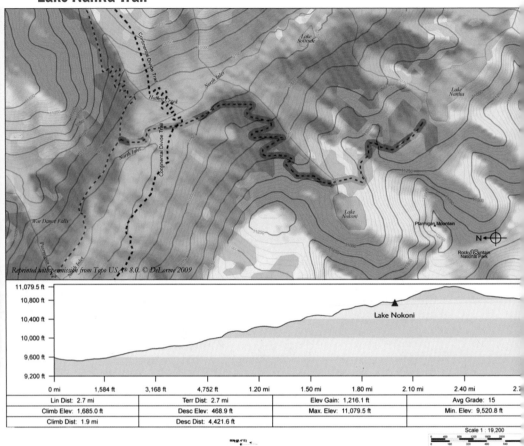

Reprinted with permission from Topo USA® 8.0. © DeLorme 2009

Lin Dist: 2.7 mi		Terr Dist: 2.7 mi		Elev Gain: 1,216.1 ft			Avg Grade: 15	
Climb Elev: 1,685.0 ft		Desc Elev: 468.9 ft		Max. Elev: 11,079.5 ft			Min. Elev: 9,520.8 ft	
Climb Dist: 1.9 mi		Desc Dist: 4,421.6 ft						

Scale 1 : 19,200

Trailhead: *Tonahutu / North Inlet*   **USGS Quad(s):**   *McHenry's Peak*

Trail Overview

🥾🥾🥾 - 🥾🥾🥾🥾

Note the orientation of the topographic map above. From North Inlet Trail, Lake Nanita Trail is noticeably steeper. Several switchbacks wind in and out of wonderful views of the valley where North Inlet Creek originates. The trail gains 1,700 feet of elevation over 2.7 miles. You'll pass Lake Nokoni, which by all accounts should have fish, but doesn't. From Lake Nokoni to Lake Nanita, the trail again gets steeper warranting a few rest stops; you're almost there. The saving grace of this healthy hike is that the last third of a mile is downhill to the lake. These waters are considered barren: Lake Nokoni and drainage, Lake Powell and drainage.

Lake Nanita and Drainage 🐟 10,797 ft

Lake Nanita is a rather large alpine lake for the Park. It's just shy of thirty-five acres whereas the average lake size in the Park is seven acres. At 10,797 feet, it's one of the highest lakes in the Park as well. The lake is flanked to the north by picturesque Ptarmigan Mountain. The lake fishes well by simply walking the shoreline looking for cruising trout

Fishing Lake Nanita Trail

seeking blown down ants, hoppers and beetles. It's easy to see the cruisers well in advance since the water is quite clear most of the year. If dry flies don't entice rises, fling a streamer or Woolly Bugger through deeper drop-offs. Expect average-sized cutthroat in the 11" to 16" range. The hike around the lake is gorgeous by itself. Without a doubt, this is one of my favorite lakes in the Park.

Solitude Lake 9,726 ft

Following North Inlet Creek off trail to Solitude Lake will take a fly fisher hours to reach the lake simply due to the good fishing in the creek along the way. The off-trail trek is only 1.3 miles and aside from a few downed trees, is easy to navigate. Follow several game trails and a few cairns to the open meadow where moose congregate in the evenings. Solitude Lake is tucked in a stand of pines to the west of the creek. The lake is like an inverted bowler hat - it has an extended shallow muddy shoreline with a rather deep bowl in the middle just out of reasonable casting range. Smallish cutthroat cruise the flats and run down the lake's outlet which drains into North Inlet Creek. The lake itself isn't necessarily reason to hike back into the meadow, but fishing the creek and the moose sightings make it worth the effort.

ABOVE: Kollin Evens and Max Moree fish Lake Nanita from the small rock island on the north shore. The swim over was chilly.

BELOW: Solitude Lake sits in an opening protected by tall pines on three sides. This is a favorite place for moose in the evening.

Tonahutu Creek and Haynach Lakes Trail

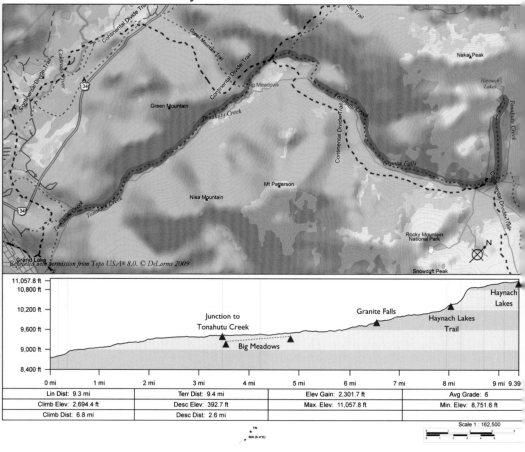

Reprinted with permission from Topo U.S.A.® 8.0. © DeLorme 2009

Lin Dist: 9.3 mi	Terr Dist: 9.4 mi	Elev Gain: 2,301.7 ft	Avg Grade: 6
Climb Elev: 2,694.4 ft	Desc Elev: 392.7 ft	Max. Elev: 11,057.8 ft	Min. Elev: 8,751.6 ft
Climb Dist: 6.8 mi	Desc Dist: 2.6 mi		

Scale 1 : 162,500

Trailhead: *Tonahutu/North Inlet*   **USGS Quad(s):** *Grand Lake*
McHenry's Peak

Trail Overview

🚶🚶 - 🚶🚶🚶🚶

Note the orientation of the topographic map above. The average trail slope of grade 6 for the map above can be deceiving. It is weighted more towards the section of trail below Granite Falls. From Granite Falls to Haynach Lakes the average grade is nine, with the Haynach Lakes Trail a steeper grade eleven. The closer you get to Haynach Lakes, the steeper the trail becomes. The first five miles of the trail offers a gentle rise following picturesque Tonahutu Creek. Big Meadows is aptly named – it seems to take forever traversing from one end to the other. The trail meets up with Tonahutu Creek again just after west Big Meadows, and follows the creek closely until Granite Falls, where the trail and creek meet intermittently until the trail breaks northward to Haynach Lakes Trail. **A note about Haynach Lakes Trail:** *Many current topographic maps do not show Haynach Lakes horse trail and Haynach campsite. This is also the foot trail to Haynach Lakes. The trail is decisively steep from the junction of Tonahutu Creek Trail and will warrant a few rest breaks for even the fit. These waters are considered barren: Murphy Lake and drainage, Eureka Ditch, Tonahutu Creek above 10,167 ft, most forks and drainages into Tonahutu Creek, and the unnamed lake near headwaters of Tonahutu Creek.*

Fishing Tonahutu Creek and Haynach Lakes Trail

Tonahutu Creek (Trailhead to Granite Falls) 🐟 🐟 🐟

This creek offers the day hiker the chance at a trout trifecta of brookies, browns and generic cutthroat (most likely of Colorado River cutthroat strain). From the trail's beginnings near the northeast side of the town of Grand Lake, brookies and browns dominate. After about a half mile up the stream, brookies predominate for several miles through Big Meadows. The closer to Granite Falls you hike you'll run into more cutthroat. The creek takes on many different faces throughout this six mile stretch, from small pockets and pools to gently moving meadow flows. An easier approach to Tonahutu Creek is to hike in from Green Mountain trailhead, cutting off about 2.5 miles of trail distance to reach the prime fishing waters of Big Meadows and beyond. This is not to say the water below Big Meadows is not fishable, it certainly is, but there are plenty other brookie waters in the Park worth more exploration.

Tonahutu Creek (Granite Falls to 10,167 ft) 🐟

Above Granite Falls, Tonahutu Creek takes on the appearance and feel of North Inlet Creek. Plunge pools, tail-outs, pocket water behind boulders and short riffles dominate this steeper section of the stream. It would be easy to consume an entire day fishing in just this section of stream. The trail loosely follows the stream to the north, but at times is considerably higher than the streambed, so pick a spot to enter the stream and fish your way up until you see a good vantage point to return to the trail again. Generic cutthroat rise eagerly to PMDs and caddis dries. Most will be in the 10-11" size with a 14" cutt a prize catch.

Haynach Lakes (upper and lower) 🐟 11,103 ft

With no hesitation in saying, this is one of the most beautiful lakes in the Park and one of my favorites, but the hike in may not be for everyone. From the Green Mountain trailhead, the hike in is 7.4 miles one-way, with the last 1.4 miles (Haynach Lakes Trail) being quite steep. Large Yellowstone cutthroat trout peruse the shore banks looking for any morsel blown in with the wind. The wind picks up during mid-day, so plan your hike to get there early, or make an overnight of it and camp at Haynach Lakes campsite and fish early mornings and late evenings for mirror-smooth water dimpled with rises. The main lake is unlike any other in the Park. It is a series of interconnected 'lake-ettes' with clearly seen streambed channels braiding throughout. The cutthroat cruise the channels and occasionally swim to the surface or to the lake's edge looking for any floating treat.

There are several other smaller ponds down from the main Haynach Lake. Sometimes they contain fish, but only seasonally. They are too shallow to hold fish year round.

Yellowstone cutthroat of Haynach Lakes are a finicky and easily-spooked bunch. You won't get away with slapping a fly on the water and expecting a cruising cutt to take interest. More often than not, the cutt will dart to the bottom of a channel in a blink of an eye. The best strategy is to find a high spot on a bank side boulder and look for cruising fish. Prepare your cast and delicately place a small Adams, PMD, ant or beetle. Larger dry flies or general attractor flies can work, but not as well as more drab colored and realistic looking flies.

Haynach Lakes Drainage 🐟

Don't bypass the Haynach Lakes outlet thinking it is too small for fish. In the outlet you will find gorgeous resident Yellowstone cutthroat in the 5-8" range. Dap a size 14 caddis dry or a hopper behind rocks and over the small slicks in the meadow below the lakes.

Fishing Tonahutu Creek and Haynach Lakes Trail

UPPER LEFT: *Kerry Evens fights a brisk wind to place a dry fly inside a small section of the Haynach Lakes drainage to holding Yellowstone River cutthroat.*

UPPER RIGHT: *Tonahutu Creek in Big Meadows runs crystal clear. During bright sunny days, expect to find brook trout quickly looking for cover as you walk near.*

BELOW: *Yellowstone River cutthroat have characteristic hazy blue vertical parr marks across a red stripe. In stream resident Yellowstone cuts, parr marks may remain even into adulthood.*

Fishing Tonahutu Creek and Haynach Lakes Trail

ABOVE: Upper Haynach Lake sits in a picturesque bowl, making this location one of the most beautiful in the Park.

BELOW: A closer look at one of the fingers of upper Haynach Lake reveals the many deeper and darker 'river' channels where the cutthroat find protection and a source of travel from one area to another.

"We stood on the mountain looking down at the headwaters of Little Thompson Creek, where the Park spread out before us. No words can describe our surprise, wonder and joy at beholding such a sight."
- Milton Estes, on the discovery of Estes Park, October 15, 1859

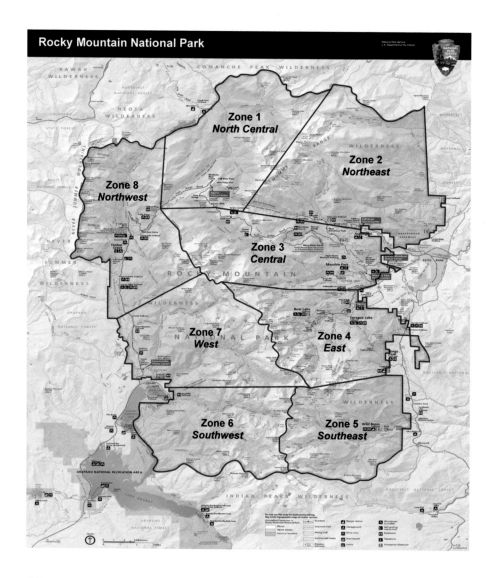

Zone 8 - Northwest

Kawuneeche Valley

La Poudre Pass Trail

Little Yellowstone Trail

Timber Lake Trail

Onahu Creek Trail

Rocky Mountain National Park

Kawuneeche Valley

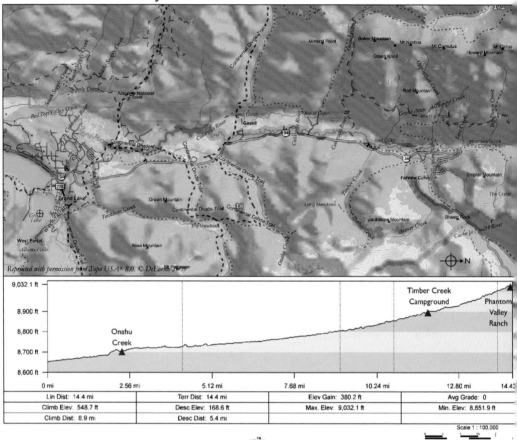

Reprinted with permission from Topo USA® 8.0. © DeLorme 2009

Lin Dist: 14.4 mi	Terr Dist: 14.4 mi	Elev Gain: 380.2 ft	Avg Grade: 0
Climb Elev: 548.7 ft	Desc Elev: 168.6 ft	Max. Elev: 9,032.1 ft	Min. Elev: 8,651.9 ft
Climb Dist: 8.9 mi	Desc Dist: 5.4 mi		

Scale 1 : 100,000

Trailhead: *US 34 Roadside*   **USGS Quad(s):**   *Grand Lake*
Fall River Pass

Trail Overview

Note the orientation of the map above. It is hard to state the official start and end of the valley. It generally starts at the Kawuneeche Visitor Center just north of Grand Lake and ends near Lulu City. The map above does not show the far north end to Lulu City. Trail Ridge Road spans this distance for about 13.25 miles, while the Colorado River weaves its way for over fifteen miles. The entire valley has a nominal gradient, making the hiking some of the easiest in the Park. Some of the Kawuneeche Valley is in Zone 7 but its entirety is discussed here.

One could literally spend days fishing the "Coyote" Valley (*kawuneeche* roughly translated means 'coyote' in Arapahoe). The creeks and rivers that spill into this vast expanse offer plenty of cuts, bends, pools, eddies, riffles and glides to keep one busy for days. Too often, I have fished the valley where I found myself lost in time and quite a bit farther away from my vehicle than I imagined. It's easy to lose track of time and distance fished - the valley can be *that* good. The water in the valley is comparable in size to the Big

Fishing Kawuneeche Valley

Thompson River in Moraine Park, or to the North St. Vrain in the southeast of the Park. And like those two rivers, the valley drains a considerable amount of surface land each spring, so expect run-off to affect fishing well into the summer months. While the Colorado River in the valley doesn't mirror the same river that cut the Grand Canyon, it's not a tiny mountain trickle like its meager beginnings some 15 miles upstream. It's the perfect sized stream for the fly fisher. If you have a day to fish the Park and have a difficult time hiking in altitude, this can be your ticket to dry fly nirvana, especially during the *magical months* (discussed below).

At that precarious time of the year where things warm up but before run-off starts, you'll find exquisite nymphing - that is if you take on the challenge of trekking across the valley floor covered in crusty snow and semi-frozen wetlands. Trail a size 16 or 18 blue-winged olive nymph imitation such as a Pheasant Tail or Hare's Ear nymph behind a larger attractor fly such as a Prince Nymph or San Juan Worm.

During run-off, it's best to find a stream or thawed lake in the higher country - the valley will be blown out. Run-off typically lasts to the first or second week of July. Fishing a streamer during run-off can be productive, especially in and around undercut banks. But generally fish are so well fed during run-off due to the water dislodging food from the banks that they really aren't easily enticed to a fly.

Then the magical months come - late July through mid-fall. The streamside vegetation is in full growth and the terrestrial action brings the fish's attention upward. As a rule-of-thumb, the second week of July is typically the beginning of the magical time. But really, the key is when the river flows subside, the water clears and as you walk through the meadow hoppers bound out of your way. Then you know you've hit the magical time. Wet wading becomes the norm as you cast upstream to working fish in the textbook feeding lies. A size 12 or 14 hopper imitation is the go-to fly of choice. Alternatively, a size 14 or 16 Elk-Hair Caddis or X-caddis cast close to the bank will bring plenty of fish to hand. While hoppers and caddis are essential fly box patterns, don't forget to fish large ants either. A size 12 is easy to see and imitates the large ants you'll notice stream side.

Many streams and creeks are seasonal and may contain fish, but are generally considered barren: Crater Gulch, Lady Creek, Lulu Creek, Little and Middle and Big Dutch Creeks, Green Valley Stream, Lost Creek, Opposition Creek, Mosquito Creek, Phantom Creek, Sawmill Creek, Specimen Creek and Squeak Creek.

Colorado River (Park Boundary to 8,800 ft) 🐟 🐟 🐟

The lower section of the Colorado River starts just northeast of Grand Lake and extends to Gaskil, just north of Bowen Gulch. Most of the fish you'll find are brook trout, with some brown trout. Rainbow trout are sparse during the summer months, but are more prevalent just prior to run-off.

Colorado River (8,800 ft to 9,200 ft) 🐟 🐟

This mid-section extends from the Bowen-Baker Gulch area to just north of the northern-most bend in Trail Ridge Road. The area is often called Shipler Park. This is a fun and scenic section of river to fish, especially above the Colorado River trailhead. There's plenty of winding river in and out of forested land giving way to a small, open winding stream as you work upstream. Don't forget to explore the ponds to the western side of the valley; trout migrate in and out of these ponds from the river. Expect to catch mostly brook trout and expect to hear the sound of Trail Ridge Road traffic. This section of the valley has easy access throughout via the Colorado River Trail.

Fishing Kawuneeche Valley

Colorado River (above 9,200 ft)

(Note: this section is not highlighted in blue on the section topo map) Once you get to Lulu City via the river or the Colorado River Trail, you'll notice the gradient increase dramatically towards the headwaters some two miles upstream. Brook trout continue to dominate, however you'll find the river's namesake fish, smallish in size, mixed in with pods of brookies. The water is more small creek in nature and has plenty of gradient to create pockets and pools. The Colorado River Trail provides easy access to this section of stream.

Baker Creek (Baker Gulch)

From the Bowen-Baker trailhead, follow the dirt path to the foot trail that follows the creek up Baker Gulch. The trail up Baker Gulch is two and a half miles long; all but the first few hundred feet are outside the Park boundaries. Baker Creek along the trail up the gulch is a beautiful mountain stream, but has too many natural barriers to allow fish upstream. Instead, focus your fishing from where the trail meets up with the creek and follow it off-trail downstream to the Gaskil area. The creek parallels the Colorado River on the western side of the valley, going in and out of wooded areas. It is slightly smaller than the Colorado, but has the same characteristics and fishes the same. You'll likely not run across another angler as most focus on the Colorado River in the valley and forget this stream is tucked just a few hundred yards to the west. In the spring and early summer, it's best to wear waders as the area gets marshy.

Bowen Gulch (near Gaskil)

A trail loosely follows Bowen Gulch to Bowen Lake; the first 3.5 miles of the trail follow the Gulch closely. Only the first 2,000 feet of the trail are within Park boundaries. The best way to access this water is to walk across the valley to find the confluence of Baker Creek and Bowen Gulch. Another fine way is to take the Baker Gulch trail (as discussed

The Colorado River in Kawuneeche Valley is a classic meandering meadow stream. Summertime flows can reduce to a trickle in drought years. Pictured below is what the stream looks like just after run-off during a good snow-pack year. Like the Big Thompson, undercut banks can extend inward for several feet, giving larger trout good protection.

Fishing Kawuneeche Valley

ABOVE: *The upper valley contains beaver dams and ponds on the western side. Don't miss fishing the ponds during the dog days of summer.*

BELOW: *At the Park boundary, Baker Creek offers plenty of small plunge pools and slicks to hold very wary brook trout.*

above) to Baker Creek as it flows out of the gulch and fish it downstream to the confluence of Bowen Gulch. You could spend all day fishing just this stretch.

Red Gulch (below 9,100 ft)

There is no formal trail to Red Gulch, but it can be accessed by following the winding Colorado River about 2,500 feet north of Timber Creek Campground. If you fish the Colorado River upstream from the campground, you can't miss it.

Beaver Creek

Like Red Gulch, you can't help but find Beaver Creek on the east side of the Colorado River as you fish the Colorado upstream. It has populations of small brook trout which find their way up from the Colorado. It is heavily covered with willows and you have a good chance of spotting moose along this natural corridor between the hills and the valley.

La Poudre Pass Trail

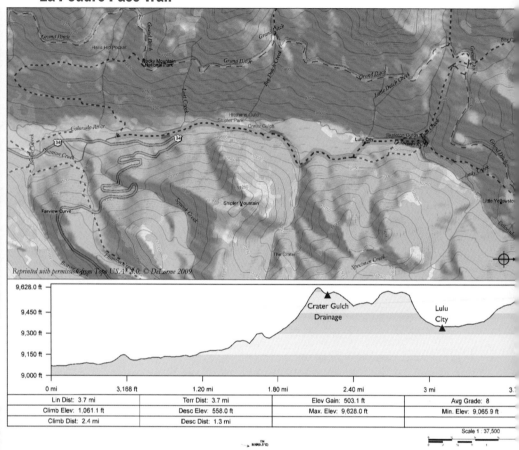

Lin Dist: 3.7 mi	Terr Dist: 3.7 mi	Elev Gain: 503.1 ft	Avg Grade: 8
Climb Elev: 1,061.1 ft	Desc Elev: 558.0 ft	Max. Elev: 9,628.0 ft	Min. Elev: 9,065.9 ft
Climb Dist: 2.4 mi	Desc Dist: 1.3 mi		

Scale 1 : 37,500

Trailhead: *Colorado River*   **USGS Quad(s):** *Fall River Pass*

Trail Overview

🚶 - 🚶 🚶

Note the orientation of the map above. The La Poudre Pass Trail, also referred to as the Colorado River Trail on some topographic maps, starts at the Colorado River trailhead, extends through Shipler Park, Lulu City and Skeleton Gulch to the junction of Thunder Pass Trail. About a quarter mile from the trailhead is a trail spur to Red Mountain Trail. This three mile spur climbs the side of Red Mountain and leads to The Grand Ditch. Fishing for brookies and browns can be found here. The Grand Ditch is discussed in more detail in the section entitled "Little Yellowstone Trail". The La Poudre Pass Trail loosely follows the Colorado River to the east to Shipler Park, then veers northeasterly away from the meadow only to reunite with the river near the old Lulu City site. All along the way, the river weaves in and out of dense forest cover in a narrow gulch flanked by the Never Summer Mountains to the west and Mount Shipler to the east. Long shadows are cast in the spring and fall as the close by mountains prevent direct sunlight to the river until mid-day. While this is good for giving fish a sense of security in otherwise clear water, it is bad for early spring and late fall fishing as ice and snow impede fishing and line guides ice up more readily. The section of river just south of Lulu City meanders through some open meadow

Fishing La Poudre Pass Trail

and offers typical meadow fishing for brookies, browns and the occasional Colorado River cutthroat. Many feeder streams and creeks are seasonal and may contain fish, but as a general rule of thumb are considered barren, including Big Dutch Creek, Crater Gulch, Little Dutch Creek, Lost Creek, Middle Dutch Creek.

Colorado River

The Colorado River along the La Poudre Pass Trail is a pleasant river to fish for averaged sized brook trout and browns. Easy hiking along wide open trails makes this section of the Colorado a favorite for day trekkers and campers at nearby Timber Creek Campground. The usual selection of attractor dries and nymphs are all that's needed to fish this section of river.

The Colorado along the La Poudre Pass Trail has the same characteristics as it does several miles downstream in Kawuneeche Valley. The main differentiating characteristic is the river winds through tall stands of pines before reaching a small open meadow near the old Lulu City site.

Little Yellowstone Trail

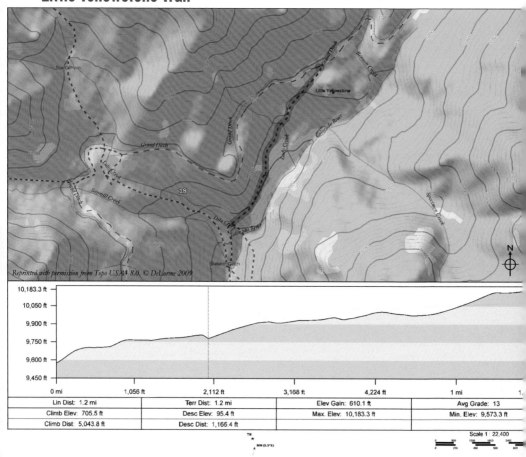

Lin Dist: 1.2 mi	Terr Dist: 1.2 mi	Elev Gain: 610.1 ft	Avg Grade: 13
Climb Elev: 705.5 ft	Desc Elev: 95.4 ft	Max. Elev: 10,183.3 ft	Min. Elev: 9,573.3 ft
Climb Dist: 5,043.8 ft	Desc Dist: 1,166.4 ft		

Trailhead: *Colorado River* **USGS Quad(s):** *Fall River Pass*

Trail Overview

The trail, combined with the forest service access road from the La Poudre Pass trail head is 2.75 miles long. The forest service access road follows the Grand Ditch. The true beginnings of the Colorado River can be found just southeast of the forest service access road only a few minutes hiking from the La Poudre Pass Trail Head. The Little Yellowstone Trail itself is 1.25 miles in length and has a respectable altitude gain of nearly 700 feet over its length with the a quarter mile section on the northerly end being the steepest. From the access road, the trail traverses through a beautifully dense pine and aspen forest clearing to an overlook in the Little Yellowstone Canyon. Following the trail doesn't get you to much fishing on the Colorado, unless you want to scramble down some rather steep and loose decaying rock to the Colorado River some 200 feet below. The easiest way to fish the headwaters is to hike downward to La Poudre Pass Trail, taking it easterly for a few hundred yards until it crosses the Colorado. Fish upstream from there. Many streams and creeks along this trail are seasonal and may contain fish, but as a general rule of thumb are barren; including Bennett Creek, LaPoudre Pass Creek below Long Draw Reservoir, La Poudre Pass Lake, Lady Creek, Lake of the Clouds, Lulu Creek, Sawmill Creek and Specimen Creek.

Fishing Little Yellowstone Trail

Grand Ditch (a.k.a. The Grand Canal) 🐟 🐟

The first eight miles of the Grand Ditch were dug by hand in 1890. It was finally finished with the aide of machinery in 1936. Fishing the Grand Ditch in the summer is a spotty proposition in the northwest corner of the Park. The water is spectacularly clear most of the year, reminiscent of a small freestone river. The bug life favors small mayflies and an occasional stonefly. Despite the healthy nature of the water, summertime flows can be low and there's not a lot of cover for fish to hide from natural predators. Springtime fishing can be exciting as the cutthroat run up the Ditch from Long Draw Reservoir.

Colorado River (above 9,200 ft) 🐟 🐟

This section of the Colorado River is considered the beginning of this fabled water that spans thousands of miles to its destination in the Gulf of California. True to its name, it contains modest populations of Colorado River cutthroat besides brook trout. Even at the start of this mighty river, it has packed enough power to erode a small canyon through prehistoric ash deposits from nearby Specimen Mountain. Accessing the river is best from the La Poudre Pass Trail and working your way upstream through the Lulu City area and up through the canyon. Fishing the canyon area has a special surreal feel to it knowing the water will eventually continue its path through the Grand Canyon and beyond.

A shorter rod, such as a 7-foot 3-weight, is ideal for the upper Colorado. Winds can howl down through the natural canyon channel, so expect to fish a shorter leader in order to gain control of your drift. A caddis dry or Adams is all that's needed to fish this section. In the spring, the canyon area drains considerable water and thus is rather unfishable. Keep an eye out for wildlife, as deer, elk and sheep are plentiful in the area.

The Grand Ditch is a beautiful specimen of flowing water cutting through the northwestern part of the Park. But due to the man-made nature of the canal, there is little structure to offer trout shelter and therefore fish populations are sparse.

Fishing Little Yellowstone Trail

ABOVE: *Sometimes the smallest fish can bring the biggest smile, as this over-achieving Colorado River cutthroat did when he aggressively attacked a CDC and Elk dry fly floating mid-stream over a riffle.*

OPPOSITE: *Just as the Colorado River gains collective momentum it tumbles down from the Poudre Pass Lake area in a small canyon that closely resembles the look and feel of canyons in Yellowstone National Park. Here, the water is 10-12' wide, to give perspective of the photograph*

BELOW: *The true beginning of the Colorado is uncertain and somewhat speculative. Just below La Poudre Pass Lake is a lush wetland where small marshy ponds begin to drain towards the canyon along Little Yellowstone Trail. With the help of a few feeder creeks, the Colorado gains momentum in rapid order.*

Timber Lake Trail

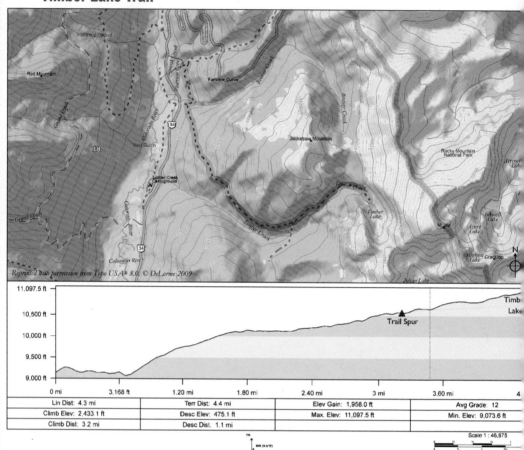

Reprinted with permission from Topo USA® 8.0. © DeLorme 2009

Lin Dist: 4.3 mi	Terr Dist: 4.4 mi	Elev Gain: 1,958.0 ft	Avg Grade: 12
Climb Elev: 2,433.1 ft	Desc Elev: 475.1 ft	Max. Elev: 11,097.5 ft	Min. Elev: 9,073.6 ft
Climb Dist: 3.2 mi	Desc Dist: 1.1 mi		

Scale 1 : 46,875

Trailhead: *Timber Lake*

USGS Quad(s): *Fall River Pass*
Grand Lake

Trail Overview

The deceptive first three-quarters of a mile lures you into thinking of an easy hike, however, the next mile brings some of the steepest yet most beautiful scenery on the trail. If you are in decent shape, this 4.4 mile (one-way) day-hike will bring you to some fine stream fishing for cutthroat trout. For some, the trail is just long and steep enough to consider making this a one-night camp-over. The trail gets plenty of day use, but only for the first mile or so. Once day hikers realize the slope of the trail gets steep around three-quarters of a mile, they take a break and turn around. The beauty of the first mile of the trail is marred by the sounds of vehicle traffic on nearby Trail Ridge Road. Continuing onward takes you through some of the most scenic sections of the trail and away from nearby traffic sounds. The trail skirts Jackstraw Mountain and, at the junction of Long Meadows Trail, follows Timber Creek to Timber Lake. There are plenty of camping sites, five to be exact, that put you within a hop-skip-jump of fine stream fishing. Many streams and creeks are seasonal and may contain fish, but as a general rule-of-thumb are barren, including Phantom Creek and Squeak Creek. Bighorn Lake is also barren.

Fishing Timber Lake Trail

Beaver Creek

While you'll cross Beaver Creek only a short distance from the trailhead, focus where the creek crosses Trail Ridge Road going into the Kawuneeche Valley. Plenty of smallish brookies can be found in this stretch.

Timber Creek (Lower)

Lower Timber Creek can be followed from Route 34 at the Timber Creek rest area upstream for a steep three quarters of a mile. Expect to find smaller brook trout in abundance in this section. Beyond three quarter of a mile, following the creek doesn't give the fly fisher any advantages. You are best to stick to the trail for easier access to fishing further upstream.

Timber Creek (Upper)

Following Timber Creek down from Timber Lake, for as long as you want to fish, arguably produces some of the finest small-stream fishing in the Park. Any well-placed attractor dry, often just dapping on the water's surface, will entice aggressive strikes from resident cutthroats. Expect smaller fish than what are found around the lake, but an occasional 12-14 incher can lurk in the deeper pools. The stream is only a few feet wide in most places and can be jumped over with little effort.

Timber Lake 11,083 ft

The lake is an on-off proposition - but when it's on, it's on. During spawning season

Timber Creek, from the outlet of Timber Lake downstream for several miles, gives easy access to unobstructed small-stream fishing. The relatively short hike and willing cutthroat makes this destination perfect for teaching young anglers the art of fly fishing.

Fishing Timber Lake Trail

(the latter half of June into the first few weeks of July) the outlet into upper Timber Creek and around the inlet to Timber Lake are the best bets for catching some of the larger cutthroats of the season. If you don't spot cruising fish, the best way to get to them is via float tube. If you have the stamina to lug a float tube up to this lake, you will most likely be rewarded with fish that you couldn't otherwise fish to. Kick-trolling a streamer is as effective as any technique on this lake.

From near the Continental Divide, the view over Timber Lake (and the drainage pond just above) is one of the more spectacular views in the Park. Behind the camera is an equally stunning view of Julian Lake (barren) and Onahu Creek Valley.

Fishing Timber Lake Trail

ABOVE: The author displays a fine Colorado River cutthroat in spawning colors.

RIGHT: A mama moose is surprised to see something floating on Timber Lake, just as the float-tubing author is to see the mama moose! Can you spot the baby moose hiding in the thicket?

www.flyfishingrmnp.com

Onahu Creek Trail

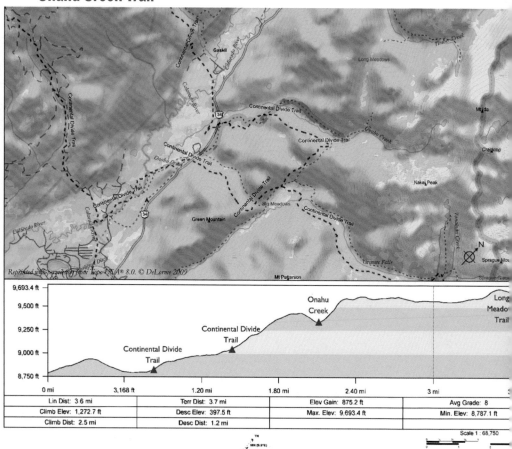

Trailhead: *Onahu Creek*   **USGS Quad(s):**   *Grand Lake*

Trail Overview

🚶🚶 - 🚶🚶🚶

Note the orientation of the map above. From the Onahu Creek trail head, the creek is close-at-hand for a majority of the way up this short two to three mile fishing journey. The creek and trail are in the heart of west slope moose country, so don't be surprised if one greets you on the trail or stream along the way. The trail is well maintained and is a popular day hike destination for fishers and non-fishers alike. A great full-day fishing 7.3 mile loop begins at Onahu Creek trailhead, fishing your way upstream to the beautiful little meadow about two miles up. Hike through the meadow to meet a trail spur at the eastern edge which takes you south to Big Meadows on Tonahutu Creek Trail. Fish Tonahutu Creek at the southern edge of the meadows, hiking out to the Tonahutu Creek trailhead. If fishing with a buddy, leave a car at both trailheads if possible, which saves you about a half mile roadside hike back to Onahu Creek trailhead. Many feeder streams and creeks to Onahu Creek may contain fish, but as a general rule of thumb are barren. Other waters considered barren are Julian Lake and Chickaree Lake.

Fishing Onahu Creek Trail

Onahu Creek (to 10,500 ft)

Essentially the first three miles of the creek is considered drive-by brookie heaven. Due to its ease of access and short trail distance, this is a popular trail amongst anglers. In the spring, the creek runs full, feeding the Colorado River in the Kawuneeche Valley below. When the Colorado River isn't fishable, try Onahu Creek. A wide variety of stream styles exist in a short distance: slow meandering meadow water, willow-choked riffles, deep undercut bends and an a few pocket pools. While dominated by brookies, an occasional Colorado River cutthroat can be caught higher up the drainage.

Onahu Creek (10,500 ft +)

If you venture up this high, Colorado River cutthroat are the norm but the trek becomes off-trail, steep and much more difficult. The stream is much smaller and choked with a canopy of tight vegetation, making fly casting difficult as well.

ABOVE: In the largest of the three meadows where Onahu Creek flows, a moose yearling nibbles on willows and watches me as I fish for brook trout mid-day.

BELOW: Just as I snapped the photo above, I realized mama moose must be nearby. I noticed her not 20 yards behind me nestled in the shady edge of the meadow, watching my every move. Note: In the spring and summer, be cautious of the cows. In the fall, be cautious of the bulls.

Effective Fly Patterns

Mayflies

Midges and Tricos

Caddis Flies

Stoneflies

Scuds and Damsels

Ants and Beetles

Crickets and Hoppers

Streamers and Worms

Attractor Patterns

May Fly Dry and Emerger Patterns

3P (Para Park PMD)

Originator	Dick Shinton
Tyer	Dick Shinton
Hook	Standard dry fly hook, size 16-18
Thread	Griffith's 14/0 Primrose
Tail	5 or 6 moose hair fibers
Body	Superfine dubbing, PMD
Wing Post	Poly Yarn, light yellow
Hackle	Whiting Farms medium dun hackle

ARF Harey Baetis Thorax

Originator	Al Ritt
Tyer	Al Ritt
Hook	TMC 101 size 14-18
Thread	Dark Olive 8/0
Tail	Olive microfibbets, tied long and split
Body	Olive goose biot
Thorax	BWO Superfine dubbing
Hackle	Whiting Farms grizzly dyed olive, tied Marinaro thorax style

Sailboat BWO

Originator	Joe Johnson
Tyer	Joe Johnson
Hook	HookDai-Riki 305 size 16-20
Thread	UTC 70, Gray
Tail	Microfibbets, dark dun
Body	Light olive goose biot
Thorax	Olive Superfine dubbing
Wing	Dun spade hackle, split
Head	Whiting Farms, medium dun

Mike's CDC Puff

Originator	Mike Kruise
Tyer	Mike Kruise
Hook	TMC 518, size 28-32
Thread	Dk Gray or black 10/0
Tail	Microfibbets, dun
Body	Wrapped tips of dark dun CDC feather
Wing	Remaining end of CDC feather, tied back and trimmed to shape
Head	Thread head

Olive Comparadun

Originator	unknown
Tyer	Rick Takahashi
Hook	TMC 100, size 12-20
Thread	Uni 8/0 olive dun
Tail	Microfibbets, dark olive, tied split style
Body	Nature's Spirit BWO
Ribbing	Stripped peacock herl
Wing	Natural deer hair, sparse

Tak's Poly Wing Tan Dun

Originator	Rick Takahashi
Tyer	Rick Takahashi
Hook	TMC 100, size 14-18
Thread	UTC 70, Dun
Tail	Microfibbets, dark dun
Body	Nature's Spirit Callibaetis stripped peacock herl
Wing	White poly yarn, colored with dark gray marker
Hackle	Whiting Farms, medium dun

Befus Para Emerger - PT

Originator	Brad Befus
Tyer	Brad Befus
Hook	TMC 2487, size 12-18
Thread	Ultra Thread 70, dark olive
Trailing Shuck	Z-lon, light brown
Body	Pheasant tail fibers
Ribbing	Ultra Wire, copper
Thorax	Peacock herl or peacock Ice Dub
Post	2mm foam, orange or yellow
Hackle	Dry fly, brown or coachman

Befus Para Emerger - Hare's Ear

Originator	Brad Befus
Tyer	Brad Befus
Hook	TMC 2487, size 12-18
Thread	Ultra Thread 70, dark olive
Trailing Shuckl	Z-lon, light brown
Body	Hare's ear, medium brown
Ribbing	Ultra Wire, gold
Thorax	Peacock herl or peacock Ice Dub, small round rubber legs
Post	2mm foam, orange or yellow
Hackle	Dry fly, brown or coachman

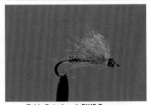

Tak's Paintbrush BWO Emerger

Originator	Rick Takahashi
Tyer	Rick Takahashi
Hook	TMC 200R size 16-20
Thread	Uni 8/0 Olive Dun
Tail	Antron fibers, brown and amber
Body	Olive polyester paintbrush fiber
Wing	Poly yarn, white
Trailing Legs	Natural CDC and ends of poly yarn colored with olive-gray marker

May Fly Dry, Emerger and Nymph Patterns

Deer Mouse Dun

Originator	Marty Staab
Tyer	Marty Staab
Hook	Dai Riki 310 size 18-20
Thread	Danville Flymaster 6/0 gray
Tail	Antron yarn, silver/gray
Abdomen	Nature's Spirit turkey biot, gray
Wing	Whiting hen, dun
Thorax	Superfine dubbing, gray
Head and Collar	Whiting Farms saddle, light dun

Hacklestack Emerger

Originator	unknown
Tyer	Mark McMillan
Hook	Daiichi 1130 size 12-22
Thread	UTC 70 brown/olive
Tail	Pheasant, church-window feather fibers
Abdomen	Stretchrite clear, tapered strip, color with marker
Thorax	Superfine dubbing, brown/olive
Legs	Same as tail, divided evenly
Thorax	Whiting hackle, dun, tied hackle-stack style

General Bou

Originator	Steve Schweitzer
Tyer	Steve Schweitzer
Hook	Daiichi 1270 size 12-18
Thread	UTC 70 tan or dun
Tail	Tips of natural Whiting Brahma Hen Chick-a-bou
Body	Whiting natural Brahma Hen Chick-a-bou
Ribbing	Stretch-Magic 5mm clear
Wing Case	Pheasant tail fibers
Thorax	Superfine dubbing, chocolate
Legs	Whiting Brahma Hen soft hackle tips

ARF Big Bird Nymph - Gray

Originator	Al Ritt
Tyer	Al Ritt
Hook	TMC 5262 size 10-18
Thread	UTC 70 Blue Dun
Tail	Pheasant tail fibers
Body	Ostrich herl, gray
Ribbing	Krystal flash, UV tan
Thorax	Pheasant tail wing case over gray ostrich herl
Head	thread

ARF Big Bird Nymph - Mahogany

Originator	Al Ritt
Tyer	Al Ritt
Hook	TMC 5262 size 10-18
Thread	UTC 70 Rust Brown
Tail	Pheasant tail fibers
Body	Ostrich herl, rusty brown
Ribbing	Krystal flash, rootbeer pearl
Thorax	Pheasant tail wing case over rusty brown ostrich herl
Head	thread

ARF Big Bird Nymph - Olive

Originator	Al Ritt
Tyer	Al Ritt
Hook	TMC 5262 size 10-18
Thread	UTC 70 Olive
Tail	Pheasant tail fibers, dyed olive
Body	Ostrich herl, olive
Ribbing	Krystal flash, olive pearl
Thorax	Olive pheasant tail wing case over olive ostrich herl
Head	thread

Lacy Baetis

Originator	Marty Staab
Tyer	Marty Staab
Hook	Dai Riki 270 size 20-22
Thread	Danville Flymaster 6/0 light olive
Tail & Back	Pheasant tail
Body	Midge tubing, light olive
Wingcase & Legs	Antron yarn, brown olive
Thorax	Hare Ice blend, light olive

Baetis Nymph

Originator	Rick Takahashi
Tyer	Rick Takahashi
Hook	TMC 200R size 18-22
Thread	UTC 70 Olive Dun
Tail	Olive partridge fibers
Body	Nature's Spirit BWO olive peacock herl, stripped
Wing Case	Larva Lace open cell foam, black
Thorax	Nature's Spirit muskrat gray peacock herl
Legs	Olive partridge fibers

Steve's Baetis

Originator	Steve Schweitzer
Tyer	Steve Schweitzer
Hook	Daiichi 1550 size 14-22
Thread	Brown 8/0
Tail	Pheasant tail fibers
Body	Stripped natural peacock herl, laquered
Wing Case	Clear Scud Back, single strand of bronze Flashabou on top
Thorax	Ice Dub, root beer
Legs	Whiting Coq de Leon hen soft hackle fibers

Midge Dry, Trico Dry and Emerger Patterns

Gunslinger

Originator	Steve Smith, Rivers Wild Flies
Tyer	Marty Staab
Hook	Dai Riki 135 size 14-18
Thread	Uni 8/0 black
Tail	Pheasant tail, natural
Ribbing	UTC Ultra Wire, copper, small
Abdomen	Pheasant tail, natural
Wingcase	Thinskin, orange bustard
Thorax	Krystal Dub, tan
Legs	Krystal Flash, black
Head	Spirit River Bright Beads, black nickel 1/8 (14), 3/32 (16-18)

Yoosta B Emerger

Originator	Dick Shinton
Tyer	Dick Shinton
Hook	TMC 206BL, size 16-24
Thread	UTC 70 brown-olive
Tail	Z-lon, amber
Body	Stripped peacock herl
Wingcase	Organza, dun with a strip of pearl flashabou on top
Legs	Organza tips, dun
Thorax	Ice Dub, olive brown
Head	thread

ARF Beadhead Swimming Baetis

Originator	Al Ritt
Tyer	Al Ritt
Hook	TMC 2488 size 14-20
Thread	Griffith's 14/0 Olive
Tail	Marabou, black-barred tan
Thorax	Peacock herl
Wing Case	Mirage tinsel, black
Head	Flymen Fishing Co RealColor bead, mayfly brown

ARF Midge Adult

Originator	Al Ritt
Tyer	Al Ritt
Hook	TMC 101 size 16-20
Thread	Griffith's 14/0 Black
Body	Quill, black
Wing	Organza, white
Wing Case and Post	Gator Hair, fluorescent orange
Hackle	Whiting grizzly

Mike's Trike

Originator	Mike Kruise
Tyer	Mike Kruise
Hook	Dry fly, size 16-22
Thread	UNI 8/0 black
Tail	Microfibbets, dun, split
Body	Superfine dubbing, black
Wing	UV Organza
Thorax	Superfine dubbing, black

Richard's Gnat
(aka Porcupine Midge)

Originator	Richard Ross
Tyer	Richard Ross
Hook	Mustad R50, size 12-20
Thread	Giorgio Benecchi Peacock 12/0
Tail	Muskrat underfur fibers
Body	Peacock herl
Hackle	Whiting grizzly

ARF Midge Pupa Blue

Originator	Al Ritt
Tyer	Al Ritt
Hook	TMC 2487
Thread	Peacock Blue
Body	Thread base, clear micro tubing
Ribbing	X-small silver wire
Wing	Organza, white
Thorax	Ice dub, UV Gray
Hackle	Starling
Head	Diamond glass bead
Antenna	Organza, white

ARF Midge Pupa Red

Originator	Al Ritt
Tyer	Al Ritt
Hook	TMC 2487
Thread	Red
Body	Thread base, clear micro tubing
Ribbing	X-small silver wire
Wing	Organza, white
Thorax	Ice dub, Peacock
Hackle	Starling
Head	Gunmetal glass bead
Antenna	Organza, white

MRE

Originator	Richard Ross
Tyer	Richard Ross
Hook	Mustad C49S, size 12-18
Thread	Giorgio Benecchi Tan 12/0
Trailing Shuck	Muskrat underfur
Body	Stripped peacock herl
Wing Post	White Poly Yarn
Wing	CDC barbs, dark dun
Thorax	Beaver dubbing

Midge Dry, Trico Emerger and Nymph Patterns

Tak's Biot Midge Adult

Originator	Rick Takahashi
Tyer	Rick Takahashi
Hook	TMC 2488
Thread	Uni 17/0, color with black marker
Body	Nature's Spirit peacock herl
Wing	Goose biot, white
Hackle	Whiting grizzly

Tak's High Post Cluster

Originator	Rick Takahashi
Tyer	Rick Takahashi
Hook	TMC 100
Thread	UTC 70 black
Body	Thread
Wing Post	Antron fibers, black
Hackle	Whiting Midge, black

Mama's Favorite

Originator	Steve Schweitzer
Tyer	Steve Schweitzer
Hook	Daiichi 1110, size 18-22
Thread	UTC 70 black
Body	thread
Ribbing	Flash-a-bou, purple
Wing	UV Organza
Hackle	Whiting Midge, black

Lime Trance Midge

Originator	Marty Staab
Tyer	Marty Staab
Hook	Dai Riki 310 size 22
Thread	Danville Flymaster 6/0 chartreuse
Wing and Post	SAAP Float Vis, white
Hackle	Whiting Farms Midge Saddle, white

Purple Dyson

Originator	Richard Ross
Tyer	Richard Ross
Hook	Mustad C49S size 18-24
Thread	Giorgio Benecchi Peacock 12/0
Body	UTC Ultra Wire, wine, small
Thorax	Hareline Ice Dub, Peacock Black
Wing	Z-lon, Light Dun
Head	Brass/Copper/Black 1/16" bead

Mama's Favorite Emerger

Originator	Steve Schweitzer
Tyer	Steve Schweitzer
Hook	Dai Riki 135, size 18-22
Thread	UTC 70 black
Body	Thread, lacquered
Thorax	Flash-a-bou, purple
Wing	UV Organza, tied V-style
Head	Black thread, lacquered

Brown Thread Midge Pupa

Originator	Rick Takahashi
Tyer	Rick Takahashi
Hook	Dai Riki 060 size 18-22
Thread	Uni 8/0 Black
Body	Coats and Clark 54A Summer Brown sewing thread
Head	Tying hread

Cream Thread Midge Pupa

Originator	Rick Takahashi
Tyer	Rick Takahashi
Hook	Dai Riki 060 size 18-22
Thread	Uni 8/0 Black
Body	Coats and Clark Cream sewing thread
Head	Tying thread

Holiday Midge

Originator	Tyler Befus
Tyer	Tyler Befus
Hook	TMC 2487 size 16-22
Thread	Ultra Thread 70 white
Body	Red Ultra wire over white thread base
Thorax	Pearl Ice Dub or Prism Dubbing
Head	Red glass bead

Midge Nymph and Caddis Dry Patterns

Yamauchi's Black Fly Larva

Originator	Brian Yamauchi
Tyer	Rick Takahashi
Hook	TMC 100 or Dai Riki 060 size 18-22
Thread	Uni 17/0 white
Body	Natural latex colored with marker to match naturals
Head	Thread colored with brown marker
Coating	UV Knot Sense

Karl's UV Red Midge Larva

Originator	Chris Karl
Tyer	Rick Takahashi
Hook	TMC 200R size 12-18
Thread	Uni 8/0 red
Body	UV Pearl tinsel over thread base
Head	Thread colored with red marker

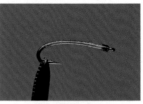

Karl's UV Midge Larva

Originator	Chris Karl
Tyer	Rick Takahashi
Hook	TMC 200R size 12-18
Thread	Uni 8/0 white
Body	UV Pearl tinsel over thread base
Head	Thread colored with tan marker

Checkers

Originator	unknown
Tyer	Marty Staab
Hook	Dai Riki 135 size 18
Thread	Unithread 6/0 red Unithread 6/0 black
Ribbing	UTC Ultra Wire, copper, small
Head	Spirit River, copper, 5/64
Coating	Sally Hansen's Hard As Nails

Tak's Mini Bowtie Buzzer

Originator	Rick Takahashi
Tyer	Rick Takahashi
Hook	TMC 100, size 16-20
Thread	UTC 70 black
Body	Black superfine
Ribbing	Silver wire, X-small
Thorax	Latex strip colored with marker over Ice Dub, peacock
Gills	Oral B Ultra Floss
Finish	UV glue over entire fly except for head filaments

Chickabou Emergent - Olive

Originator	Marty Staab
Tyer	Marty Staab
Hook	Dai Riki 070 size 14
Thread	UTC 140, olive
Tail & Body	Whiting Chick-a-bou, pale yellow
Ribbing	Danville single-strand floss, yellow
Wing	Deer Hair, dyed olive

ARF Trailing Bubble Harey Caddis

Originator	Al Ritt
Tyer	Al Ritt
Hook	TMC 101 size 14-18
Thread	UTC 70 Tan
Tail	Mirage Flash, opal
Body	Superfine dubbing, tan
Underwing	Mirage Flash, opal
Wing	Snowshoe hare, tan
Hackle	Whiting light-barred ginger, trimmed V-style on bottom

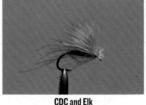

CDC and Elk

Originator	Hans Weilenmann
Tyer	Hans Weilenmann
Hook	TMC 102Y size 11 - 17 or equivalent dry fly hook
Thread	Tan/Brown 6/0
Body	Wrapped CDC tips, allowing loose fibers to flow backwards
Wing	Fine-tipped deer hair

Tak's Split Wing Caddis

Originator	A version of Craig Matthew's X-caddis
Tyer	Rick Takahashi
Hook	TMC 2302 size 12-16
Thread	Olive 8/0
Tail	Antron, amber
Body	Superfine dubbing, caddis green
Wing	Nature's Spirit natural mule deer hair

Caddis Dry, Emerger and Nymph Patterns

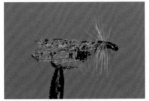

Web Wing Caddis

Originator	Rick Takahashi
Tyer	Rick Takahashi
Hook	TMC 2302 size 14-18
Thread	UTC 70 rusty dun
Body	Stripped peacock herl
Wing	D's tan web wing
Hackle	Whiting light dun

Billy Goat Caddis

Originator	Marty Staab
Tyer	Marty Staab
Hook	Dai Riki 300 size 14-16
Thread	Uni 6/0, tan
Body	Ultra Chenille, gray
Wing	CDC dun under sparse elk
Hackle	Whiting Saddle, brown
Antenna	Moose body, bleached

CDC Caddis Pupa

Originator	Brad Befus
Tyer	Brad Befus
Hook	TMC 3761 size 14-18
Thread	Ultra thread 70 to match body
Body	Nymph Skin colored with marker (tan or olive)
Legs	Centipede legs, small
Thorax	Ice Dub, peacock or Prism dubbing
Hackle	CDC, medium dun or natural

Glass Bead Cased Caddis

Originator	Brad Befus
Tyer	Brad Befus
Hook	TMC 3761 size 12-18
Thread	Ultra thread 70, black
Body	Hare's mask, medium brown
Ribbing	Ultra wire, copper, small
Wing	wing
Collar	Ostrich herl, natural
Head	Glass bead, green

Tarheel Caddis Larva

Originator	Josh Stephens
Tyer	Dick Shinton
Hook	Standard nymph, size 14-18
Thread	UTC 70 Fl. Orange
Tail	Olive soft hackle fibers
Tag	Tying thread
Body	Hare's mask
Ribbing	Copper wire, fine
Collar	Hareline Dubbin, insect green
Head	Black or copper bead

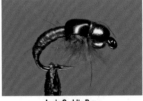

Joe's Caddis Pupa

Originator	Joe Johnson
Tyer	Joe Johnson
Hook	Dai Riki 135, size 14-18
Thread	UTC 70, white
Body	Scud back, olive
Legs	India hen back
Thorax	Any darker colored dubbing
Wing Case	Thin Skin, black
Head	Gold tungsten

Tan Flex Caddis Emerger

Originator	Larry O Jurgens
Tyer	Larry O Jurgens
Hook	Dai Riki 070 or 075 size 16-20
Thread	Uni Dark Brown 8/0
Trailing Shuck	Poly bear fiber
Under Body	UTC 70, white
Body	Spanflex floss, tan
Wing	Goose biots, natural
Head	Superfine dubbing, mahogany brown

Tan Flex Caddis Rock Worm

Originator	Larry O Jurgens
Tyer	Larry O Jurgens
Hook	TMC 2302 or Dai Riki 280 size 12-20
Thread	UTC 70 white
Body	Spanflex floss, tan
Thorax	Superfine dubbing, mahogany brown
Head	Mill Hill glass bead, matte chocolate 11/0

Rubber-Legged Go2 Caddis

Originator	Rick Takahashi
Tyer	Rick Takahashi
Hook	TMC 9300, 3769, 3761 size 14-18
Thread	UNI 8/0 Olive dun
Tail	Whiting hen hackle, brown
Body	Diamond midge braid, charteuse
Hackle	Whiting midge, brown
Wing	Poly Yarn, white
Legs	Round rubber, black, small
Thorax	Ice Dub, peacock

Caddis Emerger and Stonefly Dry Patterns

Tabou Caddis Emerger

Originator	Steve Schweitzer
Tyer	Steve Schweitzer
Hook	Daiichi 1270, size 14-16
Thread	Brown 8/0
Tail Tip and Body	Whiting Brahma hen chick-a-bou, pale yellow
Ribbing	Stretch Magic, 0.5mm clear
Wing	Whiting Brahma hen soft hackle feather
Head	Ice Dub, peacock

T's Wee Pupa: Olive

Originator	Tim Drummond
Tyer	Tim Drummond
Hook	Dai Riki 135 size 14-18
Thread	White for body, black for thorax
Butt	Krystal Flash, gray ghost
Body	Wee Wool, olive
Ribbing	D-Rib, dark brown
Thorax	Tan ostrich herl and Peacock Ice Dub
Wing Bud	Hungarian Partridge, dark brown
Legs	Hungarian Partridge, light gray, peacock Sulky thread
Antennae	Hungarian Partridge feather

T's Wee Pupa: October Caddis

Originator	Tim Drummond
Tyer	Tim Drummond
Hook	Dai Riki 135 size 14-18
Thread	White for body, tan for thorax
Butt	Krystal Flash, gray ghost
Body	Wee Wool, tan
Ribbing	D-Rib, amber
Thorax	Tan ostrich herl and Golden Brown Ice Dub
Wing Bud	Hungarian Partridge, dark brown
Legs	Hungarian Partridge, light gray and Tan Sulky thread
Antennae	Hungarian Partridge feather

Richard's Pupa

Originator	Richard Ross
Tyer	Richard Ross
Hook	Mustad R50, size 12-18
Thread	UTC 70 Ultra Olive
Body	A mix of Hareline Hare's Ear Plus and Wapsi Sow-Scud, smoky olive
Hackle	Whiting Coq de Leon Hen
Head	Tungsten bead

Go2 Caddis

Originator	Rick Takahashi
Tyer	Rick Takahashi
Hook	TMC 9300, 3769, 3761 size 14-18
Thread	UNI 8/0 Olive dun
Tail	Whiting hen hackle, brown
Body	Diamond midge braid, charteuse
Hackle	Whiting midge, brown
Wing	Poly Yarn, white
Thorax	Ice Dub, peacock

Achy Brachy

Originator	Marty Staab
Tyer	Marty Staab
Hook	Dai Riki 135 size 14-16
Thread	Uni 6/0 black
Abdomen	Flex Floss, insect green
Ribbing	Flex Floss, chartreuse
Highlight	Black Sharpie
Legs	Partridge, brown
Antenna	Wood duck (optional)
Thorax	Ostrich, olive
Head	Hareline Ice Dub, black peacock

ARF Humpulator Orange/Yellow

Originator	Al Ritt
Tyer	Al Ritt
Hook	TMC 5212 size 6-10
Thread	UTC 70 Yellow
Tail	Squirrel
Back	Brown foam
Abdomen	Poly Yarn, Orange
Ribbing	Whiting grizzly hackle
Underwing	Mirage Flash, Opal
Wing	Squirrel
Post	Para Post yarn, Fl. Orange
Thorax	Ice Dub, Holographic yellow
Hackle	Whiting grizzly

ARF Trailing Bubble Harey Yellow Stone

Originator	Al Ritt
Tyer	Al Ritt
Hook	TMC 101 size 14-18
Thread	UTC 70 Yellow
Tail	Mirage Flash, Opal
Egg Sack	Closed cell foam, red
Abdomen	Superfine dubbing, yellow
Ribbing	Whiting grizzly dyed yellow, trimmed
Underwing	Mirage Flash, Opal
Wing	Snowshoe hare, natural cream
Post	Closed cell foam, red
Thorax	Superfine dubbing, yellow
Head	Whiting barred light ginger

Slow Water Sally

Originator	Brad Befus
Tyer	Brad Befus
Hook	TMC 2302 size 14-16
Thread	Ultra thread 70 neutral
Tail	Goose biots, ginger
Butt	Superfine dubbing, orange
Underbody	Superfine dubbing, pale yellow
Abdomen	Turkey biot, PMD, wrapped over underbody
Wing	Medallion sheet, golden stone
Thorax	Superfine dubbing, pale yellow
Indicator	2mm foam, pink or red
Hackle	Whiting grizzly dyed yellow

Stonefly Dry and Nymph Patterns

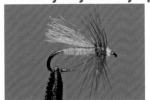

Dick's Little Green Stone

Originator	Dick Shinton
Tyer	Dick Shinton
Hook	Standard dry fly size 18-22
Thread	UTC 70 Fl. Green
Body	Superfine dubbing, fl. chartreuse
Wing	Float-Vis chartreuse
Hackle	Whiting light dun

PMS

Originator	Dick Shinton
Tyer	Dick Shinton
Hook	Standard dry fly size 18-22
Thread	Gordon Griffith Primrose 14/0
Body	Superfine dubbing, PMD
Wing	Float-Vis yellow
Hackle	Whiting light dun

Tak's Yellow Sally

Originator	Rick Takahashi
Tyer	Rick Takahashi
Hook	TMC 2302 size 12-16
Thread	Yellow 3/0 monocord or 140 UTC Hopper Yellow
Butt	8/0 red thread
Body	Flyrite dubbing, golden yellow
Wing	MFC wing, tan
Indicator	McFly Foam, fl. yellow
Wing	Mule deer, natural
Legs	MFC clear legs

Tak's Stonefly Nymph

Originator	Rick Takahashi
Tyer	Rick Takahashi
Hook	TMC 2302 size 6-10
Thread	Brown monocord, 3/0
Tail	Goose biots, tan
Body and Thorax	Golden Stonefly dubbing or mix yellow and tan acrylic yarn
Back and Wing Case	Pallon strip colored with tan marker
Ribbing	Brassie wire, brown
Legs	Whiting brown hackle
Gills	Ostrich herl, light dun

Golden Prince

Originator	Joe Johnson
Tyer	Joe Johnson
Hook	Dai Riki 730 size 12-18
Thread	UTC 70, yellow
Tail	Goose biots, ginger
Back	Lateral Scale, black
Ribbing	Gold wire, small
Legs	India hen back
Abdomen	Scud Dub, amber
Head	Tungsten bead, gold

Frank's Flashy Stone

Originator	Frank Drummond
Tyer	Tim Drummond
Hook	Dai Riki 280 size 10-12
Thread	Burnt Orange 8/0
Tail & Back	Pheasant tail
Abdomen	Krystal Flash, Golden Olive
Rib	Copper wire, medium
Thoraxes	Krystal Flash, hot orange
Wing Cases	Pheasant tail
Legs	Krystal Flash, hot orange and pheasant tail
Head	Tungsten bead, black

Steve's Wee Little Black Stone

Originator	Steve Schweitzer
Tyer	Steve Schweitzer
Hook	Daiichi 1270 size 16-20
Thread	UTC 70, black
Tail	Goose biots, black
Body	Stretch Magic, black 0.5mm
Back	Scud Back, black with 1 strand of holographic fiber on top
Thorax	Superfine dubbing, black
Legs	Brahma hen soft hackle feather (Whiting)

Steve's Wee Little Golden Stone

Originator	Steve Schweitzer
Tyer	Steve Schweitzer
Hook	Daiichi 1270 size 14-18
Thread	UTC 70, golden
Tail	Goose biots, golden
Body	Stretch Magic, clear 0.5mm, brown marker on top
Back	Scud Back, golden with 1 strand of holographic fiber on top
Thorax	Superfine dubbing, golden
Legs	Brahma hen soft hackle feather (Whiting)

Steve's Flimsy Damsel

Originator	Steve Schweitzer
Tyer	Steve Schweitzer
Hook	Daiichi 1270 size 14
Thread	UTC 70 Golden Olive
Tail	Micro Pearl Core Braid, chartreuse or olive, tied at hook halfway point
Body	Ice Dub, chartreuse or olive
Back	Loon UV Knot Sense
Eyes	Mono eyes, olive or black

Damselfly, Scud and Ant Patterns

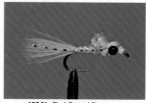

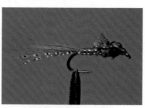

ARF SlimFlash Damsel Tan

Originator	Al Ritt
Tyer	Al Ritt
Hook	TMC 3761 size 12 - 16
Thread	UTC 70 Tan
Tail	Marabou, tan with Mirage Flash, Opal
Body	Marabou, tan
Ribbing	Mirage Flash, Opal, single strand
Wingcase	Mirage Flash (opal) and antron yarn (tan)
Eyes	Plastic bead chain, black

ARF SlimFlash Damsel Chartreuse

Originator	Al Ritt
Tyer	Al Ritt
Hook	TMC 3761 size 12 - 16
Thread	UTC 70 Fl. Chartreuse
Tail	Marabou, chartreuse with Mirage Flash, Opal
Body	Marabou, chartreuse
Ribbing	Mirage Flash, Opal, single strand
Wingcase	Mirage Flash (opal) and antron yarn (chartreuse)
Eyes	Plastic bead chain, black

ARF SlimFlash Damsel Olive

Originator	Al Ritt
Tyer	Al Ritt
Hook	TMC 3761 size 12 - 16
Thread	UTC 70 Olive
Tail	Marabou, Olive with Mirage Flash, Opal
Body	Marabou, olive
Ribbing	Mirage Flash, Opal, single strand
Wingcase	Mirage Flash (opal) and antron yarn (olive)
Eyes	Plastic bead chain, black

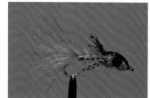

Ziggy Damsel

Originator	Marty Staab
Tyer	Marty Staab
Hook	Dai Riki 270 size 10-12
Thread	Danville Flymaster 70 lt. olive
Tail & Body	Stillwater Creations Marabou, light olive
Ribbing	Stretch Magic, 0.5mm
Legs	Spirit River TarantuLegs, mini, olive barred
Wing Buds	Pheasant tail with Loon's UV Knot Sense over the top
Thorax	Ice Dub, UV light olive
Eyes	Bead chain, black

Simple Scud Alive (Olive)

Originator	Steve Schweitzer
Tyer	Steve Schweitzer
Hook	Daiichi 1130 size 12-18
Thread	UTC 70 Gray
Tail	Whiting Coq de Leon tailing fibers with 1 strand of pearl krystal flash
Back	Scud Back, clear
Dubbing	UV Ice Dub gray and olive mixed
Ribbing	Silver wire, thin

Simple Scud Dead (Rust)

Originator	Steve Schweitzer
Tyer	Steve Schweitzer
Hook	Daiichi 1130 size 12-18
Thread	UTC 70 Gray
Tail	Whiting Coq de Leon tailing fibers with 1 strand of pearl krystal flash
Back	Scud Back, clear
Dubbing	UV Ice Dub rust and tan mixed
Ribbing	Silver wire, thin

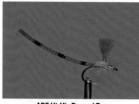

ARF Hi-Vis Damsel Tan

Originator	Al Ritt
Tyer	Al Ritt
Hook	TMC 2488 size 12-16
Thread	UTC 70 tan
Tail	Braided leader dyed tan, colored with black marker (add a drop of super glue to prevent fraying)
Thorax	Superfine dubbing, tan
Post	Para Post Yarn, Hi-Vis orange
Wing Case	2mm foam, tan
Wing	Organza, clear white

Flying Flip-Flop Ant

Originator	Harrison Steeves
Tyer	Dick Shinton
Hook	Standard dry fly size 14-18
Thread	Black 8/0
Body	Foam cylinder cut from closed-cell foam
Wing	Float Vis, UV white
Hackle	Whiting grizzly, sparse

Tak's Big Butt Ant

Originator	Rick Takahashi
Tyer	Rick Takahashi
Hook	TMC 100 size 16-20
Thread	UTC 70 black
Rear Body	Black glass bead covered with UV Knot Sense
Front Body	Superfine dubbing, black
Wing	Poly yarn, white
Hackle	Whiting black saddle

Ant and Beetle Patterns

Para-Cupboard Ant

Originator	Kruise / Schweitzer
Tyer	Steve Schweitzer
Hook	Standard dry fly hook size 14-16
Thread	UTC 70 black
Body	Two connected "pillow" segments from shelf lining; pull the segments from the sheet to obtain the antenna effect
Post	2mm foam, green
Hackle	Whiting grizzly, over-sized

Cupboard Ant

Originator	Davidson / Kruise
Tyer	Mike Kruise
Hook	Standard dry fly hook size 14-16
Thread	UTC 70 black
Body	Two connected "pillow" segments from shelf lining; pull the segments from the sheet to obtain the antenna effect
Hackle	Whiting black saddle

MK Flip-Flop Ant

Originator	Harrison Steeves
Tyer	Mike Kruise
Hook	Standard dry fly hook size 14-16
Thread	Black 8/0
Tail	Krystal Flash, pearl
Body	Foam cylinder cut from a black flip-flop sandal
Hackle	Whiting grizzly saddle

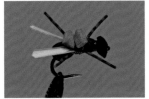

Winged Foam Ant

Originator	Rick Takahashi
Tyer	Rick Takahashi
Hook	TMC 100
Thread	UTC 70 black
Body	Rainy's float foam, black
Indicator	Thin foam, orange
Wing	Goose biot, white
Legs	MFC Centipede Legs, brown

Ishiwata's Poodle Ant

Originator	Kazuhiko Tani
Tyer	Eric Ishiwata
Hook	Gamakatsu C-14BV, size 16
Thread	UTC 70 black
Body	Superfine dubbing, black
Wing Post	TMC Aero Dry Wing, fl. white
Hackle	Whiting grizzly saddle

Hi-Vis Ant

Originator	Eric Ishiwata
Tyer	Eric Ishiwata
Hook	Tiemco 212Y
Thread	Rust 8/0
Body	Peacock herl
Overbody	2mm foam strip, black
Indicator	TMC Aero Dry Wing, fl. green
Hackle	Whiting black saddle

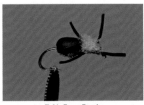

Tak's Foam Beetle

Originator	Rick Takahashi
Tyer	Rick Takahashi
Hook	TMC 100
Thread	UTC 70 black
Under Body	Peacock herl
Body	Rainy's Float Foam, black
Indicator	McFly yarn, pink
Legs	MFC Sili Legs, brown

Fathead Beetle

Originator	Dennis Potter, Riverhouse Flies
Tyer	Marty Staab
Hook	Dai Riki 730 size 12-14
Thread	Danville Flymaster Plus 210, black
Back	Foam, 2mm black
Abdomen	Peacock or Ice Dub, holographic copper
Wing	H2O Fluoro Fiber, gray
Legs	Round rubber, medium black
Spotlight	McFlyFoam, chartreuse or orange

Mark's Beetle

Originator	Mark McMillan
Tyer	Mark McMillan
Hook	Mustad 3906 heavy shank size 8 - 16
Thread	UTC 140 Denier, black
Underbody	Ostrich herl, tan
Body	Craft foam, 2mm cut to shape using River Road Creations Caddis Wing Cutter
Legs	Poly rope fibers, black
Head	Shelf liner, single "pillow" segment hand-pulled apart, black

Beetle, Hopper and Cricket Patterns

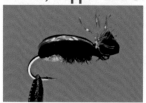

Bright Butt Beetle

Originator	Harrison Steeves
Tyer	Mike Kruise
Hook	Standard dry fly size 12-18
Thread	Black 8/0
Body	2mm foam, black
Under Body, Butt	Micro Pearl Core Braid, chartreuse
Under Body, Front	Peacock herl
Indicator	Micro Flash fibers, pearl

LA Hopper

Originator	Mark McMillan
Tyer	Mark Tracy
Hook	Standard dry fly size 8-12
Thread	Brown 8/0
Tail Legs	Rubber legs, round, coral snake barring
Body	2mm tan foam cut with caddis wing cutters
Under Wing	Deer hair, natural
Over Wing	2mm tan foam cut with caddis wing cutters
Front Legs	Round rubber, orange

LA Stimi

Originator	Mark McMillan
Tyer	Mark Tracy
Hook	Standard dry fly size 16-22
Thread	Brown 8/0
Tail	Deer hair tips, fine
Body	Whiting grizzly hackle, tightly palmered
Foam Body	1-2mm foam, light tan cut with caddis wing cutters
Collar	Whiting grizzly hackle
Eyes	Black marker

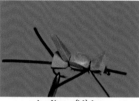

Los Alamos (LA) Ant

Originator	Harrison Steeves
Tyer	Harrison Steeves
Hook	Dry fly, size 8-12, 2X long
Thread	Brown 6/0
Tail Legs	Rubber Legs, brown
Body	Locofoam tan, two triangles tied in opposite direction
Under Body	Peacock herl

Mark's Spider

Originator	Mark McMillan
Tyer	Mark McMillan
Hook	Mustad 3906 size 8 - 16
Thread	UTC 140 Denier, brown
Underbody	Sulky mylar thread contrasting to color of foam
Body	Craft foam, 2mm cut to shape using River Road Creations Caddis Wing Cutter, many colors applicable
Legs	Centipede legs, med and sm
Head	Superfine dubbing, match color of foam

Brad's Cricket

Originator	Brad Befus
Tyer	Brad Befus
Hook	TMC 100, size 10-16
Thread	Ultra Thread 70, black
Body	Superfine dubbing, black
Wing	Peacock sword fibers
Hackle	Whiting black

Takahopper

Originator	A version of Ed Shenk's Letort Hopper
Tyer	Rick Takahashi
Hook	TMC 2302 size 12-16
Thread	UTC 140 Hopper Yellow
Body	Flyrite dubbing, golden yellow
Under Wing	MFC wing, tan
Over Wing	Mule deer, natural

Baby Boy Hopper

Originator	Charlie Craven
Tyer	Charlie Craven
Hook	TMC 2499SP-BL size 12-16
Thread	Tan 3/0 monocord
Body	2mm Thin Fly Foam
Legs	Medium round rubber, brown
Wing	Natural deer hair
Eyes	Black marker

Chernobyl Ant

Originator	Mark Forslund
Tyer	Rick Takahashi
Hook	TMC 5212 size 10-16
Thread	UTC 70 black
Body	2mm foam, tan, cut with salmonfly wing cutters
Under Body	Whiting brown saddle hackle
Legs	Sili Legs, olive brown
Indicator	2mm foam, chartreuse

Streamers, Worm and Attractor Dry Patterns

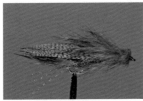

Spun Bunny Muddler

Originator	Steve Schweitzer
Tyer	Steve Schweitzer
Hook	Daiichi 1750 size 4-10
Thread	Brown 6/0
Tail	Rabbit fur, tan
Body	Hare'e Ice Dub, peacock
Ribbing	ribbing
Wing	Mallard flank, dyed wood duck with pearl krystal flash strands
Head and Collar	Spun rabbit hair in dubbing loop, tan. Trim head area short.

Little Spruce Matuka

Originator	unknown
Tyer	Scott Stisser
Hook	Dia Riki 700 size 12
Thread	Danville 6/0, black
Rib	Gold wire, fine
Aft Body	Danville A bright orange or red
Fore Body	Peacock herl
Wing	Coq de Leon hen feathers, 4 back-to-back, stripped on bottom, tied matuka style
Collar	Coq de Leon, folded

Secret Weapon

Originator	Tyler Befus
Tyer	Tyler Befus
Hook	TMC 2487 size 8-12
Thread	Ultra Thread, olive
Tail	Marabou, grizzly dyed olive and pearl Krystal Flash
Body	Marabou, grizzly dyed olive, twisted and wrapped
Ribbing	Ultra Wire, copper
Legs	Barred Sili-Legs, olive
Wing	Marabou, grizzly dyed olive
Thorax	Ice Dub, olive
Head	Gold bead

Chamois Leech

Originator	unknown
Tyer	Mike Kruise
Hook	Standard wet fly size 8-12
Thread	Wine 8/0
Body	Chamois leather strip, tan

Mike's Worm

Originator	Mike Kruise
Tyer	Mike Kruise
Hook	Daiichi 1770 swimming nymph hook size 12-18
Thread	Black 8/0
Body	Ultra wire, small, wine, covered with tying cement

Purple San Juan Worm

Originator	unknown
Tyer	Rick Takahashi
Hook	TMC 2457 size 12-16
Thread	Fire Orange or fl. red 8/0
Body	Purple vernille

Go-To-Hell Variant

Originator	Charlie Craven
Tyer	Charlie Craven
Hook	Standard dry fly, size 12-14
Thread	UTC 70 black
Tail	Calf tail, white
Body	Back half: UTC 70 chartreuse , front half: Ice Dub, black peacock
Wings	Calf tail, white, in a 'V'
Hackle	Whiting brown and grizzly neck

Red Humpy

Originator	unknown
Tyer	Rick Takahashi
Hook	TMC 100, size 10-16
Thread	UNI 8/0, red
Body	Bleached elk hair over tying thread
Tail	Moose body hair
Wing	Mule deer tips or white poly yarn
Hackle	Whiting brown or furnace

Brookie Buster

Originator	Steve Schweitzer
Tyer	Steve Schweitzer
Hook	Daiichi 1190 barbless size 12-14
Thread	Tan 8/0
Body	Whiting grizzly; 2 feathers, dyed olive, dyed orange
Ribbing	Silver wire, ultra fine, counter wrapped from rear

Attractor Dry and Nymph Patterns

Kirk's Green Foam Bug

Originator	Kirk Bien
Tyer	Kirk Bien
Hook	Daiichi 1270 size 10-16
Thread	Green 8/0
Under body	2mm foam, lime green, extended for tail and head
Body	Whiting brown saddle palmered with a pearl Flashabou strand
Wing	Deer hair, natural
Hackle	Whiting grizzly
Eyes	3D Holographic eyes

ARF Egg Sucking Gnat

Originator	Al Ritt
Tyer	Al Ritt
Hook	TMC 5212 size 8-12
Thread	UTC 70 brown
Abdomen	Peacock herl
Ribbing	Whiting grizzly, sized to half of the hook gape
Head/Wing	Fl. Orange deer hair
Legs	Round rubber legs, yellow-black

CDC Cranefly Adult

Originator	Brad Befus
Tyer	Brad Befus
Hook	TMC 206BL size 14-18
Thread	UTC 70 cream
Body and Thorax	Superfine dubbing, yellow, tan, olive or brown
Wings	Whiting hen neck tips
Hackle	CDC, tan, cream or yellow

Beefmo Coachman

Originator	Brad Befus
Tyer	Brad Befus
Hook	TMC 3761 size 10-16
Thread	Ultra Thread 70, black
Tail	Golden pheasant crest dyed black
Body	Rear 1/3 silver holographic tinsel, front 2/3 peacock herl
Ribbing	Ultra wire, copper
Collar	Hen neck, badger
Wing	Calf tail, white

Deep Blue Poison Tung

Originator	Charlie Craven
Tyer	Charlie Craven
Hook	TMC 2488 size 16-22
Thread	Uni Thread gray
Body	Tying thread
Ribbing	Lagartun wire, blue
Thorax	UV Ice Dub, gray
Head	2mm Tungsten silver

Jumpin' Black Flash

Originator	Dick Shinton
Tyer	Dick Shinton
Hook	Dai-Riki 135
Thread	UTC 70 black
Tail	Lagartun Midge Braid, black
Body	Holographic tinsel, black, medium
Shellback, Wingcase	Mirage Tinsel, ice blue pearl
Ribbing	UTC Wire, silver, small
Thorax	Ice Dub, UV Black
Legs	Lagartun Midge Braid
Head	Silver bead

Boulder Creek Nymph

Originator	Joe Johnson
Tyer	Joe Johnson
Hook	Dai Riki 135 size 14-18
Thread	UTC 70 black
Tail	Krystal Flash, hot orange
Shellback	Scud Back, olive
Thorax	Ice Dub, olive
Ribbing	Wire, small red
Head	Tungsten bead, copper

RK Emerger

Originator	Mike Kruise
Tyer	Mike Kruise
Hook	TMC 2487 size 16-20
Thread	UTC 70 Blue Dun
Body	Tying thread
Ribbing	Sulky Thread, caddis green
Wing	Poly yarn, white, with motor oil Sulky Thread
Thorax	UV Ice Dub, tan
Head	Silver bead

Fakey Nymph

Originator	Tyler Befus
Tyer	Tyler Befus
Hook	TMC 2457 size 10-16
Thread	Ultra Thread 70, black
Tail	Pheasant tail
Abdomen	Pheasant tail, wrapped with flat pearl mylar over top
Thorax	Ice Dub, peacock
Ribbing	Ultra Wire, copper
Legs	Centipede legs
Hackle	Whiting hen, brown
Head	Gold bead

ABOVE: Greenback cutthroat stage for spawning in a small outlet creek of one of the highest lakes in the Park. The larger fish was approximately 11"-12" long, for perspective.

BELOW: This male brook trout is the most colorful brook trout the author has ever caught. A vibrant orange belly, black and white laced fins, a dark green back, blue-halos around red dots and yellow spots glowing like stars in the night make this brook trout unforgettable.

Appendix

Area Fly Shops

Hatch Seasons

Hatch Charts

Creeks, Streams, Rivers and Lakes in RMNP

20-Year Average Snow-Free Dates

Lakes Over 10,000 feet

Trails Ranked By Difficulty

References

Visit the Book's Website

OPPOSITE: Echo Creek after a summer morning rain. The first quarter mile up from East Inlet Creek harbors some nice brook trout. Beyond a quarter mile, fish are scarce and the creek is considered barren. All of Echo Creek is off trail, steep and rugged.

Area Fly Shops

Fly Shop	Address	Phone	Website	Fly Shop	RMNP Guide Svc
Charlie's Fly Box	7513 Grandview Ave Arvada, CO 80002	303.403.8880	www.charliesflybox.com	•	
Elkhorn Fly Rod & Reel	3121 West Eisenhower Blvd Loveland, CO 80538	970.227.4707	www.elkhornflyrodandreel.com	•	•
Estes Angler	338 W Riverside Estes Park, CO 80517	970.586.2110	www.estesangler.com	•	•
Estes Park Mountain Shop	2050 Big Thompson Ave. Estes Park, CO 80517	866.303.6548	www.estesparkmountainshop.com	•	•
Front Range Anglers	2344 Pearl Street Boulder, CO 80302	303.494.1375	www.frontrangeanglers.com	•	•
Hook Fly Fishing	2030 E. County Line Road Highlands Ranch, CO 80126	720.920.9780	www.hookflyfishing.com	•	•
Jax Outdoor - Ft. Collins, CO	1200 North College Fort Collins, CO 80525	970.221.0544	www.jaxmerchantile.com	•	
Jax Outdoor - Loveland, CO	950 E. Eisenhower Loveland, CO 80537	970.776.4540	www.jaxmerchantile.com	•	
Kinsley Outfitters (aka Sunrise Outfitters)	2070 Broadway Boulder, CO 80302	303.442.6204	--		•
Kirk's Fly Shop	230 E Elkhorn Ave Estes Park, CO 80517	970.577.0790	www.kirksflyshop.com	•	•
Laughing Grizzly Fly Shop	10675 Ute Highway Longmont, CO 80504	303.772.9110	www.laughinggrizzlyflyshop.net	•	•
Rocky Mountain Anglers	1904 Arapahoe Boulder, CO 80302	303.447.2400	www.rockymtnanglers.com	•	•
Sasquatch Fly Fishing	2515 Tunnel Road Estes Park, CO 80511	970.586.3341 ext 1153	www.frontrangeanglers.com	•	•
Scot's Sporting Goods	870 Moraine Avenue Estes Park, CO 80517	970.586.2877	www.scotssportinggoods.com	•	•
Sportsman's Warehouse	1675 Rocky Mountain Avenue Loveland, CO 80538	970.461.5000	www.sportsmanswarehouse.com	•	
St. Peter's Fly Shop	202 Remington Street Fort Collins, CO 80524	970.498.8968	www.stpetes.com	•	•

Hatch Seasons

January and February (and December)

Essentially, every water that contains fish is frozen solid in January. Fishing outside the Park below the town of Estes Park on the Big Thompson River is your best bet, but expect crowds on the weekends and sunny week days. The warming sun brings out good hatches of small 22 through 24 midges around 10AM to 1PM daily.

March

If the weather patterns give unseasonably warm days, some of the water in the valleys can be open and fishable. As the month progresses, there is open water at the lowest elevations, but trekking much above 9,000 feet may not be too productive. Nymphing is your best bet, with small size 18 to 20 BWO nymphs, midge larvae and San Juan Worms. Occasionally you'll see some small dark-bodied caddis; this is your clue to fish a caddis nymph or emerger as fish will not usually rise to this sporadic hatch. Same applies for the small winter stonefly hatch; fish a small black stonefly nymph.

April and May

This is the time of the year when the locals get excited to fish the Park. Longer and warmer days open most streams up to 9,800 feet or so. At the end of May, searching for ice-out lakes is a possibility, however there will still be plenty of snow pack above 9,500 feet, warranting snowshoes. Ice-out lake fishing has become a irrevocable passion for some; it can be that good, but difficult to time perfectly (refer to the Appendix *Twenty-Year Snow-Free Average Dates* for predicted snow-free dates). Fishing lower elevation streams can be exciting as fish start to look up and take the smaller mayflies and midges which hatch in sometimes epic numbers on a sunny warm day.

June

Snow pack will still exist the first half of June above 9,800 feet, trails will be slushy and slick. Lakes will begin thawing rapidly during the longer days and plentiful sunshine. Ice-out fishing is prime. By the end of June, summer conditions are in full swing. Expect PMDs and BWOs to be the primary mayflies. Don't overlook stoneflies and caddis nymphs and emergers as a trailer to a dry fly. Backpacking is in full swing and the fish that have been under ice for 5-7 months are now looking up for easy shoreline meals.

July, August

This is the prime time in the Park, both for fishing and for tourists. Expect easily accessible water to be, well, easily accessed by the surge in visitor traffic. Planning a hike of an hour or two to reach higher elevation water will pay off. Fishing a terrestrial this time of year is essential, but don't forget to bring your caddis dries as well. Along with the terrestrials come the mosquitos. Be sure to bring bug dope to ward off those annoying critters.

September, October and November

In early September, the crowds wane and the fishing remains spectacular with summer day weather and cooler nights. At the end of September, you might find thin sheets of ice along the edges of streams and certainly on lakes, but by mid-afternoon they have melted. Prime fishing time is from 11am to 3pm this time of year. In November, lakes will have started their deep freeze, but some creeks, streams and rivers can be fishable. Caddis and midges continue to hatch well into October.

Hatch Charts

Stonefly & Caddis Hatches

Stoneflies are often an overlooked fish food source in the Park. While the dry fly hatches won't be as prolific and fish-stirring as they are on larger Colorado rivers, the nymphs are just as active and prevalent. Caddis are some of the most dense food sources in the Park's waters. Green free living caddis nymphs, caddis emergers and the classic Elk-Hair caddis should all be in your fly box arsenal.

Stonefly Hatches - *Rocky Mountain National Park*

■ Prime hatch period
□ Marginal hatch period

Common Name	Size	Color	Hatch Time	J	F	M	A	M	J	J	A	S	O	N	D
Tiny Winter Black Stone	16 - 18	Black body, medium dun wings	40°- 44°F water temps	■	■	■	■	□							□
Early Brown Stone	10 - 12	Light to dark brown bodies with clear to yellow-clear wings	44°- 48°F water temps				■	■	□						
Salmon Fly	4 - 6	Black body top with reddish-brown to orange underside	55°- 58°F water temps, cloudy days					□	■	□					
Small Western Stone	8 - 12	Dark brown to black	–					□	■	□					
Golden Stonefly	6 - 10	Golden brown body with yellowish dun wings	–						■	■					
Little Yellow Stonefly	12 -16	Pale yellow to yellow-green body with dun wing	mornings						□	■	□				
Medium Brown and Yellow Stonefly	10 - 12	Brown to yellow body; brown dun wings	50°F water temp, early mornings to 2pm						□	■	■				
Green Stonefly	12 -16	Light olive to green body; clear to yellow-clear wing	–						□	■	■				

Caddis Hatches - *Rocky Mountain National Park*

■ Prime hatch period
□ Marginal hatch period

Common/Scientific Name	Size	Color	Hatch Time	J	F	M	A	M	J	J	A	S	O	N	D
Short-Horn Sedge	14	Dark brown/yellow body with tan wing	Sporadic throughout day			□	■	■	■	■	■	■	□		
Classic Grannom Caddis	10 - 14	Bright green to dun green body with light tan dun wing	Early AM and PM			■	■	□							
Little Sister Sedge	14	Green to brown/green body with mottled tan wing	Late afternoons into evening						□	■	■	■			
Spotted Sedge	10 -12	Yellow/brown body with mottled tan wing	Througout the day						□	■	■	■	■		
Gray Spotted Sedge	10 - 12	Green or olive/brown body with mottled gray wing	Throughout the day							■	□				
Little Dark Sedge	16	Dark brown body with dark brown/black wing	Noon to 3pm							■	■	□			
Little Brown Sedge	14	Brown body with tan wing	Throughout the day								■	■			
Micro Caddis	20 - 22	Yellow/brown/reddish body with dun brown wing	Throughout the day							■	■	■			
Green Sedge	12	Olive/yellow body with mottled dun brown wings	Throughout the day								■	■			
Giant Orange Sedge	6 - 8	Orange body with translucent brown wing	Late afternoon until dark									■	■		

Hatch Charts

May Fly and Midge Hatches

From June through October, a plethora of mayflies hatch in the Park's lakes and streams. They most often are a convenient and visible size 14 and 16. A Para-Adams or traditional Adams is the go-to fly. Classic quill-bodied Catskill-style dry flies such as the Gordon and Red Quill service those mid-summer hatches well. Having a selection of pale yellow, cream and pinkish-red PMD's tied comparadun-style also is a good choice. Over-hackle quills and PMDs by a few wraps to ensure they float high over riffles and fast water. Midges are a year-round good bet, particularly for early spring streams and mid-summer lakes. Often you will see rises to apparently nothing at all. Tie on a size 20 to 24 black-bodied, white-hackled midge dry to feed these fish.

May Fly and Midge Hatches - *Rocky Mountain National Park*

■ Prime hatch period
□ Marginal hatch period

Common/Scientific Name	Size	Color	Hatch Time	J	F	M	A	M	J	J	A	S	O	N	D
Midge and Snow Fly	22 - 28	Gray to Black	Warmest part of day	■	■	■	■	■	■	■	■	■	■	■	■
Blue-Winged Olive	16 -18	Olive brown	Warmest part of day; spinner fall in evening			■	■	■	■	■	■	■	■	■	□
Black Quill	12	Black w/ dun wing	10-11am; spinner fall in evening				□	■	■	□					
Pale Morning Dun	16 -18	Cream olive with light dun wing	10am - 5pm						■						
Iron Blue Quill	20	Light Olive-tan with mottled wing	2-5pm; spinner falls in morning and eve						■	■					
Western Green Drake	8 - 12	Dark olive with medium dun wing	1-4pm on cloudy days; spinner fall in evenings							■	□				
Slate-Winged Drake Mahogany Dun Brown Drake	12 -16	Brown body with med-dun wing	1-3pm; spinner fall in evening							□	■				
Gordon Quill	12 - 16	Brown dun body with clear wing	Late afternoon hatches with evening spinner falls							□	■				
Small Western Green Drake	14 - 16	Olive body with dark dun wing	Evening hatches with late eve spinner falls							□	■	■			
Red Quill	16	Reddish-brown body with medium dun wing	Mid-morning; spinner fall in evenings							□	■	□			
Pale Morning Dun	16 - 22	Green-Yellow-Olive body with light dun wing	10am - 2pm						■	■	■	□			
Speckled Wing Quill	14 - 16	Gray body and speckled wing	Late morning on cloudy days							□	■	■	■		
Dark Hedrickson Rusty Spinner	14	Reddish brown body with med dun wing	Late PM hatch; spinner fall in late evening								■	■			
Western Gray Drake	12 - 14	Gray body with medium dun wing	Late PM hatch; spinner fall in late evening							■	■	■	■	■	
Trico	20 - 22	Black body with white wing	Late PM hatch; spinner fall in late evening								□	■	■		
Pink Quill	10 - 12	Cream body with red/pink tint, clear wing	Late PM hatch; spinner fall in late evening									□	■		

Creeks, Streams, Rivers and RMNP

Creeks, Streams, Rivers & Lakes — Rocky Mountain National Park

Fishing Destination	Zone	Book Section	Acres	Mi	Elev (ft)	Regs	Barren	BKT	BNT	RBT	CRC	GBC	YCT	CUT
Adams Lake	6	East Inlet Trail	4.5	0	11217						•			
Adams Lake drainage	6	East Inlet Trail	0	3.2	0						•			
Alpine Brook	4	Chasm Lake Trail	0	12.3	0		•							
Andrews Creek	4	Sky Pond Trail	0	1	0		unknown							
Arrowhead Lake	3	Gorge Lakes	34.5	0	11158							•		
Aspen Brook	4	Lily Lake	0	1.7	0		•							
Azure Lake	3	Gorge Lakes	13.6	0	8552		•							
Baker Creek	8	Kawuneeche Valley	0	2.5	0				•					
Bear Lake	4	Glacier Gorge Trail	11	0	9481	1						•		
Beaver Brook	2	n/a	0	6.1	0		•							
Beaver Creek	8	Kawuneeche Valley	0	3.4	0			•						
Beaver Creek, unnamed lake near Colorado River junction	8	Timber Lake Trail	0	0	9001			•						
Bench Lake	7	North Inlet Trail	6.3	0	10157	2					•			
Bennett Creek	8	Little Yellowstone Trail	0	1.8	0		•							
Bierstadt Lake	4	n/a	7.3	0	9406		•							
Big Dutch Creek	8	La Poudre Pass Trail	0	2.4	0		•							
Big Thompson (The Pool)	3	Fern Lake Trail	0	0	8305			•	•	•		•		
Big Thompson River	3	Moraine Park	0	3.3	0			•	•	•		•		
Big Thompson River (above The Pool)	3	Fern Lake Trail	0	7.8	0							•		
Big Thompson River (along Fern Lake Trail)	3	Fern Lake Trail	0	2	0			•		•		•		

Creeks, Streams, Rivers and Lakes in RMNP

Creeks, Streams, Rivers & Lakes — Rocky Mountain National Park

Fishing Destination	Zone	Book Section	Acres	Mi	Elev (ft)	Regs	Barren	BKT	BNT	RBT	CRC	GBC	YCT	CUT
Bighorn Creek	2	n/a	0	2.1	0		•							
Bighorn Lake	8	Timber Lake Trail	0.9	0	10937	2	•							
Black Canyon Creek, above McGregor Falls	2	Black Canyon Trail / McGregor Falls Trail	0	5.1	0		•							
Black Canyon Creek, below McGregor Falls	2	Black Canyon Trail / McGregor Falls Trail	0	1.3	0			•						
Black Lake	4	Glacier Gorge Trail	9.1	0	10634			•						
Blue Lake	4	Glacier Gorge Trail	2.7	0	11147		•							
Bluebird Lake	5	Bluebird Lake & Ouzel Lake Trail	21.7	0	10985		•							
Boulder Brook (near Sprague Lake)	4	Sprague Lake Nature Trail	0	0.7	0			•	•					
Boulder Brook (upper)	4	Sprague Lake Nature Trail	0	4.6	0		•							
Bowen Gulch drainage, near Gaskil	8	Kawuneeche Valley	0	0.5	0				•	•				
Box / Eagle Lake Drainage (below Mertensia Falls to N. St. Vrain)	5	Thunder Lake Trail	0	0.2	0			•						
Box Canyon Creek	8	n/a	0	0	0		•							
Box Lake	5	Thunder Lake Trail	6.3	0	10767			•						
Box Lake Drainage	5	Thunder Lake Trail	0	0.4	0			•						
Box Lake Drainage (Mertensia Falls to Box Lake)	5	Thunder Lake Trail	0	0.3	0			•						
Cabin Creek (above 9,400 ft)	5	Cabin Creek	0	1.5	0		•							
Cabin Creek (below 9,400 ft)	5	Cabin Creek	0	1.2	0			•						
Cache La Poudre River	1	Cache La Poudre River Trail	0	10	0	5		•						•
Cache La Poudre River, South Fork (above 9,500)	1	Cache La Poudre River Trail	0	4.9	0	5	•							
Cache La Poudre River, South Fork (below 9,500)	1	Cache La Poudre River Trail	0	0.1	0	5						•		

Creeks, Streams, Rivers and Lakes in RMNP

Creeks, Streams, Rivers & Lakes — Rocky Mountain National Park

Fishing Destination	Zone	Book Section	Acres	Mi	Elev (ft)	Regs	Barren	BKT	BNT	RBT	CRC	GBC	YCT	CUT
Caddis Lake (see Fay Lakes Lower)		Ypsilon Lake Trail												
Camper's Creek	5	Sandbeach Lake Trail	0	1.9	0		•							
Cascade Creek (above Mirror Lake)	1	Mirror Lake Trail	0	0.4	0		•							
Cascade Creek (below Mirror Lake)	1	Cache La Poudre River Trail, Mirror Lake Trail	0	4	0			•	•					
Cascade Lake	2	Horseshoe Park	0	0	0	unknown								
Castle Lake	5	Thunder Lake Trail	1.8	0	11167		•							
Castle Lakes (S of Castle Lake, E)	5	Thunder Lake Trail	0	0	10627	unknown								
Castle Lakes (S of Castle Lake, W)	5	Thunder Lake Trail	0	0	10627	unknown								
Chaos Creek (lower)	4	Lake Haiyaha, Dream Lake, Emerald Lake Trails	0	0.9	0							•		
Chaos Creek (middle)	4	Lake Haiyaha, Dream Lake, Emerald Lake Trails	0	0.4	0								•	
Chaos Creek (upper)	4	Lake Haiyaha, Dream Lake, Emerald Lake Trails	0	1.4	0		•							
Chapin Creek	1	Chapin Creek Trail	0	3	0			•						
Chasm Lake	4	Chasm Lake Trail	19.1	0	11768		•							
Chickadee Pond	5	Bluebird Lake & Ouzel Lake Trail	0.9	0	10017		•							
Chickaree Lake	7	Onahu Creek Trail	4.5	0	9296		•							
Chipmunk Lake	2	Ypsilon Lake Trail	0.1	0	10657		•							
Chiquita Creek	2	Horseshoe Park	0	2.9	0		•							
Chiquita Lake	2	Ypsilon Lake Trail	3.7	0	11357		•							
Colorado River (8,800 ft to 9,200 ft)	8	Kawuneeche Valley	0	8.8	0			•	•					
Colorado River (above 9,200 ft)	8	La Poudre Pass Trail	0	3.5	0			•			•			

Creeks, Streams, Rivers and Lakes in RMNP

Creeks, Streams, Rivers & Lakes — Rocky Mountain National Park

Fishing Destination	Zone	Book Section	Acres	Mi	Elev (ft)	Regs	Barren	BKT	BNT	RBT	CRC	GBC	YCT	CUT
Colorado River (below Shadow Mountain Dam)	8	Outlet Trail	0	1.4	0			•	•					
Colorado River (Park Boundary to 8,800 ft)	8	Kawuneeche Valley	0	6.5	0			•	•	•				
Columbine Creek (9,000 ft to 9,200 ft)	6	Outlet Trail	0	0.7	0	6					•			
Columbine Creek (above 9,200 ft)	6	Outlet Trail	0	2.4	0	6	•							
Columbine Creek (Colorado River to 9,000 ft)	6	Outlet Trail	0	1.3	0			•						
Cony Creek (above upper Hutcheson Lake)	5	Finch Lake, Pear Lake Trail	0	0.5	0		•							
Cony Creek (Calypso Cascades to Upper Hutcheson Lake)	5	Finch Lake, Pear Lake Trail	0	3.6	0			•				•		
Cony Creek (N. St. Vrain to Calypso Cascades)	5	Wild Basin Trail	0	0.3	0			•	•					
Cony Lake	5	Finch Lake, Pear Lake Trail	16.3	0	11520		may have fish							
Copeland Lake	5	Sandbeach Lake Trail	0	0	8326					•				
Corral Creek	1	Corral Creek Trail	0	1.8	0		•							
Cow Creek (above Bridal Veil Falls)	2	Cow Creek Trail	0	2.8	0		•							
Cow Creek (below Bridal Veil Falls)	2	Cow Creek Trail	0	2.4	0			•						
Crater Gulch drainage (from Shipler Mtn)	8	La Poudre Pass Trail	0	2.1	0		•							
Crystal Lake (Big Crystal Lake)	2	Lawn Lake Trail	24.5	0	11528				•			•		
Cub Creek	3	Moraine Park	0	1.2	0			•						
Cub Lake	3	Fern Lake Trail	10	0	8646		•							
Desolation Peaks Lake	1	Mummy Pass Trail	0	0	11918		•							
Doughnut Lake	3	Gorge Lakes	7.3	0	11257		•							
Dream Lake	4	Lake Haiyaha, Dream Lake, Emerald Lake Trails	5.4	0	9916							•		

Creeks, Streams, Rivers and Lakes in RMNP

Creeks, Streams, Rivers & Lakes — Rocky Mountain National Park

Fishing Destination	Zone	Book Section	Acres	Mi	Elev (ft)	Regs	Barren	BKT	BNT	RBT	CRC	GBC	YCT	CUT
Dunraven, Lake (Lost Lake)	2	North Fork (Lost Lake) Trail	11	0	11367		•							
Dunraven, Lake (lower lake above Dunraven)	2	North Fork (Lost Lake) Trail	2.7	0	11628		•					•		
Dunraven, Lake (lower lake below Dunraven)	2	North Fork (Lost Lake) Trail	0	0	10987									
Dunraven, Lake (upper lake above Dunraven)	2	North Fork (Lost Lake) Trail	3.3	0	11548		•					•		
Dunraven, Lake (upper lake below Dunraven)	2	North Fork (Lost Lake) Trail	0	0	10997									
Eagle Lake	5	Thunder Lake Trail	11.8	0	10847		•							
Eagle Lake Drainage (above 10,600 ft)	5	Thunder Lake Trail	0	0.7	0		•							
East Inlet Creek (10,800 to Fifth Lake)	6	East Inlet Trail	0	0.1	0			•						
East Inlet Creek (9,000 ft to 10,800 ft)	6	East Inlet Trail	0	3.6	0						•			
East Inlet Creek (above Fifth Lake)	6	East Inlet Trail	0	0.5	0		•							
East Inlet Creek (Adams Falls to 9,000 ft)	6	East Inlet Trail	0	2.6	0			•						
East Inlet Creek (below Adams Falls)	6	East Inlet Trail	0	0.1	0			•	•					
Echo Creek (above 9,600 ft)	6	East Inlet Trail	0	1.7	0		•							
Echo Creek (below 9,600 ft)	6	East Inlet Trail	0	1.1	0			•						
Embryo Lake	4	n/a	0.1	0	10367		•							
Emerald Lake	4	Lake Haiyaha, Dream Lake, Emerald Lake Trails	6.3	0	10117							•		
Eureka Ditch	7	Tonahutu Creek Trail	0	0.8	0		•							
Falcon Lake	5	Thunder Lake Trail	4.5	0	11067		•							
Fall River (above 9,500 ft)	2	Horseshoe Park	0	3.6	0		•							
Fall River (below Sheep Lakes)	2	Horseshoe Park	0	2	0				•					

Creeks, Streams, Rivers and Lakes in RMNP

Creeks, Streams, Rivers & Lakes — Rocky Mountain National Park

Fishing Destination	Zone	Book Section	Acres	Mi	Elev (ft)	Regs	Barren	BKT	BNT	RBT	CRC	GBC	YCT	CUT
Fall River (Chasm Falls to 9,500 ft)	2	Horseshoe Park	0	1.2	0			•		•				•
Fall River (Fan Lake to Chasm Falls)	2	Horseshoe Park	0	2.2	0			•				•		
Fall River (Sheep Lake to Fan Lake)	2	Horseshoe Park	0	1	0			•		•		•		
Fan Lake	2	Horseshoe Park	0	0	8556			•				•		
Fay Lakes Drainage (10,200 ft to 10,800 ft)	2	Ypsilon Lake Trail	0	0.8	0			•						
Fay Lakes Drainage (above 10,800 ft)	2	Ypsilon Lake Trail	0	1.4	0		•							
Fay Lakes Drainage (below 10,200 ft)	2	Ypsilon Lake Trail	0	0.2	0						•			
Fay Lakes, Lower (aka Caddis Lake)	2	Ypsilon Lake Trail	0.7	0	10757		•							
Fay Lakes, Upper	2	Ypsilon Lake Trail	4.5	0	11029							•		
Faylene Lake	2	n/a	4.5	0	11217		•							
Fern Creek, lower	4	Fern Lake Trail	0	0.4	0		unknown							
Fern Creek, middle	4	Fern Lake Trail	0	1.4	0		•							
Fern Creek, upper	4	Fern Lake Trail	0	1.1	0									
Fern Lake	3	Fern Lake Trail	9.1	0	9547							•		
Fifth Lake	6	East Inlet Trail	7.3	0	10867						•			
Finch Lake	5	Finch Lake, Pear Lake Trail	7.3	0	9916		•							
Finch Lake Drainage	5	Finch Lake, Pear Lake Trail	0	0.1	0		•							
Fish Creek	4	Lily Lake	0	0	8933	7								
Forest Lake	3	Gorge Lakes	7.3	0	10307		may have fish					•		
Fourth Lake	6	East Inlet Trail	7.3	0	10397			•						

Creeks, Streams, Rivers and Lakes in RMNP

Creeks, Streams, Rivers & Lakes — Rocky Mountain National Park

Fishing Destination	Zone	Book Section	Acres	Mi	Elev (ft)	Regs	Barren	BKT	BNT	RBT	CRC	GBC	YCT	CUT
Fox Creek	2	North Boundary Trail	0	3.2	0		•							
Frigid Lake	5	Finch Lake, Pear Lake Trail	11.8	0	11808		•							
Frozen Lake	4	Glacier Gorge Trail	7.3	0	11568									•
Gem Lake	3	n/a	0.2	0	8836		•							
Glacier Creek (10,100 ft to 10,200 ft, halfway to Black Lake)	4	Glacier Gorge Trail	0	0.2	0			•		•				•
Glacier Creek (10,200 ft to Black Lake)	4	Glacier Gorge Trail	0	0.7	0			•						•
Glacier Creek (below Prospect Canyon)	4	Glacier Gorge Trail	0	4.6	0			•	•	•				
Glacier Creek (Black Lake to Green Lake)	4	Glacier Gorge Trail	0	1	0		•							
Glacier Creek (Glacier Falls to 10,100 ft, just above Jewel Lake)	4	Glacier Gorge Trail	0	0.7	0			•		•				•
Glacier Creek (Prospect Canyon to Glacier Falls)	4	Glacier Gorge Trail	0	1.4	0			•		•				
Glass Lake	4	Sky Pond Trail	4.5	0	10827			•				•		
Grand Ditch	8	Little Yellowstone Trail	0	14.5	0		•		•					•
Green Lake	4	Glacier Gorge Trail	3.7	0	11588		•							
Green Valley Stream	8	Kawuneeche Valley	0	2	0		•							
Grouse Creek	2	North Boundary Trail	0	1.4	0		•							
Hague Creek	1	Mummy Pass Trail	0	3.6	0		•	•						
Hallet Creek	7	North Inlet Trail	0	2.1	0			•						
Hayden Creek	3	Gorge Lakes	0	4.3	0		•							
Hayden Lake	3	Gorge Lakes	2.7	0	10607									
Haynach Lakes	7	Tonahutu Creek Trail	2.6	0	11103								•	

Creeks, Streams, Rivers and Lakes in RMNP

Creeks, Streams, Rivers & Lakes — Rocky Mountain National Park

Fishing Destination	Zone	Book Section	Acres	Mi	Elev (ft)	Regs	Barren	BKT	BNT	RBT	CRC	GBC	YCT	CUT
Haynach Lakes drainage	7	Tonahutu Creek Trail	0	1.5	0								●	
Hazeline Lake	1	Mummy Pass Trail	7.3	0	11117		●							
Hazeline Lake Drainage (unnamed stream above 10,068 ft)	1	Mummy Pass Trail	0	1.8	0		●							●
Hazeline Lake Drainage (unnamed stream below 10,068 ft)	1	Mummy Pass Trail	0	0.2	0			●						
Helene, Lake	3	Fern Lake Trail	2.7	0	10607		●							
Hiayaha, Lake	4	Lake Haiyaha, Dream Lake, Emerald Lake Trails	15.4	0	10227								●	
Hidden River	3	n/a	0	1.4	0		unknown							
Hidden Valley Creek (9,000 ft to 9,200 ft)	2	Horseshoe Park	0	1.8	0			●	●			●		
Hidden Valley Creek (above 9,200 ft)	2	Horseshoe Park	0	2.1	0		●							
Hidden Valley Creek (all lakes along Hidden Valley Creek)	3	Horseshoe Park	0	0	0			●						
Hidden Valley Creek (Fall River to 9,000 ft)	2	Horseshoe Park	0	0.7	0			●	●			●		
Hidden Valley Creek (West branch)	2	Horseshoe Park	0	0.5	0		●							
Highest Lake	3	Gorge Lakes	7.3	0	12433		unknown							
Horse Creek	5	n/a	0	1.6	0		●							
Hourglass Lake	3	Gorge Lakes	9.1	0	11207		unknown							
Hunter's Creek (Lyric Falls to Keplinger Lake)	5	Sandbeach Lake Trail	0	0.1	0	3	unknown							
Hunter's Creek (North St. Vrain Creek to Wild Basin TH)	5	Sandbeach Lake Trail	0	0.1	0	3	unknown							
Hunter's Creek (Wild Basin TH to Lyric Falls)	5	Sandbeach Lake Trail	0	0.1	0	3						●		
Husted, Lake	2	North Fork (Lost Lake) Trail	10	0	11093							●		
Hutcheson Lake, Lower	5	Finch Lake, Pear Lake Trail	4.2	0	10859							●		

Creeks, Streams, Rivers and Lakes in RMNP

Creeks, Streams, Rivers & Lakes — Rocky Mountain National Park

Fishing Destination	Zone	Book Section	Acres	Mi	Elev (ft)	Regs	Barren	BKT	BNT	RBT	CRC	GBC	YCT	CUT
Hutcheson Lake, Middle	5	Finch Lake, Pear Lake Trail	2.4	0	11067							●		
Hutcheson Lake, Upper	5	Finch Lake, Pear Lake Trail	7.3	0	11490							●		
Iceburg Lake	1	n/a	0.2	0	11998		●							
Icy Brook (above Sky Pond)	4	Sky Pond Trail	0	0.3	0		●							
Icy Brook (lower, from Glacier Creek)	4	Sky Pond Trail, Loch Vale Trail	0	0.3	0			●	●					
Icy Brook (middle to Timberline Falls, along Loch Vale Trail)	4	Loch Vale Trail	0	0.8	0							●		
Icy Brook (upper, to Sky Pond)	4	Sky Pond Trail	0	0.4	0			●				●		
Indigo Pond	5	Thunder Lake Trail	0.7	0	11167		●							
Indigo Pond Drainage	5	Thunder Lake Trail	0	0.7	0		●							
Inkwell Lake	3	Gorge Lakes	29.9	0	11508		●							
Inn Brook	4	n/a	0	2	0		●							
Irene Lake	3	Gorge Lakes	1.8	0	11848		●							
Irene, Lake	1	n/a	0.7	0	10607		●							
Isolation Lake	5	Bluebird Lake & Ouzel Lake Trail	0	0	12008	unknown								
Jewel Lake	4	Glacier Gorge Trail	4.5	0	9946					●				
Julian Lake	8	Onahu Creek Trail, Gorge Lakes	5.4	0	11107		●							
Junco Lake	5	Bluebird Lake & Ouzel Lake Trail	9.1	0	10637		●							
Junco Lake Drainage	5	Bluebird Lake & Ouzel Lake Trail	0	1.2	0		●							
Kepplinger Lake	5	Sandbeach Lake Trail	9.1	0	11694			●						
La Poudre Pass Creek (above Long Draw Reservoir)	1	Corral Creek Trail	0	1.4	0									●

Creeks, Streams, Rivers and Lakes in RMNP

Creeks, Streams, Rivers & Lakes — Rocky Mountain National Park

Fishing Destination	Zone	Book Section	Acres	Mi	Elev (ft)	Regs	Barren	BKT	BNT	RBT	CRC	GBC	YCT	CUT
La Poudre Pass Creek (below Long Draw Reservoir)	8	Little Yellowstone Trail	0	3.5	0		seasonal							
La Poudre Pass Lake	8	Little Yellowstone Trail	0	0	10180		•							
La Poudre Pass Lake (unnamed creek below)	8	Little Yellowstone Trail	0	0	0		•							
Lady Creek	8	Little Yellowstone Trail	0	0.8	0		•							
Lake of Many Winds	5	Thunder Lake Trail	0.9	0	11618		•							
Lake of Many Winds Drainage	5	Thunder Lake Trail	0	1	0		•							
Lake of the Clouds	8	Little Yellowstone Trail	11	0	11438		•							
Lark Pond	5	Bluebird Lake & Ouzel Lake Trail	4.5	0	11327		•							
Larkspur Creek	4	n/a	0	0.6	0		•							
Lawn Lake	2	Lawn Lake Trail	19.7	0	11007		•							
Lily Lake	4	Lily Lake	16.8	0	8933	7								
Lion Lake Number 1	5	Thunder Lake Trail	7.3	0	11072		•							
Lion Lake Number 2	5	Thunder Lake Trail	3.7	0	11407		•							
Lion Lakes Drainage (above Thunder Falls)	5	Thunder Lake Trail	0	1.4	0		•							
Lion Lakes Drainage (below Thunder Falls)	5	Thunder Lake Trail	0	0.7	0			•						
Little Crystal Lake	2	Lawn Lake Trail	3.7	0	11518		•					•		
Little Dutch Creek	8	La Poudre Pass Trail	0	1	0		•					•		
Little Rock Lake	3	Gorge Lakes	0.7	0	10308									
Loch, The	4	Loch Vale Trail	14.5	0	10184			•				•		
Lone Pine Lake	6	East Inlet Trail	12.8	0	9891			•						•

Creeks, Streams, Rivers and Lakes in RMNP

Creeks, Streams, Rivers & Lakes — Rocky Mountain National Park

Fishing Destination	Zone	Book Section	Acres	Mi	Elev (ft)	Regs	Barren	BKT	BNT	RBT	CRC	GBC	YCT	CUT
Lonesome Lake	3	Gorge Lakes	7.3	0	11708		•							
Long Draw Reservoir	8	Little Yellowstone Trail	0	0	10112		n/a					•		
Loomis Lake	3	Fern Lake Trail	2.7	0	10247									
Lost Brook	3	Fern Lake Trail	0	0.9	0		unknown							
Lost Creek	8	La Poudre Pass Trail	0	0.9	0		•							
Lost Lake	2	North Fork (Lost Lake) Trail	9.1	0	10747							•		
Lost Lake Drainage	2	North Fork (Lost Lake) Trail	0	2.4	0									
Louise, Lake	2	North Fork (Lost Lake) Trail	6.3	0	11040							•		
Louise, Lake Drainage	2	North Fork (Lost Lake) Trail	0	1.2	0							•		
Love Lake	3	Gorge Lakes	1.8	0	11287		•							
Lulu Creek	8	Little Yellowstone Trail	0	2.7	0		•							
Marigold Lake	3	Fern Lake Trail	0.2	0	10227		•							
Marigold Pond	3	Fern Lake Trail	0.1	0	10587		•							
Middle Dutch Creek	8	La Poudre Pass Trail	0	0.5	0		•							
Mill Creek (lower)	4	Moraine Park	0	1.5	0			•	•	•				
Mill Creek (middle)	4	Moraine Park	0	1.5	0			•						
Mill Creek (upper)	4	Moraine Park	0	2.5	0									
Mills Lake	4	Glacier Gorge Trail	15.4	0	9952		•			•				
Mirror Lake	1	Mirror Lake Trail	5.2	0	11020			•	•					
Mosquito Creek	8	Kawuneeche Valley	0	2.2	0		•							

Creeks, Streams, Rivers and Lakes in RMNP

Creeks, Streams, Rivers & Lakes — Rocky Mountain National Park

Fishing Destination	Zone	Book Section	Acres	Mi	Elev (ft)	Regs	Barren	BKT	BNT	RBT	CRC	GBC	YCT	CUT
Mummy Pass Creek, lower	1	Mummy Pass Trail	0	1.2	0			•						
Mummy Pass Creek, upper	1	Mummy Pass Trail	0	0.8	0									
Murphy Lake	7	Tonahutu Creek Trail	7.3	0	11227		•							
Murphy Lake drainage	7	Tonahutu Creek Trail	0	0	0		•							
Nanita, Lake	7	Lake Nanita Trail	33.6	0	10797						•			
Nanita, Lake drainage (10,780 ft to Lake Nanita)	7	Lake Nanita Trail	0	0.1	0	4					•			
Nanita, Lake drainage (above Lake Nanita)	7	Lake Nanita Trail	0	0.4	0		•							
Nanita, Lake drainage (below 10,780 ft)	7	Lake Nanita Trail	0	0.7	0		unknown							
Nokoni, Lake	7	Lake Nanita Trail	24.6	0	10787		•							
Nokoni, Lake drainage	7	Lake Nanita Trail	0	0.9	0		•							
North Fork of the Big Thompson River (above 11,050 ft)	2	North Fork (Lost Lake) Trail	0	2.1	0		•							
North Fork of the Big Thompson River (below Lost Falls)	2	North Fork (Lost Lake) Trail	0	3	0							•		
North Fork of the Big Thompson River (Lost Falls to 11,050 ft)	2	North Fork (Lost Lake) Trail	0	2.9	0							•		
North Inlet Creek (9,485 ft to 9,925 ft) (Lake Nanita Trail to CD Trail)	7	North Inlet Trail	0	2.3	0						•			
North Inlet Creek (9,925 ft to Lake Powell) (CD Trail to Lake Powell)	7	North Inlet Trail	0	1.7	0		•							
North Inlet Creek (below Cascade Falls) (Summerland Park area)	7	North Inlet Trail	0	2.5	0			•	•					
North Inlet Creek (Cascade Falls to falls at 9,485 ft) (Cascade Falls to Lake Nanita Trail)	7	North Inlet Trail	0	4	0			•			•			
North Saint Vrain Creek (below Copeland Falls)	5	Wild Basin Trail	0	1.5	0			•	•					•
North Saint Vrain Creek (Copeland Falls to Falcon Lake)	5	Wild Basin Trail, Thunder Lake Trail	0	5.6	0			•	•					•
Nymph Lake	4	Lake Haiyaha, Dream Lake, Emerald Lake Trails	0.9	0	9706		•							

Creeks, Streams, Rivers and Lakes in RMNP

Creeks, Streams, Rivers & Lakes — Rocky Mountain National Park

Fishing Destination	Zone	Book Section	Acres	Mi	Elev (ft)	Regs	Barren	BKT	BNT	RBT	CRC	GBC	YCT	CUT
Odessa Lake	3	Fern Lake Trail	11	0	10023							•		
Onahu Creek (10,500 ft to 10,800 ft)	8	Onahu Creek Trail	0	0.7	0						•			
Onahu Creek (10,800 ft to Julian Lake)	8	Onahu Creek Trail	0	0.4	0						•			
Onahu Creek (9,000 ft to 10,500 ft)	8	Onahu Creek Trail	0	3.2	0			•						
Onahu Creek (Colorado River to 9,000 ft)	7	Kawuneeche Valley	0	2.6	0			•	•					
Onahu Creek, fork #4 through Long Meadows	7	Onahu Creek Trail	0	1.4	0		unknown							
Opposition Creek	8	Kawuneeche Valley	0	2.2	0		•							
Ouzel Creek (above 10,600 ft)	5	Bluebird Lake & Ouzel Lake Trail	0	0.7	0		•							
Ouzel Creek (North St Vrain to Ouzel Falls)	5	Wild Basin Trail	0	0.3	0			•	•					
Ouzel Creek (Ouzel Falls to Ouzel Lake)	5	Bluebird Lake & Ouzel Lake Trail	0	0.7	0			•						
Ouzel Creek (Ouzel Lake to 10,600 ft)	5	Bluebird Lake & Ouzel Lake Trail	0	0.6	0							•		
Ouzel Lake	5	Bluebird Lake & Ouzel Lake Trail	6.3	0	10107			•				•		
Pale Creek	6	Outlet Trail	0	0	0		unknown							
Paradise Creek (9,500 ft to Boundary Lake)	6	East Inlet Trail	0	5	0						•	•		
Paradise Creek (East Inlet to 9,500 ft)	6	East Inlet Trail	0	0.5	0			•						
Paradise Creek, all 4 unnamed lakes off fork #4	6	East Inlet Trail	0	0	11001		•							
Paradise Creek, lake between forks #4 and #5	6	East Inlet Trail	0	0	0									
Peacock Pool	4	Chasm Lake Trail	4.5	0	11309			•			•			
Pear Creek	5	Finch Lake, Pear Lake Trail	0	0.7	0									
Pear Lake (Reservoir)	5	Finch Lake, Pear Lake Trail	16.3	0	10587							•		

Creeks, Streams, Rivers and Lakes in RMNP

Creeks, Streams, Rivers & Lakes — Rocky Mountain National Park

Fishing Destination	Zone	Book Section	Acres	Mi	Elev (ft)	Regs	Barren	BKT	BNT	RBT	CRC	GBC	YCT	CUT
Pettingell Lake	7	North Inlet Trail	10	0	10517						•			
Pettingell Lake drainage	7	North Inlet Trail	0	1.4	0		•							
Phantom Creek	8	Timber Lake Trail, Kawuneeche Valley	0	2	0		•							
Pinnacle Pool	8	n/a	3.6	0	11307		•							
Pipit Lake	5	Bluebird Lake & Ouzel Lake Trail	12.8	0	11407		•							
Pole Creek	6	n/a	0	1.5	0		•							
Potts Puddle	2	n/a	3.7	0	10907		•							
Poudre Lake	1	Cache La Poudre River Trail	3.2	0	11047		•							
Powell, Lake	7	North Inlet Trail	12.8	0	11558		•							
Primrose Pond	3	Fern Lake Trail	0.9	0	10137		•							
Ptarmigan Creek (above 10,400 ft)	7	North Inlet Trail	0	1	0		•							
Ptarmigan Creek (Fork #4 above 10,400 ft)	7	North Inlet Trail	0	0.6	0		•							
Ptarmigan Creek (Fork #4 below 10,400 ft)	7	North Inlet Trail	0	1	0									
Ptarmigan Creek (North Inlet to War Dance Falls)	7	North Inlet Trail	0	0.4	0									
Ptarmigan Creek (War Dance Falls to 10,400 ft)	7	North Inlet Trail	0	1.2	0	2								
Ptarmigan Lake	7	North Inlet Trail	20.9	0	11467		•							
Rainbow Lake	3	Gorge Lakes	12.8	0	11748		•							
Ranger Creek	6	n/a	0	1.6	0		•							
Red Gulch (above 9,100 ft)	8	Kawuneeche Valley	0	2	0	unknown								
Red Gulch (below 9,100 ft)	8	Kawuneeche Valley	0	0.2	0			•						

Creeks, Streams, Rivers and Lakes in RMNP

Creeks, Streams, Rivers & Lakes — Rocky Mountain National Park

Fishing Destination	Zone	Book Section	Acres	Mi	Elev (ft)	Regs	Barren	BKT	BNT	RBT	CRC	GBC	YCT	CUT
Roaring Fork (above Peacock Pool)	4	Chasm Lake Trail	0	0.5	0		•							
Roaring Fork (below Peacock Pool)	4	Chasm Lake Trail	0	4.7	0			•						
Roaring River (above 9,200 ft)	2	Lawn Lake Trail	0	3.6	0							•		
Roaring River (below Horseshoe Falls)	2	Lawn Lake Trail	0	0.3	0			•	•	•		•		
Roaring River (Horseshoe Falls to 9,200 ft)	2	Lawn Lake Trail	0	1.3	0							•		
Rock Cut Lake	3	Gorge Lakes	5.4	0	10307									•
Round Pond	3	Fern Lake Trail	0.2	0	10347		•							
Rowe Glacier Lake	2	n/a	7.3	0	13109		•							
Sandbeach Creek (10,300 ft to Sandbeach Lake)	5	Sandbeach Lake Trail	0	0.1	0							•		
Sandbeach Creek (8,725 ft to 9,000 ft)	5	Sandbeach Lake Trail	0	0.4	0							•		
Sandbeach Creek (9,000 ft to 10,300 ft)	5	Sandbeach Lake Trail	0	1.6	0							•		
Sandbeach Creek (North St. Vrain to 8,725 ft)	5	Sandbeach Lake Trail, Wild Basin Trail	0	0.2	0							•		
Sandbeach Lake	5	Sandbeach Lake Trail	16.3	0	10307							•		
Sawmill Creek	8	Little Yellowstone Trail	0	3.3	0		•							
Sheep Lakes (both)	2	Horseshoe Park	0	0	8519		•							
Shelf Creek	4	n/a	0	1.3	0		•							
Shelf Lake	4	n/a	3.6	0	11227		•							
Sky Pond	4	Sky Pond Trail	11	0	10887			•						
Snow Drift Lake	7	North Inlet Trail	9.1	0	11167		•							
Snow Drift Lake drainage, above 10,400 ft	7	North Inlet Trail	0	0.5	0		•							

Creeks, Streams, Rivers and Lakes in RMNP

Creeks, Streams, Rivers & Lakes — Rocky Mountain National Park

Fishing Destination	Zone	Book Section	Acres	Mi	Elev (ft)	Regs	Barren	BKT	BNT	RBT	CRC	GBC	YCT	CUT
Snow Drift Lake drainage, below 10,400 ft	7	North Inlet Trail	0	0.1	0									
Snowbank Lake	5	Thunder Lake Trail	7.3	0	11529		•				•			
Solitude, Lake	7	Lake Nanita Trail	7.3	0	9726						•			
Specimen Creek	8	Little Yellowstone Trail	0	2.1	0		•							
Spectacle Lakes (lower)	2	Ypsilon Lake Trail	7.3	0	11357		•							
Spectacle Lakes (upper)	2	Ypsilon Lake Trail	11	0	11407		•							
Spectacle Lakes Drainage	2	Ypsilon Lake Trail	0	0.3	0		•							
Spirit Lake	6	East Inlet Trail	18.2	0	10297			•			•			
Sprague Lake	4	Sprague Lake Nature Trail	5.4	0	8688			•	•	•				
Spruce Creek (lower)	3	Fern Lake Trail	0	0.8	0		•							
Spruce Creek (middle)	3	Fern Lake Trail	0	0.1	0			•						
Spruce Creek (upper)	3	Fern Lake Trail	0	2.7	0		•							
Spruce Lake	3	Fern Lake Trail	3.7	0	9646							•		
Squeak Creek	8	Timber Lake Trail	0	2.6	0		•							
Sundance Creek (above Thousand Falls)	2	Horseshoe Park	0	2.2	0		•							
Sundance Creek (below Thousand Falls)	3	Horseshoe Park	0	0.2	0			•						
Ten Lake Park Lake	6	East Inlet Trail	12	0	11076						•			
Thunder Lake	5	Thunder Lake Trail	16.5	0	10574			•				•		•
Timber Creek (lower)	8	Timber Lake Trail	0	2.6	0									•

Creeks, Streams, Rivers and Lakes in RMNP

Creeks, Streams, Rivers & Lakes — Rocky Mountain National Park

Fishing Destination	Zone	Book Section	Acres	Mi	Elev (ft)	Regs	Barren	BKT	BNT	RBT	CRC	GBC	YCT	CUT
Timber Creek (upper)	8	Timber Lake Trail	0	0.6	0			•						
Timber Lake	8	Timber Lake Trail	10	0	11083									•
Tonahutu Creek (above 10,167 ft)	7	Tonahutu Creek Trail	0	1.2	0		•							
Tonahutu Creek (Granite Falls to 10,167 ft)	7	Tonahutu Creek Trail	0	1.4	0									•
Tonahutu Creek (trailhead to Granite Falls)	7	Tonahutu Creek Trail	0	3.9	0			•	•		•			
Tonahutu Creek, Fork #8	7	Tonahutu Creek Trail	0	1.3	0		•							
Tonahutu Creek, Fork #9	7	Tonahutu Creek Trail	0	0.8	0		•							
Tonahutu Creek, Fork of Fork #6	7	Tonahutu Creek Trail	0	0.7	0		•							
Tourmaline Lake	4	n/a	1.8	0	0		•							
Twin Lakes (East)	5	Thunder Lake Trail	1.8	0	9876		•							
Twin Lakes (West)	5	Thunder Lake Trail	4.5	0	9776		•							
Two Rivers Lake	3	Fern Lake Trail	4.5	0	10607		•							
Tyndall Creek (above Dream Lake)	4	Lake Haiyaha, Dream Lake, Emerald Lake Trails	0	1.4	0		•							
Tyndall Creek (below Dream Lake)	4	Lake Haiyaha, Dream Lake, Emerald Lake Trails	0	0.2	0							•		
Unnamed lake below Lake of the Clouds	8	n/a	0	0	10707		•	•						
Unnamed lake near headwaters of Tonahutu Creek	7	n/a	0	0	10707		•	•						
Verna, Lake	6	East Inlet Trail	32.7	0	10187		•							
West Creek (above 8,925 ft)	2	North Boundary Trail	0	3.9	0									
West Creek (below West Creek Falls)	2	North Boundary Trail	0	0.3	0							•		
West Creek (West Creek Falls to 8,925 ft)	2	North Boundary Trail	0	1.9	0							•		

Creeks, Streams, Rivers and Lakes in RMNP

Creeks, Streams, Rivers & Lakes — Rocky Mountain National Park

Fishing Destination	Zone	Book Section	Acres	Mi	Elev (ft)	Regs	Barren	BKT	BNT	RBT	CRC	GBC	YCT	CUT
Willow Creek (above 10,500 ft)	1	Corral Creek Trail	0	2	0			•						•
Willow Creek (below 10,500 ft)	1	Corral Creek Trail	0	3.1	0			•						
Wind River (lower)	4	Wind River Trail	0	1.2	0			•						
Wind River (upper)	4	Wind River Trail	0	0.8	0		•							
Ypsilon Creek (10,400 ft to Ypsilon Lake)	2	Ypsilon Lake Trail	0	1.7	0						•			
Ypsilon Creek (above Ypsilon Lake)	2	Ypsilon Lake Trail	0	1.5	0		•							
Ypsilon Lake	2	Ypsilon Lake Trail	7.3	0	10547						•			

Key to Fish Species

BKT = Brook trout
BNT = Brown trout
RBT = Rainbow trout
CRC = Colorado River Cutthroat
GBC = Greenback Cutthroat
YCT = Yellowstone River Cutthroat
CUT = Cutthroat of general origin, unspecified

Key to Fishing Regulations, column 'Regs' in tables

1. No fishing in Bear Lake; inlet streams and 200 yards downstream
2. No fishing in Bench Lake and Ptarmigan Creek above War Dance Falls
3. No fishing above Wild Basin Ranger Station, as posted
4. No fishing in outlet stream or 100 yards downstream
5. No fishing above Pingree Park
6. No fishing above 9,000 feet
7. No fishing on the East shore, May-June annually

Twenty-Year Snow-Free Date Averages by Back Country Campsite

Predicting Snow-Free Dates by Elevation

Twenty year averages for snow free dates are provided on the following pages, sorted by back country campsite (source: The National Park Service - Rocky Mountain National Park Back Country Office). This data is valuable for predicting average snow-free dates by elevation.

Figure 6 plots the relationship of elevation (x-axis) and 20-year average snow-free date (y-axis) via a scatter diagram. Using regression analysis, we can reasonably predict the average snow-free date by elevation For math buffs, the R^2 value of the regression line tells us that if we know one variable, say date, we can predict the other variable (elevation) with 85% accuracy, according to this data set.

Table 6 below uses some fancy math (polynomial regression, removing outliers) to predict snow-free dates at 500 foot elevation intervals. This can be important to the fly fisher in order to plan fishing and seasonable camping at higher altitudes. Please note this data doesn't predict lake *ice-out dates*, which happens many weeks before snow-free dates.

Figure 6. - 20 Year Average Snow Melt Dates by Elevation

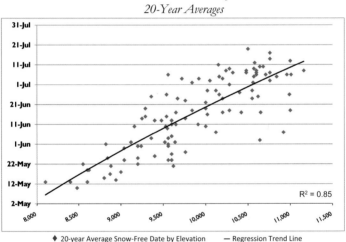

Table 6. - Predicted Snow-Free Date by Elevation

Predicted Snow-Free Date by Elevation	
Elevation (ft)	**Snow Melt Date**
8000	5/12
8500	5/21
9000	5/31
9500	6/9
10000	6/19
10500	6/28
11000	7/7
11500	7/17
12000	7/26

Twenty-Year Average Snow-Free Dates by Back Country Campsite

Campsite	Site #	# of Pads	Current Status	Privy	Food Storage Box	Group Site	Wood Fire Ring	Llama Site	Stock Site	EIDCZ	20 Year Avg Snow-Free	Distance from TH	Elev Gain	Site Elev
Andrews Creek	40	1		•							2-Jul	3.6	1320	10560
Arch Rock	26	1	Closed											
Aspen Knoll	52	1						•			26-May	2.3	900	9400
Aspen Meadow	5	1		•		•	•				31-May	5.9	1600	9560
Battle Mountain	43	1				•					18-Jun	2.8	1600	11000
Beaver Mill	47	1									2-Jun	3	1330	9640
Big Meadows	85	1		•		•					13-Jun	1.9	600	9400
Big Pool	72	2									10-Jun	5	620	9160
Bighorn Mountain	16	1		•		•	•		•		25-Jun	6.5	2700	10620
Boulder Brook	38	1		•							17-Jun	3.9	960	10200
Boulder Brook	38	2		•							17-Jun	3.9	960	10200
Boulderfield	44	9		•	•		•				19-Jun	6	3360	12760
Boundary Creek	1	2									2-Jun	4.6	1160	9120
Box Canyon	111	2									8-Jul	5.5	1470	10480
Cache	113	2									11-Jul	5.6	(600)	10150
Camper's Creek	46	1									5-Jun	2.3	1290	9600
Cascade Falls	71	1		•							25-May	3.5	300	8840
Cat's Lair	63	3				•				•	31-May	4	810	9200
Chapin Creek	114	1		•							8-Jul	6.1	(510)	10240
Cub Creek	32	2		•							13-May	2.2	520	8600
Cutbank	21	1		•							21-May	2.3	1080	9620

Rocky Mountain National Park

Twenty-Year Average Snow-Free Date by Back Country Campsite

Rocky Mountain National Park

Campsite	Site #	# of Pads	Current Status	Privy	Food Storage Box	Group Site	Wood Fire Ring	Llama Site	Stock Site	EIDCZ	20 Year Avg Snow-Free	Distance from TH	Elev Gain	Site Elev
Desolation	116	1									2-Jul	2.3	(160)	9840
Ditch Camp	109	1				•			•		26-Jun	4.6	1130	10160
Ditch Camp	109	2		•							26-Jun	4.6	1130	10160
Dutch Town	107	1									17-Jul	6	1750	10760
East Meadow	61	2		•		•				•	22-May	1.5	160	8550
Fern Lake	28	1		•							10-Jun	3.8	1380	9530
Fern Lake	28	4		•		•					10-Jun	3.8	1380	9530
Finch Lake	58	1		•		•			•		11-Jun	4.6	1440	9910
Finch Lake	58	2		•							11-Jun	4.6	1440	9910
Flatiron	117	1					•				4-Jul	2.8	(80)	9920
Footbridge	75	1		•			•				15-Jun	6.5	750	9290
Glacier Gorge	39	1		•							19-Jun	3.8	760	10000
Goblin's Forest	42	6		•							7-Jun	1.2	720	10120
Golden Banner	22	1		•							24-May	2.6	1060	9600
Granite Falls	89	2									18-Jun	5.4	1040	9840
Gray Jay	64	1		•		•					11-Jun	4.9	1260	9650
Grouseberry	73	2							•		14-Jun	6.2	710	9250
Hague Creek	115	1		•		•					4-Jul	1.6	(280)	9720
Hague Creek	115	2		•							4-Jul	1.6	(280)	9720
Halfway	4	2		•			•				2-Jun	5.6	1560	9520
Happily Lost	6	1		•			•				4-Jun	6.2	1600	9560

Twenty-Year Average Snow-Free Dates by Back Country Campsite

Rocky Mountain National Park

Campsite	Site #	# of Pads	Current Status	Privy	Food Storage Box	Group Site	Wood Fire Ring	Llama Site	Stock Site	EIDCZ	20 Year Avg Snow-Free	Distance from TH	Elev Gain	Site Elev
Haynach	93	2						1L			7-Jul	7.2	1960	10760
Hitchins Gulch	106	2									7-Jul	5.8	1470	10480
Hole in the Wall	45	1									31-May	1.9	930	9240
Hunter's Creek	48	1									14-Jun	3.3	1450	9760
Jackstraw	99	2		•		•					3-Jul	4	1760	10760
July	81	1		•							14-Jul	9.7	2220	10760
July	81	3		•							14-Jul	9.7	2220	10760
Kettle Tarn	2	2		•							25-May	4.9	1240	9200
Koenig	119	1							•		10-Jul	5.2	1040	10680
La Poudre Pass	112	3		•							24-Jun	6.7	750	10200
Lake Verna	68	1									9-Jul	6.9	1890	10280
Lawn Lake	23	5		•					1S		26-Jun	6.2	2450	10990
Little Rock Lake	24	1									1-Jul	6	(470)	10280
Lodgepole	82		Closed											
Lost Falls	7	2		•							11-Jun	6.7	1640	9600
Lost Lake	12	4		•							6-Jul	9.7	2750	10710
Lost Meadow	11	1		•		•	•		•		17-Jun	8.4	2460	10420
Lost Meadow	11	1		•							17-Jun	8.4	2460	10420
Lower Granite Falls	88	2									23-Jun	5.1	960	9760
Lower Tileston	17	1		•							17-Jun	6.3	2090	10650
McGregor Mountain	15	2		•			•				30-May	4.1	1190	9040

Twenty-Year Average Snow-Free Date by Back Country Campsite

Campsite	Site #	# of Pads	Current Status	Privy	Food Storage Box	Group Site	Wood Fire Ring	Llama Site	Stock Site	EIDCZ	20 Year Avg Snow-Free	Distance from TH	Elev Gain	Site Elev
Mill Creek Basin	33	2		•							18-May	1.8	600	9000
Mirror Lake	120	3									13-Jul	6	1020	11000
Moore Park	41	2		•							28-May	1.7	360	9760
Mummy Pass	118	2					•		•		10-Jul	4.6	1000	10640
North Inlet	74	1		•		•					19-Jun	6.5	750	9290
North Inlet Falls	79	1									26-Jun	7.6	1000	9540
North Inlet Junction	78	3		•							11-Jun	7.5	1060	9600
North St. Vrain	54	2		•							1-Jun	3.5	1060	9560
Odessa Lake	30	2		•							28-Jun	4.1	550	10020
Old Forest Inn	27	2		•							13-May	1.7	250	8400
Onahu Bridge	97	1									17-Jun	2.9	890	9650
Onahu Creek	95	1									13-Jun	2.4	720	9480
Opposition Creek	104		Closed											
Ouzel Lake	56	1		•							16-Jun	4.9	1520	10020
Over the Hill	36	1		•							17-May	1.3	550	8870
Paint Brush	83	1									9-Jun	1.8	750	9550
Pear Creek	59	3									28-Jun	6.4	2080	10550
Pear Lake	60	1									12-Jul	6.6	2110	10580
Peregrine	14	1		•							10-May	2	640	8480
Pine Marten	80	2									6-Jul	7.8	1020	9560
Pine Ridge	50	2		•							21-May	1.4	380	8880

Twenty-Year Average Snow-Free Dates by Back Country Campsite

Rocky Mountain National Park

Campsite	Site #	# of Pads	Current Status	Privy	Food Storage Box	Group Site	Wood Fire Ring	Llama Site	Stock Site	EIDCZ	20 Year Avg Snow-Free	Distance from TH	Elev Gain	Site Elev
Porcupine	77	2					•				25-Jun	6.8	820	9360
Ptarmigan	76		Temporarily closed due to Pine Beetle kill											
Rabbit Ears	13	1		•							13-May	1.4	260	8100
Red Gulch	105	1		•		•					7-Jul	5.8	1310	10320
Renegade	92	1									19-Jul	7.3	1700	10500
Rockslide	100	1									6-Jul	4.5	1960	10960
Sandbeach Lake	49	1		•		•					18-Jun	4.2	1970	10280
Sandbeach Lake	49	4		•							18-Jun	4.2	1970	10280
Silvanmere	3	2					•				4-Jun	5.6	1400	9360
Siskin	53	1									27-May	3.7	1100	9600
Skeleton Gulch	110	1									8-Jul	6.7	1590	10600
Slickrock	65	1									22-Jun	6	1610	10000
Snowbird	101	2									6-Jul	4.6	2010	11010
Solitaire	66	1									28-Jun	6.2	1730	10120
Sourdough	31	1		•							7-Jul	2.5	1130	10600
South Meadows	84	1									15-Jun	2	650	9540
Sprague Lake	A1	1		•	•	•	•				1-Jun	5	20	8820
Spruce Lake	29	2		•							24-Jun	4.6	1520	9670
Stage Road	108		Temporarily closed due to Pine Beetle kill											
Stormy Peaks	10	1		•		•					8-Jul	11	2800	11160
Stormy Peaks	10	2		•							8-Jul	11	2800	11160

Twenty-Year Average Snow-Free Date by Back Country Campsite

Rocky Mountain National Park

Campsite	Site #	# of Pads	Current Status	Privy	Food Storage Box	Group Site	Wood Fire Ring	Llama Site	Stock Site	EIDCZ	20 Year Avg Snow-Free	Distance from TH	Elev Gain	Site Elev
Stormy Peaks South	9	1		•							5-Jul	8.6	2880	10840
Sugarloaf	8	1		•							7-Jun	8.2	2330	10920
Summerland Park	69	1		•		•					19-May	1.5	60	8600
Summerland Park	69	1		•							19-May	1.7	80	8620
Sunrise	87	1									11-Jun	3.5	800	9600
Sunset	86		Temporarily closed due to Pine Beetle kill											
Tahosa	51	1		•							24-May	1.7	540	9040
Thunder Lake	55	2		•					1		5-Jul	6.8	2070	10570
Thunder Lake	55	3		•		1					5-Jul	6.8	2070	10570
Tileston Meadow	18	2		•							24-Jun	6	2260	10550
Timber Creek	98	2									27-Jun	3	1400	10400
Timberline	94	1		•		•					9-Jul	7.4	1780	10570
Tonahutu	91	1		•		•	•		•		5-Jul	6.6	1360	10160
Tonahutu Meadow	90	2									3-Jul	6.2	1260	10050
Twinberry	70		Temporarily closed due to Pine Beetle kill	•										
Upper Chipmunk	19	2									3-Jun	4.2	2100	10640
Upper East Inlet	67	1									4-Jul	6.6	1810	10200
Upper Mill Creek	34	2		•							22-May	1.7	800	9200
Upper Onahu	96	1									13-Jun	2.8	840	9600
Upper Ouzel Creek	57	1									6-Jul	5.6	2100	10600
Upper Wind River	37	2		•							14-May	1.6	620	8940

Twenty-Year Average Snow-Free Dates by Back Country Campsite

Rocky Mountain National Park

Campsite	Site #	# of Pads	Current Status	Privy	Food Storage Box	Group Site	Wood Fire Ring	Llama Site	Stock Site	EIDCZ	20 Year Avg Snow-Free	Distance from TH	Elev Gain	Site Elev
Ute Meadow	25	1						●			10-Jun	2.7	1320	10000
Valley View	102	1	Temporarily closed due to Pine Beetle kill											
Wind River Bluff	35	1		●								15-May	1	480	8800
Ypsilon Creek	20	1		●								24-May	2.6	1020	9560

Lakes Over 10,000 Feet Which Contain Fish

The Park contains approximately 139 lakes (not counting seasonal water). There are currently 54 lakes in the Park which have known populations of fish. Of the 54 lakes, 42 are above 10,000 feet in altitude. Sorting the lakes by altitude reveals two interesting characteristics. First, if you intend on fishing a high mountain lake for rainbows or browns, you'll find none. Lakes over 10,000 feet in altitude predominantly hold cutthroat, primarily greenback cutthroat trout. Secondly, all but four contain only one species of fish. Glass Lake (BKT, GBT), Spirit Lake (BKT, CRC), The Loch (BKT, GBT) and Ouzel Lake (BKT, GBT) are the exceptions.

Rocky Mountain National Park
Lakes over 10,000 Which Feet Contain Fish   (n=42)

Fishing Destination	Acres	Elev (ft)	BKT	BNT	RBT	CRC	GBC	YCT	CUT
Crystal Lake (Big Crystal Lake)	24.5	11528					•		
Hutcheson Lake, Upper	7.3	11490					•		
Solitude Lake	7.3	11427				•			
Peacock Pool	4.5	11309	•						
Adams Lake	4.5	11217				•			
Arrowhead Lake	34.5	11158					•		
Haynach Lakes	2.6	11103						•	
Husted, Lake	10	11093					•		
Timber Lake	10	11083							•
Ten Lake Park Lake	12	11076				•			
Hutcheson Lake, Middle	2.4	11067					•		
Louise, Lake	6.3	11040					•		
Mirror Lake	5.2	11020	•	•					
Lawn Lake	19.7	11007					•		
Dunraven, Lake (upper)		10997					•		
Dunraven, Lake (lower)		10987					•		
Sky Pond	11	10887	•						
Fifth Lake	7.3	10867				•			
Hutcheson Lake, Lower	4.2	10859					•		
Glass Lake	4.5	10827	•				•		
Nanita, Lake	33.6	10797				•			
Box Lake	6.3	10767	•						
Fay Lakes, Lower (aka Caddis Lake)	0.7	10757					•		
Lost Lake	9.1	10747					•		
Black Lake	9.1	10634	•						
Pear Lake (Reservoir)	16.3	10587					•		
Thunder Lake	16.5	10574	•						•
Ypsilon Lake	7.3	10547				•			
Pettingell Lake	10	10517				•			
Fourth Lake	7.3	10397	•						
Little Rock Lake	0.7	10308							•
Rock Cut Lake	5.4	10307							•
Sandbeach Lake	16.3	10307					•		
Spirit Lake	18.2	10297	•			•			
Loomis Lake	2.7	10247					•		
Hiayaha, Lake	15.4	10227						•	
Verna, Lake	32.7	10187	•						
Loch, The	14.5	10184	•				•		
Bench Lake	6.3	10157				•			
Emerald Lake	6.3	10117					•		
Ouzel Lake	6.3	10107	•				•		
Odessa Lake	11	10023					•		
Average/Count	**10.2**	**10,734**	**12**	**1**	**0**	**9**	**20**	**2**	**4**

Trails Ranked by Difficulty

Rocky Mountain National Park
Trails Ranked by Difficulty

Trail	Side	USGS Quad(s)	Difficulty	Approx Trail Len (mi)	Notes	Zone	Page
Cow Creek Trail	E	Estes Park, Glen Haven	🚶	1.2		2	84
Horseshoe Park (Fall River)	E	Estes Park, Trail Ridge	🚶	3.2		2	88
Horseshoe Park (Hidden Valley Creek)	E	Estes Park, Trail Ridge	🚶	2.4	♿ (in sections)	2	90
Kawuneeche Valley	W	Grand Lake, Fall River Pass	🚶	13.5		8	178
Lily Lake	E	Longs Peak	🚶	0.75	♿	4	114
Moraine Park	E	Longs Peak, McHenry's Peak	🚶	3.5	♿ (in sections)	3	100
Outlet Trail	W	Shadow Mountain	🚶	1.9		6	158
Sprague Lake	E	Longs Peak	🚶		♿	4	116
Wind River	E	Longs Peak	🚶	1.8		4	118
Black Canyon - MacGregor Falls Trail	E	Estes Park	🚶 - 🚶🚶	3		2	86
Cache La Poudre River Trail	E	Comanche Peak, Trail Ridge, Fall River Pass	🚶 - 🚶🚶	4		1	66
Colorado River Trail	W	Fall River Pass	🚶 - 🚶🚶	3.7		8	182
Corral Creek Trail	E	Chambers Lake, Comanche Peak	🚶 - 🚶🚶	1		1	64
La Poudre Pass Trail	E	Fall River Pass	🚶 - 🚶🚶	4.5		8	182
Glacier Gorge Trail	E	McHenry's Peak	🚶 - 🚶🚶🚶	3		4	120
Glacier Creek Trail	E	McHenry's Peak	🚶 - 🚶🚶🚶	2		4	120
Little Yellowstone Trail	E	Fall River Pass	🚶 - 🚶🚶🚶	3.1		8	184
Wild Basin Trail	E	Allenspark	🚶 - 🚶🚶🚶	1.9		5	138
Bluebird, Ouzel Lake Trails	E	Allenspark, Isolation Peak	🚶🚶 - 🚶🚶🚶	4.3		5	148
Chapin Creek Trail	E	Trail Ridge	🚶🚶 - 🚶🚶🚶	0.85		1	68
Finch Lake, Pear Lake Trail	E	Allenspark, Isolation Peak	🚶🚶 - 🚶🚶🚶	6.2		5	144
Loch Vale Trail	E	McHenry's Peak	🚶🚶 - 🚶🚶🚶	1.3		4	124
Mirror Lake Trail	E	Comanche Peak	🚶🚶 - 🚶🚶🚶	0.8		1	72
North Inlet Trail	W	Grand Lake, McHenry's Peak	🚶🚶 - 🚶🚶🚶	5.5		7	164
Onahu Creek Trail	W	Grand Lake	🚶🚶 - 🚶🚶🚶	2.8		8	192
Fern Lake Trail	E	McHenry's Peak	🚶🚶 - 🚶🚶🚶🚶	7.2		3	102
Timber Lake Trail	W	Fall River Pass, Grand Lake	🚶🚶 - 🚶🚶🚶🚶	4.4		8	188
Haynach Lakes Trail	W	Grand Lake, McHenry's Peak	🚶🚶 - 🚶🚶🚶🚶	1.2		7	170
Tonahutu Creek Trail	W	Grand Lake, McHenry's Peak	🚶🚶 - 🚶🚶🚶🚶	6.7		7	170
North Fork (Lost Lake Trail)	E	Glen Haven, Estes Park, Pingree Park	🚶🚶🚶	10.1		2	78
Chasm Lake Trail (Peacock Pool)	E	Longs Peak	🚶🚶🚶 - 🚶🚶🚶🚶	4		4	130
East Inlet Trail	W	Shadow Mountain, Isolation Peak	🚶🚶🚶 - 🚶🚶🚶🚶	8.3		6	154
Lake Nanita Trail	W	McHenry's Peak	🚶🚶🚶 - 🚶🚶🚶🚶	3.2		7	168
Lawn Lake Trail	E	Estes Park, Trail Ridge	🚶🚶🚶 - 🚶🚶🚶🚶	7.4		2	92
Mummy Pass Trail	E	Pingree Park, Comanche Peak	🚶🚶🚶 - 🚶🚶🚶🚶	3.1		1	70
Sandbeach Lake Trail	E	Allenspark	🚶🚶🚶 - 🚶🚶🚶🚶	4		5	136
Sky Pond Trail	E	McHenry's Peak	🚶🚶🚶 - 🚶🚶🚶🚶	0.6		4	126
Thunder Lake Trail	E	Allenspark, Isolation Peak	🚶🚶🚶 - 🚶🚶🚶🚶	3.2		5	140
Ypsilon Lake Trail	E	Trail Ridge	🚶🚶🚶 - 🚶🚶🚶🚶	2.8		2	94
Lake Haiyaha, Dream Lake, Emerald Lake Trails	E	McHenry's Peak	🚶🚶🚶 - 🚶🚶🚶🚶	2.5		4	128
Gorge Lakes	E/W	Fall River Pass, Grand Lake	🚶🚶🚶🚶	6		3	106
North Boundary Trail	E	Estes Park	🚶🚶🚶🚶	2		2	82

Index

Index

Index

Index

Index

H

I

J

K

L

Index

Index

Index

Index

References

Below is a selected list of published electronic and printed resources consulted when writing this book.

- Bergman, Ray. *Trout.* New York, NY. Alfred A. Knopf, Inc., 1988

- Buchholtz, C.W. *Rocky Mountain National Park - A History.* Boulder, Colorado. Colorado Associated University Press, 1983.

- Burns, Ken. *"The National Parks: America's Best Idea",* a PBS documentary video series, 2009.

- Carey, Kip. *Official Colorado Fishing Guide.* Littleton, CO. Kip Carey Publications, 2001, 2003.

- Cordes, Ron and Kaufmann, Randall. *Lake Fishing With A Fly.* Portland, OR. Frank Amato Publications, 1984.

- Dannen, Kent and Donna. *Hiking Rocky Mountain National Park.* Guilford, CT. The Globe Pequot Press, 1978 - 2002.

- Engle, Ed. *Fishing Small Flies.* Mechanicsburg, PA. Stackpole Books, 2005.

- Foster, Lisa. *Rocky Mountain National Park - The Complete Hiking Guide.* Englewood, CO. Westcliffe Publishers, 2005.

- Gierach, John. *Fly Fishing the High Country.* Boulder, CO. Pruett Publishing Co., 1984.

- Hughes, Dave. *Handbook of Hatches.* Mechanicsburg, PA. Stackpole Books, 2005.

- Hughes, Dave. *Trout From Small Streams.* Mechanicsburg, PA. Stackpole Books, 2002.

- Judy, John. *Slack Line Strategies For Fly Fishing.* Harrisburg, PA. Stackpole Books, 1995.

- LaFontaine, Gary. *Fly Fishing The Mountain Lakes.* Guilford, CT. The Lyons Press, 1998, 2003.

- National Park Service Public Use Statistics Office - *http://www.nature.nps.gov/stats/*

- National Park Service, Rocky Mountain National Park - *http://www.nps.gov/romo/*

- Osthoff, Rich. *Fly Fishing the Rocky Mountain Backcountry.* Harrisburg, PA. Stackpole Books, 1999.

- Rubingh, J., and Fritz, R. *Colorado Greenback Cutthroat Trout, A Fisherman's Guide.* Portland, OR. Frank Amato Publications, 2009.

- Schollmeyer, Jim. *Hatch Guide For Lakes.* Portland, OR. Frank Amato Publications, 1995.

- Shewey, John. *Alpine Angler.* Portland, OR. Frank Amato Publications, 1985.

- U.S. Board on Geographic Names - http://geonames.usgs.gov/ (used to search names of streams and lakes)

- Ward, J. V., and Kondratieff, B. C. *An Illustrated Guide to the Mountain Stream Insects of Colorado.* Niwot, CO. University Press of Colorado, 1992.

- Willard, Beatrice E. and Foster, Susan Q. *A Roadside Guide To Rocky Mountain National Park.* Boulder, CO. Johnson Publishing Co., 1990.

Visit the Book's Website

Additional Content Online

Be sure to visit *A Fly Fishing Guide to Rocky Mountain National Park* on the web at www.flyfishingrmnp.com. On the website, you'll find additional content which cannot be easily shared in a printed book such as videos and current conditions in the Park.

Share Your Thoughts About The Book

Help make *A Fly Fishing Guide to Rocky Mountain National Park* a better book for future printings. Take a moment to participate in a brief online survey which is designed to capture your thoughts on the book and what could be done to make it better. In appreciation of your time, you will automatically be entered into a drawing for an autographed copy of the book for you or a friend. Visit www.flyfishingrmnp.com/booksurvey.html for more details and to complete the survey.

Errata and Etcetera

Correction to errors and omissions can be found by visiting the book's website at www.flyfishingrmnp.com.

Kurt Legerski casts a nymph rig to actively feeding brown trout in the Big Thompson River in Moraine Park. The river is swollen to the top of its banks due to spring run-off (early June).